A Taste of Paradise

A Feast of Authentic Caribbean Cuisine and Refreshing Tropical Beverages for Health and Vitality

Susana Lewis
and Charles Lewis MD

Psy Press
Est. 1978

Psy Press
Revised June 2017
Carrabelle Florida
PsyPress\~email.com
IBSN 978-1-938318-00-9

Table of Contents

A Taste of Paradise

CUISINE OF THE CARIBBEAN

A Taste of Paradise is written to teach the preparation of foods with rich and authentic Caribbean flavors. These traditional foods form a natural and healthy diet where the meal is highly flavored and satisfying and usually served with fresh cut fruit. Well over 200 traditional recipes for great tasting food are given, many prepared with coconut cream.

This book is more than a collection of traditional Caribbean recipes. Not only does it explain how to prepare dishes, but it also teaches the selection and storage of tropical fruit, how to prepare plantains and cassava for cooking, and how to obtain the most health benefit from foods. Tricks are given on how to avoid the formation of intestinal gas from beans.

This book's co-authored is a medical doctor, board certified in preventive medicine. A section is dedicated to healthy weight loss (never calorie counting) and enjoying food. Along with the recipes are notes explaining why mangoes can cause allergic reactions in individuals susceptible to poison oak and how to avoid the reaction while enjoying the fruit, why some smoothies get bitter and how to prevent it, which tropical foods are likely to trigger migraines, which foods can be toxic if not correctly prepared. It provides instructions for safe preparation of ceviche, meats, and seafood. The section on meats explains how to avoid creation of carcinogens during cooking, and it teaches how to prepare vegetables to maximize anti-carcinogenic compounds.

Most of the recipes are gluten-free, and to extend this benefit, instructions are given for the use of gluten free pasta. Many recipes use coconut rather than milk and thus are lactose-free; there are milk free recipes for flan, cake and smoothies made using coconut cream. There is a traditional recipe for cookies that uses no milk or eggs, and a recipe for molasses "brownies" made without milk, eggs or chocolate.

The Spanish-speaking Caribbean islands (Cuba, Dominican Republic, and Puerto Rico) share climate, language, geography, and not surprisingly, many elements of traditional cuisine. Many traditional dishes from the islands originated with the native residents, the Taíno people. These include cornbread, roast turkey, and root beer. Other recipes can be traced back to Moorish casserole, fufu and elephant ear soup from Africa, bread and war paint used by the Arawak Indians, and spicy hot cocoa drink from the Aztecs. Early in their history, these islands were the crossroads for the development of the Americas, and this is reflected in the diversity of their tropical cuisine.

This book gives traditional recipes and also provides shortcuts and modern adaptations so that the authentic flavors can be enjoyed using ingredients that can be found in most American and Canadian cities. Also included are recipes for the "fast foods" sold by street vendors on the islands.

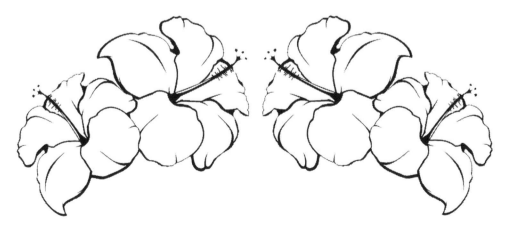

Picking Fresh Fruit and Other Produce

SELECTING TROPICAL FRUIT:

The first secret to preparing delicious food is to start with great tasting ingredients. This section gives guidance on selecting the raw materials for great tasting food and keeping them at their best.

Most fruits picked for the market are picked unripe so that they will be hard enough to survive transport. This does not make for the best-flavored fruit. Some types of fruits will continue to ripen after being picked; their flavor matures, and their sugars increase. Other fruit just gets soft. The flavor of a peach that is picked too early and is allowed to soften has little in common with the glorious sweet essence of summer contained within a tree-ripened peach. Fruits that have been subjected to cold injury will be mealy and unpleasant. A banana, on the other hand, continues to ripen after being picked, thus allowing bananas to have long been among the most common of all fruits eaten in Europe and the United States, even though they must be transported from the tropics.

Generally, if a fruit does not have a good aroma in the market, it is unlikely to have much flavor at home. To get juicy fresh fruit, weigh the fruit in your hand. It should feel heavy for its size, meaning that it has plenty of water and dissolved sugars. Fruit that was not allowed to mature enough will be less juicy, and fruit that is old or has been stored without enough humidity can become dehydrated on the shelf. Most fruits should show the blossom of youth, with unblemished, smooth, shiny skin indicating its freshness.

It is important how fruit is stored. You can't change what happened to the produce before you purchase it, but you can easily ruin it by storing it wrong. *Most tropical and subtropical fruits are damaged by chilling*, and thus storage at low temperatures should be avoided. Some exceptions are dates, figs, kiwifruit and Fuyu persimmons. Most fruits do not freeze at 32°F, because of sugars that prevent freezing until getting to a bit lower temperature. Refrigerators are set to maintain temperatures between 35°F and 38°F. This is cold enough to damage most tropical fruits.

The best temperature for ripening most fruits is between 67°F and 75°F, a comfortable room temperature.

Many fruits can be frozen, but I cannot think of one that can be thawed and eaten out of hand. Freezing destroys the texture and alters the flavor of the fruit. Frozen fruit can be eaten frozen, put into smoothies, used for ice cream, or for cooking and baking.

SCIENCE ALERT: Many fruits contain the enzyme amylase that breaks starches in the fruit down into simple, sweet sugars, and pectinase that breaks pectin down, thus softening the fruit. Ethylene, a gas that is formed from the amino acid methionine, acts as a hormone to increase the activity of amylase and pectinase. Ethylene from one fruit can act to accelerate the ripening of other fruit. Other enzymes break down chlorophyll and thus reduce the green coloration of the fruit. Fruit that continues to ripen after separation from the plant is known as *climacteric* fruit. Oddly, the term *climacteric* also refers to menopause.

ETHYLENE PRODUCING FRUITS:
The fruits that produce the most ethylene gas are: Apples, Apricots, Avocados, Banana, Nectarines, Kiwi fruit Papayas, Peaches, Pears, and Plums, Passion Fruit, Zapote, and Guanábana. These fruits can be used to help ripen other fruit by putting them in a closed bag together.

There is well-researched science guiding the harvest, curing, and storage of produce. Professional produce producers and distributors have a lot at stake in delivering high-quality produce to grocery stores without excessive losses.

Professional distributors have temperature and humidity controlled environments for storage and shipping of the produce to keep each type of produce in its best possible condition.

Retail outlets are often not such experts and have much less control. Once the produce is on the display counter, it is at the room temperature of the store, or in a cooling display. Markets can't keep produce in the dark and on display at the same time, and they have only a couple of different temperatures to store the produce. Most produce is best stored at 85 to 95 percent relative humidity to keep it from drying out This is why you see mist sprayers in the vegetable sections of many grocery stores. This is hard to maintain in your home.

Your best bet is to try to buy as fresh from the distributor as possible and use the produce within a few days. The grocer wants to sell what he buys, but may have produce sitting on display for more than a few days. I have seen mummified produce on the shelf at stores all too often.

REFRIGERATION: Home freezers are designed to maintain a freezer compartment temperature between -5°F and +5°F (-20.6°C and -15°C). Setting the freezer to +4°F (-15.6°C) will provide the same benefits as lower temperatures for food storage, but will use less energy and have the compressor run shorter cycles. The refrigeration compartment should be set to maintain a temperature of 34°F to 38°F (1°F to 3°C) with an optimal temperature of 36°F (2°C) to preserve freshness while conserving energy and minimizing running time.

Since colder air is denser, and heat rises in refrigerators without fans, the bottom section of the fridge is cooler than the upper section by a few degrees Fahrenheit. The coolest section is the (lowest) crisper drawer, which should be used for vegetables. The warmest area in the refrigerator is the upper section of the door, the butter section.

BANANAS: Dominicans call eating bananas guineos. Bananos usually refers to bananas for cooking. The reason that many people don't like eating bananas is that they are uninformed, persnickety and prefer eating beautiful unblemished fruit, but a beautiful bright yellow banana is not a ripe banana and it has little flavor. Most varieties of banana need to be covered with brown speckles before they are ready to eat as a raw fruit. Many people throw bananas away just as they get ripe. A green banana has about 80 percent of its calories as starch and about seven percent as sugar. A yellow banana has about 25% of its calories as starch and 65% as sugar, and a nicely speckled banana has about 5% of its calories as starch and 90% as sugar. Which do you prefer to eat as a fruit?

A ripe banana is not to be confused with a bruised or injured fruit. Bruised bananas are slimy. An overripe banana has a poor texture, but can be used for cooking. Green bananas for use as a starchy cooked vegetable should be hard and dark green, not light green, as these are already too ripe.

Bananas are harvested for export when they are about 3/4 mature so that they will not ripen before getting to market. Bananas coming to the U.S. have a shorter boat ride and are picked riper than those going to the European market, and have a better flavor for it. Far better are bananas harvested at maturity that you can find in the tropics.

Ethylene gas is used to induce ripening and yellowing before being distributed to the grocery stores. This can make finding green bananas for cooking difficult. For cooking, look for dark green hard bananas. Usually in the U.S., I find these to be shorter than the average banana, but they should have a nearly round cross-section, and not one that is overly angular, indicating that they were picked too early.

Bananas will get chilling injury below about 56°F (13°C). This affects the skin more than the flesh, making the peel turn brown and thin. If you need to delay the use of bananas, they can be refrigerated for a day. If you have more bananas than you expect to use before they get overripe, peel the bananas when they are ripe, wrap them in plastic and freeze for use in smoothies or for other uses.

COCONUTS – COCO: Look for a coconut that is heavy for its size. Shake it. It should slosh and feel full of coconut water. Avoid coconuts that look wet around the eyes, are cracked, or smell rancid around the eyes. Coconut water (agua de coco) also called coconut juice, is the clear liquid in a fresh coconut that you drink out of a coconut with a straw while on a beach on holiday. Coconut cream is made from the flesh of the coconut (See pages 18-19).

Coconuts can be stored between 32° - 36°F (0° - 2°C) without damage, and thus can be refrigerated. Once opened, refrigerate the coconut juice and meat. The juice will be good for only about one day. Chunks or grated coconut flesh can be stored in an airtight container in the refrigerator for up to two weeks or frozen for longer periods.

MANGOES: Mangoes continue to ripen after they are picked. To pick out the best mangoes look for beautiful full fruit with smooth skin and with good color and that feel heavy for their size. They should have a strong mango fragrance, especially around the stem (but avoid touching the stem to your nose). Expect to buy mangoes that are firm and that take a few days to ripen at room temperature. When they get to the point that they look and smell delicious and you really want to eat them, they will probably need one more day. They should be starting to soften, and it is O.K to hold them until the skin just begins to shrivel some, as they will still be delicious. If they do not have fragrance when you buy them, they likely were picked too early and may never develop much flavor. You can try putting them in a bag with an ethylene gas producing fruit like an apple to get them to ripen.

GUANÁBANA: (Soursop, Prickly Custard Apple – *Annona Muricata*) This is a large tropical fruit weighing up to 4 kg with green spiny skin and white fibrous pulp with large shiny black seeds. It is luscious, creamy, sweet and tart and makes splendid smoothies. In addition to its exquisite flavor, although I have found nothing in the literature to confirm it, I am convinced from my own experience that it has pleasant mild psychopharmacologic effects. These factors make guanábana my most favored fruit. Other parts of the plant have multiple medicinal values and are being studied for anti-cancer effects. The seeds may contain toxins, and should not be eaten.

If you find fresh guanábana, the fruit should be heavy for its size. Allow it to ripen at room temperature. It must be soft and almost breaking up when it is ripe. Clean it and separate the pulp from the skin and the seeds. The pulp can be refrigerated, but should be used within a few days. The pulp will turn brown if overripe and is not much good. Chilling the fruit will also damage it.

Guanábana does not travel well and thus is not widely grown for market. Canned fruit can sometimes be found as well as the juice, but is nowhere close to the fresh fruit.

CITRUS FRUIT:

ORANGES – CHINA, NARANJA: There are many different oranges used in the Caribbean. Eating oranges are called China (pronounced cheena) in the Dominican Republic, which reflects the fact that citrus fruits are originally from the Far East.

The orange skin color of this fruit that occurs with ripening happens when cold nights are followed by warm days. This is easy in California but does not occur so much in the tropics. This is why fully ripe sweet oranges are usually at least partly greenish in the tropics. Even U.S. grown Valencia oranges will sometimes re-green after having been fully orange. This does not lower the quality of the fruit. Commercially harvested citrus fruit may be degreened by holding the fruit at room temperature and treatment with ethylene gas. Commercial oranges are often dyed with a carcinogenic coloring FD&C Citrus Red No. 2, which is approved only for this purpose and is not intended for consumption. Thus, the dyed orange peel should not be used for food use such as marmalade or zest.

Oranges do not ripen after picking, so they are ready to eat and do not get better with time. When shopping for oranges look for large dense (heavy for its size) fruit. With navel oranges (the ones with a belly button on the end), the skins should feel a bit loose. They should smell good and orangey. Valencia oranges have thinner skin, but also should be heavy and have a good fragrance.

In the Dominican Republic, a Naranja is a sour orange and is used in cooking and flavoring, or in juice, but is not eaten out of hand. Meanwhile a limón dulce (a sweet lemon) is a large yellow lemon that is eaten out of hand and tastes like lemonade. There are not separate words for lemons and limes in Spanish. In the tropics, you get the understanding that there is a wide array and great diversity of fruits. Once sitting under a mango tree with juice running down their faces a couple of my friends named over 20 varieties of mangoes that grew in the area, each with its own characteristics.

Citrus fruit can be damaged by chilling and should not be stored too cold. Grapefruit, lemons, and limes should not be stored below 50°F (10°C) to avoid chilling injury. Mandarin oranges and tangerines can be stored down to about 42°F degrees (5°C), and oranges can be stored down to about 38°F (3°C). Thus, a refrigerator is not a good place for citrus fruits.

HEALTH ALERT: Ingestion of grapefruit prevents the body from eliminating many medications, and grapefruit has caused several medications to be pulled off the market. Grapefruit (and the Asian fruit pomelo) contain furanocoumarins, compounds that inhibit the metabolism of many medications, and thus, can cause toxic, sometimes fatal, reactions. Cardiac dysrhythmias are the most common problem. A long list of medications that are affected by grapefruit include antihistamines, cholesterol lowering medications, calcium channel blockers, antidepressants, sedatives, medications for erectile dysfunction and many others. It is best to avoid consuming grapefruit with or before taking medications. Individuals taking prescription medications should ask their pharmacist if their medications are affected by grapefruit. Oranges and most other citrus do not contain sufficient levels of furanocoumarins to cause concern during normal use.

PINEAPPLE – PIÑA: Pineapples are native to South America and were introduced to Europe in the 1500s.

Pineapples do not ripen after they are harvested. This means that once cut, they only go downhill from there. If the fruit is cut with green skin, it will yellow over a few days from the base to the top, and there will be some slight change in flavor, but no increase in sweetness. Fruit harvested for export is cut earlier, so fruit found in grocery stores in non-tropical areas is not likely to have the sweetness and rich flavor of those harvested for local consumption.

When selecting a pineapple look for fruit that looks fresh with a crown of fresh looking leaves, and skin that looks plump. The fruit should be heavy for its size. The fruit should not have soft spots. To pick out a good pineapple smell it. If it does not have a good fragrance – don't buy it. The color of the skin is not a reliable indicator of the quality or ripeness of the fruit. It should not be at all mushy, but also not rock hard. In a ripe pineapple, a leaf can be pulled out of the crown without much force. Pineapples are sweetest in the warmer months, so if buying Hawaiian pineapples they should be best during the summer months. Chilling injury below 43°F (6°C), causes darkening of the flesh, especially around the core.

Don't waste the pineapple skin. There are two recipes in the beverage section you might want to consider (Mabí and Pera piña) that use the skin.

PAPAYA – LECHOSA (Carica papaya): Papaya has an unpleasant, bitter taste when not ripe. There is a short period between unripe and having mold growing on the fruit. Between the two – I prefer the first signs of mold.

Papayas will ripen after harvest, but ones that are hard and green were harvested too early and will not ripen well. Select papayas that are at least partly yellow, and that have some give to them. This fruit rots easily. Avoid papayas that are soft at the stem end of the fruit, bruised or smell fermented, or are moldy. Unlike most fruits, you cannot rely on fragrance to selecting a good papaya but only use smell to rule out bad ones.

To ripen a papaya at home, put it in a paper bag at room temperature. Ripening can be accelerated by shallowly scoring the skin in a line 1/16th inch deep (it can be done with a clean fingernail) along the long axis of the fruit, scoring it every couple of inches around the fruit. When the fruit is yellow and soft, it is ready. Don't be afraid of a few soft spots that need to be cut out. I have rarely seen a perfectly beautiful papaya that was worth eating. When the fruit is ripe, it should be peeled and seeded and refrigerated in a closed container until used within a couple of days. Discard areas that are moldy.

There are many varieties of papayas, and the Caribbean ones are large, unlike the small Hawaiian Solo variety often seen in grocery stores in the U.S. Papayas can be stored cooler than most tropical fruits and they can be kept for several days at 36°F (2°C) without injury, however, chilling increases the likelihood of fungal rot of the fruit. Chilling or heat injury from storage above 86°F (30°C) will cause uneven ripening poor color and susceptibility to decay.

Unripe papaya is sometimes used as a vegetable. A recipe for green papaya with tomatoes is given on page 139.

SCIENCE ALERT: Pineapple, papaya, guavas, kiwi fruit, melons, and figs all contain proteolytic enzymes that cut proteins into pieces, as do certain digestive enzymes. In papaya and fig, the latex contains the enzymes. As a papaya ripens, the amount of the enzyme papain decreases. In my experience, this also seems true with pineapple.

Pineapple contains proteolytic enzymes that can be used to tenderize meat, but which will also sometimes tenderize the tongue; enzymes in these fruits, especially pineapple and melons, can cause the mouth or throat to itch, burn or even bleed, especially when not fully ripened. Care should be taken not to give fresh pineapple to small children who may suck on it and get a sore mouth from it as it digests the tissue. The enzymes in pineapple have been used experimentally to remove necrotic tissue from wounds and burns. They have anti-inflammatory action and may be useful in the treatment of cancer. The meat tenderizer bromelain comes from pineapples.

Papaya enzymes (such as papain) are also used to tenderize meat. Proteolytic enzymes in these fruits also break down casein, the main protein in milk. This results in bitter tasting protein fragments. This is why pineapple and papaya smoothies get bitter if they are allowed to sit

---

even for a few minutes after making them. Any of these fruits if used raw will digest the protein in gelatin and prevent gelatin from setting.

These fruit enzymes are deactivated by heating above 149°F (65°C), so cooked or canned pineapple, for example, does not have these effects. Heating these fruits to this temperature can be used to inactivate their proteolytic enzymes.

AVOCADOS: Avocados do not ripen on the tree. Usually, it is best not to buy soft ones in the store, but rather bring them home, and allow them to soften at room temperature. This fruit is high in oils and oxidizes easily, becoming rancid and brown. A rotten avocado is so bad that it is a metaphor for a bad relationship: one taste of a bad one and you likely will not want to have anything to do with another one for a long time. So try to get good ones.

Large thin-skinned varieties will often have a loose pit that rattles inside and is a sign of a well-developed fruit. The smaller Mexican varieties (alligator pears) have a bumpy black thick skin. When the fruit softens but is not too soft, it is ready. The flesh should be a bright yellow-green. If it has brown speckles or threads, it is past its prime, but can usually still be used. If it is browned or olive color, even if only in part of the flesh, it is not worth eating – throw it out.

Avocados can be ripened more quickly by placing them in a paper bag at room temperature with an apple or other ethylene producing fruit. Avocado ripening slows at refrigerator temperatures. In the warmest areas of the refrigerator, the upper door, some ripening continues. This can be done to keep ripe or almost ripe avocados for a few days. Once an avocado is opened, it will turn brown and quickly go bad if exposed to air. Browning can be avoided by covering the exposed areas with lemon juice, covering exposed areas with plastic wrap to exclude air exposure, and then refrigerating them. Avocados should not be frozen, but guacamole can be. Guacamole should be pureed (rather than mashed to blend the citrus juice in better) with two teaspoons of lemon or lime juice for each avocado. Guacamole can be refrigerated for up to about five days if covered with plastic wrap or frozen for about five months in an airtight container.

Avocado skin and seeds are toxic to humans, and the fruit is toxic to many animals.

Temperate Climate Fruit:

APPLES – MANZANAS: Apples continue to ripen after picking. Apples can be stored at cool temperatures around 32 -36° F (0 -2 C) without freezing because of their sugar content, but will ripen much more quickly at room temperature. Do not allow them to freeze, as it will ruin their texture and flavor. They can be kept in the crisper drawer of a refrigerator. Apples will have a rich aroma at the stem end when ripe. Be careful to avoid bruised apples or to allow the bagger at the grocery store to bang them up. Many apples are coated with lac (from insect shells), or wax to make then shiny, to retain moisture and extend their shelf and storage life.

For many fruits, bigger is better as it a sign that they were allowed to mature on the plant. Small apples and pears, however, are fine, especially for eating out of hand, where a large apple can be just too much for one person.

PEARS – PERAS: A mature pear picked from a tree needs to be chilled to ripen fully and get its best flavor. If not chilled, pears often rot before they get ripe. Summer pears need about two days at 30°F and winter pears about five to seven days of chilling. Pears from the supermarket will have already been chilled.

After chilling, allow pears to ripen at room temperature (65-75° F) until the fruit at the shoulder near the stem has just a bit of softness. This takes about a week after cooling, but can be sped up by placing the pear in a closed paper bag with an apple, banana or other ethylene producing fruit.

STONE FRUIT: APRICOTS (damasco), CHERRIES (cereza) PLUMS (ciruela), PEACHES (durazno or melocotón), and NECTARINES are stone fruits that stop making sugar as soon as the fruit is picked. If they are not ripe when picked, they will not get sweeter, only softer. Some of the tartness may diminish, but mostly the post-harvest ripening is a change in texture. If the fragrance of the fruit does not entice you when you pick it up in the store, it will not improve. Chilling injury caused by cooling the fruit below 45°F, damages peaches and nectarines, causing browning and ruining the texture making them hard or mealy and destroying their juiciness. Thus, keep them out of the refrigerator.

BLUEBERRIES – ARÁNDANOS: Blueberries do not sugar up after picking. They are as ripe as they will be when you buy them, so keep them cool until you eat them. Big fat fresh berries with a good blush are most likely to be sweet. Waiting does not improve them any. Blueberries can be refrigerated for up to about ten days for eating fresh. They can be frozen for use in smoothies, or cooking, or eaten whole as a frozen treat.

GRAPES – UVAS: Grapes do not ripen after picking. Look for grapes that are large for their variety, as those are the ones most likely to have had a chance to mature and ripen on the vine. It's O.K. if the grapes are starting to fall off the stems. Avoid grapes if the stems are brown or look shriveled.

KIWIFRUIT: Kiwi ripens during storage at 32°F for at least a couple of months, increasing their sugar content and decreasing their acidity. Look for attractive fruit that are not shriveled and that have the skin intact. The fruit should give slightly to pressure, and feel heavy for its size.

MELONS – MELONES: Melons do not ripen after being picked.

HONEYDEW and most other melons do not tolerate

cold as well, are susceptible to decay and will fail to ripen normally and may show skin damage (bronzed areas) if chilled.

CANTALOUPES are an exception, as they are fairly resistant to chilling and can be stored at 36°F (2°C). Cantaloupes should have even netting and a strong pleasant melon odor at the flowering end. If the stem came off cleanly on its own, it is a good sign that it was picked ripe. Cantaloupes should not be overly soft but should have some give to pressure.

WATERMELON – PATILLA, SANDÍA: Watermelons can be just about the most frustrating fruit to select. Each choice can easily be 25 pounds of fruit, so you want to get it right. The melon should be heavy for its size. Look for a butter-yellow area where the melon was lying on the ground. If it is pale green on the ground patch – it is not ripe. The melon should have a healthy sheen, be symmetrical and have no cuts or bruised areas. The stem should be dry. There should be a melon fragrance. Avoid watermelons that are very hard.

It seems that most men cannot resist knowingly thumping a melon to approve of its quality. Here is what to look for: The thump should result in a higher pitched hollow sound, and watermelons with a dead thud sound should be rejected. Before selecting a melon at your local grocers, walk over to the laundry detergent area or cooking oil aisle. Compare the sound of thumping a plastic bottle of a heavy liquid, such as vegetable oil or laundry detergent, when held by the bottle's neck. This is the sound of a dead thud. That is what you want to avoid. What you are looking for is a tympanic, hollow sound such as you get from an empty jug. A good melon will often be so tight that it splits open when you first cut into it.

If you are picking watermelons or other melons from the vine, the tendril near the stem of the melon should be dried and shriveled.

Wash watermelon with soap and water before cutting them. Watermelons are the only melon that taste better cold and to me taste sweeter when colder. I like to cool mine before opening them, but other than that, they should be stored at room temperature until you are ready to eat them. Watermelons break another rule in that they can also be ripened some by exposure to ethylene gas, so you can try putting a watermelon in a large paper bag with an apple for a couple of days to see if it will ripen more.

STRAWBERRIES – FRESAS: Strawberries do not ripen after being picked. What happens in the field and the first hours thereafter determines the fate of the strawberry. This fruit can be easily injured, grow mold, and be a disappointment. Good harvest technique includes using forced chilled air to cool the fruit to 31 to 36 °F within an hour of picking and keeping the berries cool until they get to market. Berries should remain cooled until they are ready to be used. This suggests that they should not be purchased from roadside stands, but rather from a cooled fruit display.

Look for large strawberries without mold, with fresh green tops and without white tips. The skin of the berries should be shiny. This is a fruit that it has become hard to use your nose on as they are now generally sold in thermoplastic boxes, and the chilling reduces the perfume released by the fruit. Store the fruit in the refrigerator until ready to use or serve unless you are trying to grow penicillin mold. If the strawberries are to be eaten out of hand, in a salad, or as a garnish, allow them to warm to room temperature before serving, as it will increase the flavor and fragrance of the fruit.

Picking Vegetables:

TOMATOES - TOMATES: When shopping for tomatoes look for full, round, heavy fruit, with smooth, undamaged skin. The skin should be tight without any shriveling. Smell the flower end of the fruit – it should have a rich tomato fragrance. Vine ripened tomatoes often have a better flavor than ones picked green and ripened with ethylene gas. Almost all commercial tomatoes have a gene that induces even-ripening, but that also decreases sugar, flavor, and nutrition. Heirloom tomatoes, without the even-ripening trait, have much more flavor; but aren't as pretty on the market shelf.

Store tomatoes at room temperature with the stem down, and best in a dark area, to help develop good color. Tomatoes can be stored down to 50° F (10° C) for several days. Lower temperatures or cold temperature longer than about a week will damage the fruit. Tomatoes don't have much fragrance or flavor when they are cold. Re-warm refrigerated tomatoes to room temperature for at least an hour for use in salads.

CANNED VERSUS FRESH: If fresh ripe in-season tomatoes are available, they can be substituted for canned tomatoes. It takes about 10 minutes of simmering to cook them. During the harvest months from July to September, you are likely to get a better flavor with fresh tomatoes. Most store tomatoes, especially out of season, will not have as good flavor as those grown and harvested in the season for used in canned tomatoes. Plum or Roma tomatoes are much more likely than other tomatoes to give a good flavor outside of the summer months.

One pound of fresh tomatoes, or about 3 cups of fresh, diced tomatoes, is about equivalent to a number 1 tall 16 oz. can of tomatoes, and a number 2 can (about 28 oz.) is about 2 pounds of tomatoes. A pinch of extra salt may be needed for recipes where fresh tomatoes are replacing canned ones.

GREEN TOMATOES – TOMATES VERDES: Green tomatoes are often used in salads and sandwiches, or as a fresh vegetable in the Caribbean. The green tomato is a regular tomato at the "breaker" state; they have reached full size and are just about to change color. They are not dark green immature fruit, but also not yet yellow. They should not have a bitter taste.

Modern commercial tomatoes have been bred to be firmer for easier harvesting, but less flavorful than garden varieties. Green tomatoes are even blander. I find that the best "green tomatoes" from markets in the U.S. are those that are already beginning to have patches of pink. These give the crisp texture, green tomato flavor and are more attractive. Let the tomatoes warm to room temperature before using them and add a sprinkle of salt to enhance the flavor.

TOMATILLOS: Tomatillos will ripen after harvest – but you usually want to avoid that, as they are generally used green. Look for tomatillos with greenish brown husks and in which the husk is fairly tight over the fruit. If you peel the husk back, it should reveal a green fruit free of blemishes. The fruit should be firm. Tomatillos will ripen and get yellow, but most recipes call for green ones. Smaller tomatillos are usually sweeter and have better flavor than larger ones.

Tomatillos can be stored in the refrigerator for a couple of weeks if the husks are removed, and can even be frozen without the husks. Remove the husks and wash the fruit before using them.

SWEET CORN - MAÍZ DULCE: Corn is called Maize in much of the world. The name maize, or maíz in Spanish, comes from the Taíno word for the corn; mahiz. When selecting corn on the cob, look for ears harvested when the silk had just turned brown and that have fresh, tight dark green husks.

Pull back the husks enough to reveal the tip. The kernel should get progressively smaller at the tip and have well-filled rows. If the kernels are large at the tip, it indicates that the corn was harvested late and will be overripe and tough. If the kernels are dented, the corn has lost moisture.

Unlike fruits that ripen and get sweeter, as corn matures the sugars turn into starch. Corn is best the moment it is pulled off the stalk and gets starchier with time. Sweet corn just pulled from the corn stalk is at its sweetest. Corn can be kept in the refrigerator for a few days to slow the sugars from turning into starch, but even at 50°F over half of the sugar turns to starch in 24 hours. Warmer temperatures accelerate the process. Avoid over cooking corn, as that too toughens it. Corn can be frozen, but that also alters the flavor.

EGGPLANT – BERENJENA: Eggplant is frequently used in Dominican cooking. It is often used as a substitute for meat dishes, as there is a widely held myth on the island touting its high protein content. A cup of eggplant actually has less than a gram of protein per serving – about a quarter of that found in rice.

The eggplant most seen in the Caribbean are of the large dark purple variety that I practiced my suturing technique on when I was in med school.

Select smooth, symmetrical, eggplants that are not wrinkled, flabby or dull, as these are past their prime. The cap and stem should be green and fresh. Look for smaller, less mature eggplants as large over mature ones are likely to be tough and bitter. Ripe eggplants are soft to the touch. If you press gently on it with your finger, the mark will quickly disappear if it is ripe. Pick eggplants that are dense (heavy for their size). Bruises or tan patches indicate damage and poor flavor. Eggplant should not be bitter even when raw. (Older varieties were more often bitter, but newer eggplant varieties have been selected with less of the defensive toxins that give the bitter flavor.)

Eggplant is susceptible to chilling below 50 degrees, and chilling will cause browning around the seed area, and thus it should not be refrigerated. It is better to overcook than undercook eggplant, as undercooked eggplant is chewy and does not take up the flavor of the foods they are cooked with. Unless the recipe calls for including it, discard the skin as it is tough and often bitter.

PEELING EGGPLANTS: The peel of eggplant is tough and may contain bitter and toxic substances. It is usually not included in the meal. To peel the eggplant when you plan to dice it, cut the eggplant in half along its axis. Next, lay each half of the eggplant on the cut face and make three more lengthwise cuts – cutting each half into four long wedges. Each one eighth of the eggplant can then be easily peeled. After peeling, the eggplant can be diced.

ONION AND SHALLOTS – CEBOLLA Y CEBOLLIN: Sautéed shallots are highly prized in the Caribbean, especially when freshly harvested for their sweetness and flavor and color. Shallots are often hard to find in markets and are rarely fresh. Red onions have a similar sweetness and flavor and are more widely available. Thus, they have been used in many recipes in this book where shallots would traditionally have been used. Shallots and red onions have a health advantage over white or yellow onions, as they contain more flavonoids that act as antioxidants considered to prevent disease and promote health.

Select onions that are hard, heavy for their size, unblemished, and that have shiny, papery skin. If they have been stored correctly, they should not be sprouting. The neck (where the dry layers of skin come together) should be dry. Avoid discolored onions or any that are getting soft. Onions should not have any smell until they are cut. If they smell earthy, they are bad.

Dry onions should be stored in a cool, dry area. They do not require refrigeration, and can be kept for several weeks. Store onions in the dark as exposure to light will cause them to get bitter. Do not store onions with potatoes, as it will cause the onions to decay.

Onions can be chilled in the refrigerator for an hour before using them, to keep tears from flowing when you cut them. Using a sharp knife also helps. Once cut open, wrap the unused portion of the onion in plastic wrap and store in the refrigerator. This will keep other foods from taking up the onion flavor and keep the onion from drying out.

GREEN ONIONS AND SCALLIONS: The name scallions refers to young onions that have not yet formed a distinct bulb and that have a milder flavor, and thus are favored for use in salads. Green onions have grown enough to form a small bulb, and are more often used for cooking.

Green onions and scallions should be bought and used while fresh and unwilted. They can be stored for a couple of days in the crisper section of the refrigerator inside of a plastic bag.

GARLIC – AJO: Look for heads of garlic with large plump cloves with tight, dry paper like skin. The cloves should be dry and firm. There is nothing wrong with smaller cloves, but it is more work to remove the skin from several small cloves than from a few large ones. Smaller cloves tend to have a stronger flavor. Avoid any that are shriveled, soft or overly flaking, as these are a sign that they are getting old.

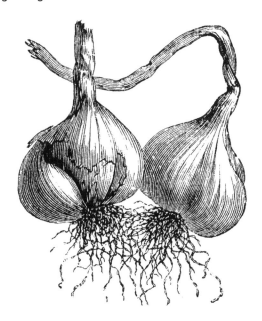

Peeling cloves: Slice off the base of the clove, and lay it on the cutting board. Lay the flat blade of a large knife over the clove with the sharp edge away from you, and give a quick downwards pop of the heel of your hand onto the flat side of the blade. The idea is to pop and free the skin, so it is easy to peel, not to crush the clove of garlic. If you need to peel many cloves of garlic, you can drop them into boiling water for ten to twenty seconds, and then quickly plunge them into cold water. The skins will soften and slide off by rubbing them between your thumb and fingers.

Commercially garlic is stored at near 32°F. Whole garlic cloves can be frozen and used as needed. Store bought whole garlic should be fine for several months if stored a cool, dry, dark area that gets some ventilation.

CAUTION: Garlic in oil needs to be refrigerated as the low-acid, low-oxygen conditions provide an excellent opportunity for the formation of botulism toxin.

GINGER – JENGIBRE: Ginger root should have a shiny skin, be plump and hard. Watch out for mold where the tubers are broken from each other and avoid these or any that are rubbery or wrinkled. Ginger should have a spicy odor.

Ginger is best stored in a closed ziplock bag in the refrigerator. It should stay in good condition for about two months.

HERBS AND SPICES: The spices trade was among the principal reasons that European explorers ventured into the Caribbean, as spices from the East were valued for preserving meats. The antioxidant phenolic compounds they contain continue to provide health benefits. These antioxidants prevent food from being oxidized, but also causes the spices themselves to be readily oxidized, giving them a short shelf life.

Fresh herbs and freshly ground spices give the best flavor and health benefits. We recommend that dried herbs and ground spices be purchased in small containers and discarded six months after opening them. Spices purchased as whole seeds, (e.g.: cinnamon sticks, peppercorns, nutmeg, and coriander) should be good for a year. Freshly ground, whole spices give the best flavor.

Reference: "Postharvest Technology of Horticultural Crops" Adel A. Kader (Editor) 2002 U.C. Davis.

Sweet Peppers

AJÍ DULCE, AJÍCE: The pepper we used most at home is ají dulce, (sweet pepper) also called ajíce in Puerto Rico. This pepper is an important ingredient in sofrito, the base for numerous dishes. Ají dulce is mildly sweet and flavorful, with only a hint of spicy heat. It is a low moisture pepper, well adapted for cooking and sautéing.

Beware: Ají dulce has an evil twin; the fiery hot Scotch bonnet pepper; they look very similar and are the same species, but they have very different effects.

Fresh ají dulce is impossible to find in most cities, so in this book I have substituted them with peppers that can be found fairly consistently; the Anaheim peppers (1st choice) and Cuban peppers, a.k.a. the cubanelle pepper, as a second choice. These peppers have a better flavor when ripe (red or turning red) but also more difficult to find.

The flavor of ají dulce is preferred. If you can find ají dulce, use six minced "sweet peppers" to replace ½ of one Anaheim or cubanelle pepper, seeds removed and minced in the recipes.

These peppers are used fresh. They keep well at room temperature for a couple of weeks. Look for fresh and plump red sweet peppers, but they are still good when they are a bit dehydrated.

> CAUTION: Never eat any pepper showing any black mold growth. The mold may be Aspergillus, a fungus that produces potent carcinogens.

ANAHEIM PEPPERS AND AJÍ CUBANO (Cubanelle Peppers): Anaheim and cubanelle peppers are similar in appearance, both about 5 inches long and 1½ inches wide. Anaheim peppers are a bit spicier. Cuban Peppers are called "pimientos de cocinara" in Puerto Rico. Both peppers have a low water content that allows using them for cooking and frying. They are used in this book as a substitute for ají dulce that are hard to find in markets in the United States. Cubanelle peppers are usually sold in markets when they are light green before they ripen completely. Anaheim peppers usually have a darker color and can more often be found in the market starting to ripen.

Look for these peppers with smooth, glossy skin and without damage. They should be crisp and not looked wilted. Green Anaheim and cubanelle peppers can be stored in a plastic bag for up to a week in a refrigerator. Yellow or red peppers, which are already ripe, should be used quickly.

BELL PEPPERS (AJÍ GRANDE): Bell peppers are large mild hollow peppers. I prefer ripe ones - yellow, orange, and red bell peppers - to the immature green peppers, for their sweet flavor and attractive colors. Green bell peppers will turn red if allowed to ripen on the plants. The colored bell peppers are more expensive, as they spend more time growing before harvest, and there is more chance of loss to the farmer and distributor, as they do not keep as long.

Bell peppers should be firm and heavy for their size, with shiny, smooth skin. The stem should look fresh. Avoid any with soft spots or that have loose seeds rattle when you shake them.

Bell peppers will last a couple of days in the refrigerator (green ones last longer than ripe ones). They can be diced and frozen for later cooking.

When using bell peppers, discard the stem and seeds, and trim the white membranes from the inside, as it can be bitter. The skin of the bell pepper causes some people to burp.

Hot Peppers:

JALAPEÑO PEPPERS: Jalapeño Peppers are medium sized cone shaped hot peppers about two inches long. They are usually sold in the market (dark) green and unripe, but are sometimes sold ripe and red ones are slightly sweet. They are sometimes stuffed and eaten, or used in salsa and other dishes to give heat. The membrane around the seeds is the hottest part.

Look for peppers with a deep color that are firm and have a smooth, shiny skin without soft spots. They can be stored in a plastic bag in the refrigerator for about 5 days.

AJÍ PIPÍ: Caribbean cuisine is not known for spicy hot foods, but that does not mean that we never dabble in this area. There is a pepper that grows wild in the Caribbean, as well as in Florida, the southwestern United States, and as far south as Columbia we call ají pipí, that is also known as chili tepin. This tiny pepper packs a lot of heat. Ají pipí is sometimes called "siete paila"; seven pots, because one pepper is said to be hot enough to spice seven pots of food. There is even a saying: "esta como un ají pipí" meaning that he is mad as hell.

These peppers are hot enough that you do need to be careful handling them as you would not want to rub your eyes after, and they can cause your fingers to have the hot pepper burning sensation that can last for hours (see section below). But if you like spicy hot, it will take more than one to season a spicy hot dish.

SUBSTITUTIONS: If you cannot find ají pipí, they can be substituted with an equal number of chili pequín (not quite as hot), or a few dried cayenne peppers. Adjust the amount of pepper to how spicy you like your food.

Chili pequín are usually sold dried, and may be found in Mexican food stores or food sections of a grocery store. Store them in a sealed container.

CAUTION: Capsaicin and some related compounds are the molecules in hot pepper that cause the hotness. This same compound is used in pepper spray used by the police. Handling hot peppers (e.g.: cleaning, deseeding, or chopping) can cause hours of agony from contact with the hands, or secondarily touching the face or other sensitive body parts. I had this happen to me by just rinsing some very hot pepper in a bowl and using my hand as a dam to strain out the water. It is best to avoid this by wearing gloves if you will be handling hot peppers. Capsaicin causes a burning sensation but does not cause tissue damage (except for those allergic to it).

HOW TO STOP THE BURNING: Capsaicin is hydrophobic, meaning it repels water, but it will mix with oils and fats. You cannot wash it off with water, so drinking water will not make it go away, but cooling it will make the burning sensation better. However, frostbite and water intoxication are not the goals here.

MOUTH, LIPS: If your mouth is burning, try sour cream, butter, buttermilk or whole milk or even vegetable oil. The idea is to get the capsaicin (and related molecules) that give the heat sensation off your tongue, lips, and mucous membranes and absorbed into the fat. The fat should absorb some of the capsaicin, and deliver it to the stomach where it will stimulate the production of stomach acid.

HANDS AND OTHER BODY PARTS: Butter will work here too, as will salad oil. The sooner the excess capsaicin is removed, the better, as it is not going to be easy to remove capsaicin that has already been absorbed. Gently anoint the area with a sufficient amount of butter or vegetable oil and then dry it off with paper towels. Repeat this a couple of times. Follow this with the use of Dawn dishwashing detergent diluted with 3 parts cold water to 1 part Dawn. Soak the area for about 15 seconds, and then rinse for 45 seconds. Repeat this for ten minutes if the burning is severe. Caution: If your hands have touched the peppers, do not touch other parts of your body until they have been cleansed, or you may worsen the situation.

EYES: If wearing contact lenses remove them if possible (with uncontaminated hands!) and discard the lenses. Do not rub your eyes, as it will spread the capsaicin. Tears will usually safely wash the capsaicin from the eyes. Saline ophthalmic solution can be used to flush the eyes. A cool damp cloth over the eyes may give some relief. Accidental capsaicin exposure from handling peppers is very unlikely to cause permanent injury to the eyes and should resolve over about 30 minutes, however scratching and rubbing can injure them.

Fruit Storage Temperatures:

Apples: Most varieties:	30-31°F	(-1.1 to - 0.6°C)
Varieties sensitive to refrigeration:	38-40°F	(3.3. to 4.4°C)
Apricots:	31-32°F	(-0.6 to 0°C)
Bananas and plantains:	56-59°F	(13.3 to 14.4°C)
Berries:	31-34°F	(-0.6 to 1°C)
Bush berries, blueberries, strawberries:	31-34°F	(-0.6 to 1°C)
Cherries:	30-32°F	(1.1 to 0°C)
Citrus fruits:		
Grapefruits:	58-60°F	(14.4 to 15.6°C)
Lemons:	50-55°F	(14. 4 to 15.6°C)
Limes:	48-50°F	(7.2 to 10°C)
Oranges:	38-44°F	(3.3 to 6.7°C)
Tangerines:	40-45°F	(0°C)
Coconuts:	32-35°F	(-0.6 to 1.7°C)
Dates:	32°F	(0°C)
Figs:	31-32°F	(-0.6 to 0°C)
Grapes:	30-31°F	(-1.1 to 0.6°C)
Mangoes:	55°F	(12.8°C)
Melons:		
Honeydew:	45-50°F	(7.2 -t o 10°C)
Cantaloupe:	32-40°F	(0 -t o 4.4°C)
Watermelon:	32-40°F	(-0.6 to 0°C)
Papayas:	31°F-32°F	(-0.6 to 0°C)
Peaches and nectarines:	32°F	(0°C)
Pears:	29-31°F	(-1.7 to -0.6°C)
Pineapples:	45-47°F	(7.6 to 8.3°C)
Prunes:	31°F-32°F	(-0.6 to 0°C)
Tomatoes:	46°F-50°F	(8 to 10°C)
Watermelon	50°F-59°F	(10 to 15°C)
Taro	45°F-50°F	(7 to 10°C)

Vegetable Storage Temperatures:

Most green vegetables can be stored at temperatures just above freezing, and maintain freshness best when kept at a relative humidity between 90 and 100 percent. Rather than list those that can, it is easier to list some vegetables that do not tolerate this storage environment.

Almost all fresh produce can be divided into 3 groups for home storage:

1. THOSE THAT SHOULD NOT BE STORED IN THE REFRIGERATOR: Tomato Family (Tomatoes, Tomatillos, Peppers, Eggplants), Squash (both summer and winter squash, including Cucumbers and Pumpkins) most Tubers (Potatoes, Sweet Potatoes, Yuca, Yams, Taro and Ginger) and Okra. These vegetables are damaged by storage in cold temperatures.

2. THOSE THAT CAN BE KEPT IN THE REFRIGERATOR AND LIKE IT DRY: Dry Onions and Garlic can be kept at cold temperatures down to just above freezing, but do not like moisture. For this reason, they are usually stored in a cool area with ventilation outside of the refrigerator. They may be stored in the refrigerator in a brown paper bag but not in a drawer with high humidity, and not with ethylene producers.

3. THOSE THAT CAN BE KEPT IN THE REFRIGERATOR AND LIKE HUMIDITY: Almost all other vegetables fall into this group. Thus, almost all vegetables can be kept in the crisper drawer in the refrigerator.

The exception is beans. Lima beans can be stored in warmer areas of the refrigerator (37 F to 41F) and snap beans are best stored at a minimum temperature of 40 F, which means that most refrigerators are set a little too cold for fresh beans. Thus, when you buy fresh beans, keep them in the warmest part of the refrigerator (the top shelf on the door) and use them quickly, or leave them out of the refrigerator and use them quickly.

Vegetables that should not be stored under refrigeration can be kept refrigerated after cooking. Cucumber, which is usually eaten raw, should not be stored in the refrigerator, but can be refrigerated after cutting it, but it will lose quality.

Fruits and vegetables that can be refrigerated can be kept fresher by storing them in the crisper section of the refrigerator and adjusting it to maintain a high humidity. In many refrigerators, there is a sliding tab on the front of the crisper drawer. Sliding the tab over to the high end closes the vent in the drawer and helps to maintain a high humidity. Opening the tab allows more dry air to vent through the drawer, which lowers the humidity.

Ethylene gas helps ripen fruit, but its effects are mostly adverse for vegetables. Ethylene gas can cause yellowing of green vegetables, spotting on lettuce, and sprouting of potatoes, and onions. It will cause asparagus to get tough and carrots to get bitter. If you store ethylene-producing fruit (page 2) in the refrigerator, they should be kept in a separate drawer from vegetables.

Cooking Oils

Cooking oil has important health impacts. Trans fats are inherently unhealthy and have been estimated by U.S. Government scientist to cause 30,000 deaths each year in the United States. They are found in hydrogenated fats, shortening, and in some cooking oils. Unfortunately, trans fats are created during the manufacturing process when some vegetable oils are made. This also occurs when cooking in fat at high temperatures.

Soy, corn, and canola oil all have some trans fats as a result of the refining process used to make them. Virgin olive oil does not, and thus is preferred in most of these recipes.

Coconut oil has very little unsaturated fats, no trans fats. Butter also contains a fat called CLA, which is thought to prevent breast cancer and have other health benefits. Corn, soy, and most other vegetable oils are high in n-6 fats that promote inflammation.

Different oils tolerate different temperatures, above which they will begin to smoke, and can burst into flame. When cooking at high temperatures these volatilized oils will coat the inside of your home and lungs with a nice sticky varnish.

SMOKE TEMPERATURES OF SOME COOKING OILS

Type of Fat	Degrees F	Degrees C	18:2 Trans Fat %
Butter	302	150	0
Coconut oil	351	177	0
Extra virgin olive oil	380 to 410	193 - 210	0
Corn oil	457	236	0.286
Soy oil	466	241	0.53
Canola oil	468	242	0.365

- Water begins to simmer at about 182°F and boils at 212°F.
- The recommended temperature for sautéing vegetables in oil is 266° to 293°F.
- The best temperature for grilling hamburgers is 320°F (See page 78).
- The recommended temperature for deep fat frying is 365° F.

When foods are cooked at excessive temperatures, bad things begin to happen. Heterocyclic amines (HCA) and polyaromatic hydrocarbons (PAH) and nitrosamines are chemicals that can form when cooking foods (especially meats) at high temperatures. The formation of HCAs accelerates with temperatures over 200°C (392°F)[1]. Flame grilling can deliver temperatures up to 1000°F. Many HCA, PAH, and nitrosamines are carcinogens.

The highest concentration of these toxic compounds is found in the drippings and pan residues from cooking meats, especially when cooked at high temperatures. For this reason, dripping and pan residues should not be used for making gravies. See the section on meats for more on avoiding carcinogen formation in foods.

Cooking oils with high smoke point temperatures allows the use of higher temperatures and for the formation of more dangerous compounds to be formed in foods.

The recipes in the book are meant to be cooked at lower temperatures than found in many other styles of cooking. This makes for slower cooking and more flavorful food. It makes for healthier food with less formation of carcinogenic compounds.

We recommend using cooking temperatures below 350°F for frying most foods. With extra virgin olive oil, you can tell when things are getting too hot as the oil thins, and at higher temperatures will start to smoke. Cooking with butter will let the cook know when it the temperature exceeds 300°F, as the butter will brown. Adding some butter to the pan when sautéing in olive oil can also be used to help signal excessive heat, for example, when sautéing vegetables.

Salad Oils

We need both n-3 and n-6 polyunsaturated fats in our diet, but most Americans get far too much n-6 fats and not enough n-3 fats. The n-6 fatty acids are needed to help the immune system function well, but an excess sets the stage for chronic inflammation, heart disease, obesity, and cancer. The n-3 fats help regulate the immune process so that it does not go too far. α-linolenic acid (ALA) is an n-3 essential fatty acid. This means that ALA is required in the diet for health.

Seafood is an important source of n-3 fats, but these are not useful as salad oils. Most vegetable oils other than canola oil are not good sources of n-3 fats.

Salad oils that are never heated can be a source for getting the n-3 fat ALA into the diet. These should be cold pressed and kept in the refrigerator. Cold pressed canola has an unpleasant flavor. Flaxseed oil goes rancid very easily even when refrigerated. It is so easily oxidized that a rag with flaxseed oil can spontaneously burst into flame. This leaves walnut oil and olive oil as desirable salad oils.

An easier choice is extra virgin olive oil and adding chopped walnuts to the salad. Chop them only when ready to use, as smaller pieces become oxidized much more easily.

Oils can become easily oxidized (rancid). When packaged, bottles of oil are top filled with nitrogen gas to get rid of the oxygen, and prevent oxidation. Once the bottle has been opened, air with oxygen gets in. Buy small bottles of oil that you will use within 1 - 2 months, so that they do not have time go rancid after opening them. Fat and oil oxidation can be accelerated by contact with metals so they should not be kept in metal containers, and butter should not be wrapped in aluminum foil, or on a metal butter tray.

Extra virgin olive oil contains antioxidants that give it some protection from oxidation; however, it can be photo-oxidized by light. This is why it is sometimes sold in dark brown glass bottles. Buy olive oil from the back of the shelf in the grocery store, where it is darker. Store the oil in a dark, closed cabinet, not out on a counter top.

Cooking with Coconut Cream

SELECTING A COCONUT: When buying coconuts, pick ones that are heavy with water. There are three eyes at one end where the coconut was attached to the palm tree. Smell the coconut. It should smell like dry rope. If it smells rancid, it is. The eyes should be dry.

COCO CONFUSION: Coconut is used for cooking in the Caribbean, as well as in Thailand, Indonesia, the Philippines and in many other tropical lands. It is not surprising that fluids made from coconut are not standardized, and the names overlap. Here are some terms used:

COCONUT WATER: The clear fluid that fills a fresh coconut

COCONUT CREAM: Also called and sold as Coconut Milk. A thick high-fat fluid made from the kernel of the coconut. In this book, coconut cream refers to unsweetened high-fat coconut milk for use in cooking, usually made fresh or purchased in cans, which may be labeled coconut cream or as coconut milk. Coconut cream is also sold as a powder.

CREAM OF COCONUT: Cream of Coconut is sweetened syrup for making sweet beverages or desserts. It is sold in cans but should not be confused with coconut cream. Cream of coconut is not utilized in any recipes in this book.

COCONUT MILK: A milky fluid made from the kernel of the coconut, similar to and sometimes identical to coconut cream, but usually prepared with more water. Coconut milk also refers to a beverage often sold in the dairy section of the grocery used as an alternative to cow's milk. To avoid confusion, the traditional "Leche de Coco" (coconut milk) is referred to as coconut cream for the recipes in this book.

COPPA: The dried kernel or flesh of a coconut.

TRADITIONAL METHOD FOR PREPARATION OF COCONUT CREAM AND MILK:

Take a ripe coconut that is heavy with water. One of the three eyes will be easy to pierce. Puncture

this and allow the coconut water to drain the water into a cup. Enjoy it now or refrigerate the coconut water for later. It is a pleasant drink that has been reported to be high in antioxidants. If the coconut water is not good, then neither will the coconut be good for milk.

After draining the coconut water, crack the coconut open. You can use a hammer to crack it, or drop it on a cement slab a couple of times. Carefully use a knife to separate out the coconut flesh from the shell. A brown skin will come away with the coconut meat.

Grate the coconut flesh with a fine grater while avoiding grating your fingers. Place the shredded coconut in a pot or large bowl with a small amount of water, and squeeze the grated 'copra' with your cleanly washed hands. Use a strainer to separate out the grated coconut flesh. Repeat this process by adding a small amount of water and expressing the milk three or four times, collecting the juice until not much more milk can be extracted. An average sized coconut can make about three cups of coconut milk and a large one about four cups. The harder you squeeze, the richer the milk will be.

CANNED COCONUT MILK OR CREAM:
When purchasing canned coconut milk or cream it is important to read the labels, as the names can be confusing. Do not get fooled into thinking that low-fat coconut milk is better; we are looking for flavor, and the flavor is in the fat. In most recipes, the fat in the coconut cream is replacing oil or butter that would have otherwise been used.

Look for cans of coconut cream with 20 grams or more fat per ½ cup serving (giving about three servings in a 13 to 14 ounce can). Brands vary greatly in their quality, so you may want to try out a selection of available brands to find the one with the best flavor. I have had the best luck with canned coconut cream from Thailand purchased in Asian markets. Coconut powder for preparing coconut cream is available and has a very good flavor.

Coconut water and coconut oil are sometimes promoted for their health benefits. Coconut oil is mostly medium chain fatty acids that are more easily digested, less dangerous for the heart and do not promote inflammation. Coconut fat may not promote abdominal obesity as much as other fats[2], may raise HDL (good) cholesterol levels[3], and coconut milk may have antidiabetic effects[4].

REPLACING COW MILK WITH COCONUT MILK:

Most adults have a limited capacity to digest the natural sugar in milk, lactose. In some people, lactose intolerance is severe and excess dietary lactose will cause "meteorism"; bloating, cramping, gassiness and sometimes diarrhea. Both adults and children can be sensitive or have allergies to the proteins in milk. Therefore is it helpful to have a substitute for cooking without cow's milk.

NOTE: Coconut cream powders often include casein as an ingredient, a protein from cow's milk. Individuals with allergy or sensitivity to cow's milk need to check the labels.

This book includes several recipes where coconut cream has been used to replace cow's milk. These include a coconut flan, coconut carrot cake, and coconut orange smoothie. Don't be afraid to experiment and invent.

Bija and Saffron

Bija, also known as Annatto or Achiote, comes from the seed of *Bixa orellana*. The Taíno word for Annatto was bija, or bixa and this name is still used in the Caribbean. The name Achiote was used by the Aztecs and is used in Mexico.

Although now used to color and flavor food, native peoples in South America originally used it for body paint and traditional medicines. Annatto is used in Caribbean cooking, to give foods a yellow to red color. Annatto is in common use as a natural yellow to red food colorant, to color cheese, butter, margarine, ice cream, microwave popcorn and other foods found in the market.

HEALTH EFFECTS: Although a natural coloring, annatto is one of the most allergenic food colorings. It has been documented as a cause of urticaria, irritable bowel syndrome and anaphylaxis in the medical literature; head banging and other behavioral disturbances in small children have also been attributed to it.

The pigments in annatto are structurally similar to carotenoids, but our bodies cannot use it as vitamin A. Annatto is relatively high in vitamin C, but the amounts of the colorant used are small, and thus it is a trivial source of antioxidants.

In the U.S., this food colorant may be variously listed on food labels as "natural color", bixin, or annatto. In Europe, it is listed as E160b.

Annatto can be prepared from achiote seeds by mixing the seeds with heated oil or in heated water, and straining out the seeds, then using the colored oil or water for cooking. Oil soluble extracts are higher in bixin, which is red. Water-soluble extracts of the seeds are higher in norbixin, which has a more yellow color. When put into highly acidic food, bija can give a pink color.

The seeds may also be ground and the powder used to color or flavor foods, but the ground bija is not commonly used in Caribbean cooking. To prepare bija from seeds in a recipe:

WATER BASED USE: Steep 1 tablespoon of bija seeds in ¼-cup boiling water, stir and allow it to cool. Strain the liquid, discarding the seeds. Reduce the amount of water in the recipe by ¼ cup.

OIL BASED USE: Heat two tablespoons of oil in a small pan and add 1 tablespoon of annatto seeds. Stir in, and when it begins to crackle turn off the heat. Strain the oil, discarding the seeds. Use the oil in the dish. (Larger amounts of annatto oil can be prepared and stored using two parts oil to 1 part annatto seeds.)

Annatto and Saffron are sometimes substituted for each other to give color to foods.

SAFFRON: Saffron is the most expensive spice in general use and costs around a thousand dollars a pound for medium quality saffron while annatto sells for a few dollars a pound. Saffron requires harvesting the stigma of 50,000 to 75,000 crocus flowers to get one pound of saffron. The fragrance of saffron is reminiscent of sweet hay while its flavor is hay like and a bit bitter. It imparts an orange-yellow color to food.

TO SUBSTITUTE BIJA WITH SAFFRON: Use about a ¼ to ½ teaspoon of saffron for 1 tablespoon of bija seeds. Crush the saffron threads between your fingers or in a pestle. Soak the crushed threads in a ¼ cup of liquid for 20-15 minutes, and add the infusion to the recipe. Saffron threads may also be gently toasted in a pan, ground and added to the recipe.

Glossary

Cooking in Water

BLANCHE: Blanching is the process of placing food in boiling water, cooking it just long enough for it to be lightly cooked, removing the food from the hot water and plunging the food into ice water to stop the cooking process. This process is intended to cook food quickly and to retain its color and texture. The food can later be reheated, but it is best to avoid recooking the food. Blanching is also used to prepare vegetables for freezing. Calamari can be blanched to avoid it from getting rubbery from overcooking. Blanching can also be used to cook shrimp that are intended to be served cold.

BOIL: Boiling refers to cooking in water heated to 100°C (212°F) where the water is bubbling forcefully. Use to reduce sauces (evaporation of the liquid helps to thicken). The boiling motion helps mix the food some. Add pasta or vegetables to boiling water to cook them quickly and avoid them getting mushy, and to retain the color of the vegetables. Remove these foods from the water as soon as they are cooked.

BRAISE: Braising is cooking in a small amount of liquid. That liquid can be water, oil, or other liquid such as juice. Usually, the food must be stirred to avoid sticking to the pan while braising.

POACH: The process of poaching is to place the food in cool water in a pot and place it on the heat until the water reaches a simmer. Poaching may be used for small pieces of fish. Poaching can also be done in milk, wine, or broth. Poaching is generally used for delicate foods that cook very quickly.

PRESSURE COOKING: A pressure cooker is a sealed cooking vessel that allows food to be boiled or steamed at a pressure above atmospheric pressure, allowing a higher cooking temperature, and thus a shorter cooking time. Most pressure cookers add 15 PSI of pressure and raise the boiling temperature to 121°C (250°F). For example, dried beans that might take 45 minutes to cook at atmospheric boiling temperature may be cooked in only 15 minutes in a pressure cooker, saving time, leaking less heat, and reducing energy use.

SIMMER: Water simmers from about 82°C to 93°C (180°F to 200° F). Simmering is useful for cooking fish and other delicate foods to keep them from breaking up, and for meat to avoid it getting tough (boiling meat will cause it to get tough). Simmering helps to release fats for separation. Simmering also helps conserve flavors that are more volatile and conserves energy. It is often easier to allow the water to come to a boil, and then lowering the heat to a point where there is only gentle and small bubble formation when simmering food. At a low simmer, there are small bubbles, but not much surface motion. A higher simmer will have small bubbles breaking the surface. A low simmer would be around 185° F at sea level.

STEAM: Steaming is used more frequently for cooking vegetables and other foods that cook quickly. Steaming refers to heating a very small amount of water in a closed pot, where food is not immersed in the water but is rather exposed to the hot vapor produced by the boiling water. This method prevents the leaching of nutrients from the food into the water. A steaming tray is usually used to elevate the food out of the boiling water. Fish and seafood can be steamed.

Cutting Terms

DICED: Dicing refers to cutting ingredients into approximate cubes. Typically dicing is understood to mean cutting into blocks about the size of playing dice; that are 16 mm on a side (about 2/3 of an inch). Large dicing would be about ¾ inch on a side, Medium about ½ inches on a side and small dicing about ¼ inch on a side. Mincing is even more finely chopped, usually less than 1/8 inch.

MINCED: Food is finely diced – 1/8 inch or smaller.

SLICED: Food cut along its axis, often forming rings or disks; onions, peppers, garlic potatoes, carrots.

QUARTERED AND SLICED: This method is used for onions to produce rings that are cut into small lengths. Cut lengthwise (root to stem) into halves and place the halves face down on the flat side. Slice again up to, but not through the root. Holding the halves together, slice the onion with narrow cuts along the other axis. This produces strips of onion of various lengths. For shorter strips, use two or three lengthwise cuts in place of one.

Elevation:

Water boils at 212°F (100°C) at sea level and simmers at about 180 to 195°F (or about 82° - 90°C). As elevation increases, the air pressure falls, and thus the vapor pressure falls, and so does the boiling point. Thus, water boils at a lower temperature at higher elevations. When baking at higher elevations a higher temperature or longer cooking time may be required.

Many of the recipes in this book call for cooking at a simmering temperature.

Here are some ways to estimate the approximate boiling temperature at different elevations that are work well for up to about 10,000 feet:

- Boiling temperature falls about 2° F for every 1000 feet of elevation
- Boiling temperature falls about 1° C for every 1000 feet of elevation
- Boiling temperature falls about 2° F for every 300 meters of elevation
- Boiling temperature falls about 1° C for every 300 meters of elevation

Thus around Denver, at an elevation of 5000 feet, the boiling temperature is about 202°F (95°C). Thus in Denver, a recipe that calls for a low simmer would require a high simmer, and a recipe that calls for a high simmer might require boiling temperature. The choice to boil also should take into consideration the effect of the boiling motion that may agitate and break up tender foods.

Canned Goods

Several recipes in this book use canned ingredients while others allow for substitution using canned goods. However, cans come in different sizes. Imported ingredients may be in metric based cans. Also, many foods are marked by weight, and thus density affects that; beans are denser than coconut cream and weigh more for a given volume. No worry though, except for baking, minor differences should be close enough for country cooking. In baked recipes, (such a coconut carrot cake) volume is used in place of calling for "a can" of coconut cream.

The chart below gives some can sizes used in this book to help get amounts correct.

Can Size	Approximate Volume	Approximate Cups	Typical Use
6Z	6 oz.	¾ cup	Frozen O.J.
No. 300	12 oz.	1½ cups	Evaporated Milk
No. 1 Tall Can	14 oz.	1¾ cups	Coconut Milk
No. 1 Tall Can	16 oz.	2 cups	Beans, tomatoes
No. 2 can	20 oz.	2½ cups	Beans
No. 2.5 can	30 oz.	3¾ cups	Whole tomatoes

Health or Obesity

People who go out of their way to learn new ways to prepare food usually do so because they love good food. But what constitutes good? We believe that food should be and can be delicious and healthful and make you feel good after the meal.

As a physician, board-certified in preventive medicine, the focus of my research and medical practice has been disease prevention through nutrition. Most of the world's population is in a health crisis because of our diets. Americans, Europeans and Asians who have adopted the Western diet are having alarmingly high rates of obesity, diabetes, heart disease, and depression and arthritis. Thus, the relation of diet and obesity is a real concern to most people. There are hundreds of diet plans, most have no long-term health benefits, and many are simply dangerous. Some work, but rob the pleasure from life.

First, if you are a bit overweight, why sweat it? What is the big deal? Being overweight does not shorten life span. Overweight may not look great in a bikini, but most adults don't look good in one anyway.

If you are obese, (a body mass index over 30) you are at risk of diabetes, atherosclerosis, heart attacks, strokes, arthritis, and probably do not feel well. A lifestyle change is in order. Body mass index can be calculated as weight in kilograms / (height in meters)^2. A better measure is your waist circumference. A healthy waist circumference is less than 36" for a man and 34" for a woman. If your waist is more than 40½ inches around for a man, or more than 38½ inches for a woman, then you are at increased disease risk.

Very few people in the Puerto Rico, Cuba, and the Dominican Republic were obese when they ate the traditional foods presented in this book, but when they started to eat like Americans, they quickly started gaining weight. To maintain a healthy weight, eat real food, and a variety of foods.

Most of the real foods are found on the inside wall of the grocery store; fruits, vegetables, dairy, seafood, and meat. They are there because they need to be kept cooler to stay fresh. If real food is good, then what are the fake foods that you should avoid? Fake foods include highly processed foods with low nutritional value. Two clear examples are potato chips and colas.

1. The best formula *for gaining weight* is meals that combine large amounts of fructose and n-6 fats such as linoleic acid. Excess fructose and linoleic acid are the two dietary components that are most responsible for obesity. Both promote inflammation.

An example is a juicy burger, extra large coke (both made with high fructose corn syrup) and fries. The cola makers add salt to the drink making you thirstier, so you drink more along with the salt on the fries or chips. It would take eating a banana, two oranges and a cup of strawberries to get close to the fructose in a 16-ounce cola (25 – 30 grams). When was the last time you tried that in one sitting and chasing it down with a couple tablespoons of lard? Fruits have antioxidants, vitamins, fiber and other nutritious factors; colas have chemicals.

A typical hamburger contains twice the calories from fat as it does from protein, and contains more than a tablespoon of fat. Add a large order of fries and add two more tablespoons of fat.

A high fructose diet alone causes weight gain. Adding fat to a high fructose meal makes it much worse. Fructose helps trigger insulin resistance, which too often progresses to diabetes. High fructose corn syrup (HFCS) is less expensive than sugar, so it is used in many processed foods. HFCS is also used as a food preservative to extend the shelf life of many packaged foods and to soften foods.

2. Fructose is a natural sugar found in fruit, how could it be bad? Fructose is limited in a natural diet, and should be thought of as a hibernation food. In nature, it is available mostly in the fall of the year and is useful for gaining weight to help survival over the lean winter months when there was not enough food.

The most successful weight loss study for teenagers simply eliminated sweet drinks.

3. Fruit and vegetables have fiber: Fiber is slowly broken down in the gut making short chain fatty

acids that are important fuels for your brain and for the large intestine. This means that dietary fiber keeps us from getting hungry as quickly, so we eat less. Fiber also serves as a prebiotic supporting the growth of helpful bacteria in the gut and decreases the growth of intestinal bacteria that promote inflammation and that increase the appetite.

Most fruit juice does not have fiber. Avoid fruit juices where the pulp has been removed. Smoothies that contain the whole fruit have the fiber that helps with a healthy diet, but still it is better to eat rather than drink your fruit. Processed foods usually have little fiber, and are easy to eat and overeat. Whole grains contain fiber that is removed to make white flour, white pasta, and white bread.

4. Drink water. Keep a pitcher of cool water in your refrigerator. In most cities, tap water is as clean and safe as bottled water while bottled water often costs more per gallon than gasoline! Water tastes better cool, a reason why people think that bottled water tastes better – they drink it cold. We have a charcoal filter system for drinking water in our home. It costs only a couple of dollars a month to maintain and supplies great water for cooking and drinking.

5. Drink milk, if you are lactose tolerant. Drinking milk causes weight loss. Drinking whole milk does not cause less weight loss than skim milk. Milk from grass fed cows is best.

6. Stay away from trans fats – they cause weight gain. Trans fats (hydrogenated fats) are used to make shortening and to increase the shelf life of food and are common in processed foods. *Trans fats look like food, and taste like food, but act more like poison.* When cooking oils are processed, some of the fats become trans fats. Fatty fast foods and processed foods often contain trans fats. The body lacks enzymes to break down trans fats, so once absorbed they stay put.

7. Avoid excessive polyunsaturated N-6 fats (corn, sunflower, safflower oils). Your body needs less than a teaspoon a day of this type of fat and more is not helpful. *Obesity is an inflammatory disease.* Consuming more than about 5 grams of n-6 fatty acids a day increases inflammation. Inflammation promotes weight gain by telling your brain to ignore hormonal signals from the fat cells that they are full. The recipes in this book mostly call for extra virgin olive oil, because it has health benefits and is low in n-6 fatty acids. See section "About Oil".

8. Eat healthy animals raised in natural conditions. Cattle's natural diet is grass. When cattle eat grass, they have high levels of n-3 fatty acids, but corn fed beef have very low levels of n-3 fats and high levels of n-6 fats. The same is true with corn fed chickens and their eggs. Feedlot (corn fed) beef cattle go to market at less than a year of age. The feedlot diet is so unhealthy that cattle become sick and cannot survive a full year on that diet. When people eat feedlot beef, the fat is mainly n-6 fats that promote inflammation. Inflammation promotes obesity. Sheep, goats and venison are usually raised on grass and have a much healthier n-3 to n-6 ratios than feedlot animals.

It is not eating meat that causes obesity, but how the animal the meat came from was fed. For most people this means they need to eat less meat to avoid weight gain. Avoid corn fed animals fat if you do eat meat. Also, avoid fatty meats.

100 grams of raw ground beef, (30% fat, and 70% lean meat) contains 14 grams of protein and 30 grams of fat. That gives 270 fat calories, and 62 protein calories.

Meat	Percent lean meat	Percent fat by weight	Percent of calories from fat
Ground beef	70	30	60
Lean ground beef	75	25	59
Ground chuck	80	20	57
Ground round	85	15	54
Ground sirloin	90	10	47

Ground meat forms higher amounts of carcinogens when cooked at grilling temperatures than whole pieces of meat; avoid it or cook it correctly (See page 78).

9. Fish contains mostly n-3 fats that are healthy for the heart and do not promote weight gain. Small fry (small fish, shrimp, scallops, and shellfish) are healthier to eat than big fish, more environmentally sustainable and contain less mercury and other toxins. The best fish in terms of healthy n-3 fats and low mercury are salmon, oysters, clams shrimp, and tilapia. Second best are mackerel, herring, sardines, trout and ocean perch, about in that order.

10. Eat foods that support CCK release. The hormone CCK helps promote satiety, the sense that we have had enough to eat. Certain proteins found in boiled and baked potatoes, peas, and soybeans trigger CCK release. Slow cooked meats have more free amino acids (see About Meat, page 75) that also trigger CCK release and promote satiety. Many types of aged cheese contain compounds that trigger CCK release, as do long-chain unsaturated fats.

Hydrogenated (and trans) fats are often used in the fast food industry and in packaged foods as they give a long shelf life and resist smoking when heated. These hydrogenated fats do not stimulate CCK release or aid in satiation but do add calories. Sweets and carbohydrates also do not stimulate CCK release and thus do not promote satiation.

Eating foods that promote the release of CCK in the early part of a meal will help promote a sense of satiation earlier, and make it less likely to overeat. Foods that are well cooked, especially slow cooked proteins, promote satiety better. Foods that increase CCK output may be eaten early in the meal. Examples include a salad with olive oil (to supply unsaturated fatty acids), or with walnuts (to supply long chain n-3 fatty acids). Boiled potatoes rather than fried, and stewed meats rather than grilled or fried increase output of CCK. Appetizers with small amounts of fermented foods such as aged cheese and capers may also help with satiation, and thus limit the amount of food eaten at a meal.

11. Take the time to enjoy meals: Relaxed, slow eating give more satiety and encourages lower intakes. Give time for the CCK to work.

12. Don't count calories! Going hungry makes things worse. The hormone ghrelin is released when blood sugar is low. This acts as a signal for the brain to eat and increases the appetite for sweet, fatty, and palatable foods that quickly increase blood sugar. These foods have less effect on satiation and are more likely to lead to storage of fat.

Skipping meals or waiting until feeling famished to eat is likely to induce consumption of junk food and increasing caloric intake. If you wait to eat until you are ravenous, it encourages rapid eating and desire for palatable sweet and fatty pleasure foods, which are easily consumed in high amounts.

13 Be Prepared. Have healthy snacks ready, such as fruits, veggies (carrots, celery and almond butter) available for when you have the urge to snack. If you don't put the junk food in your cart in the store, it won't be there to tempt you at home. Never leave a bowl of candy or cookies out - it is too easy to grab some every time you walk by. Don't snack out of a container; take the amount you think you want to eat and put it in a bowl or on a plate. That way you see how much you are eating.

14. If you drink alcohol, a glass of red wine a day will help with weight loss for most adults while beer and spirits cause weight gain. The beer belly is not a myth. Moderate red wine intake is associated with lower risk of heart disease and obesity, but saving it up and drinking a week's supply for the weekends does not. The upper daily limit for healthy red wine intake is one ounce for every 30 pounds ideal body weight.

15. About one in four women gain weight (and lose bone mass) from the use of birth control injections. A small percentage of women also gain weight from the use of birth control pills. Women who gain weight using birth control might consider changing medication or getting an IUD. Women who gain weight on the injection average a 24-pound weight gain over 3 years. (Half of these women gained more.) These are 24 pounds that are almost impossible to diet off because the medication has given your body new instructions for what is normal; that new normal is extra fat.

16. Be honest with yourself. Most overweight people did not gain the weight in 4 weeks, why would you trust a diet that promises to make it go away in that much time? That is enough time to get dehydrated, and maybe to make the fat cells depleted enough that they increase hormonal demand to the brain for food. You are unlikely to lose weight by making yourself feel hungry, but you are likely to make yourself depressed and stressed.

17. *Lack of physical activity is 10 times more dangerous to your health than being obese.* Obese individuals are 30 percent more likely to have a heart attack. Sedentary people are 300 percent more likely to have a heart attack. This includes skinny people. Get outside and walk. Exercise makes people feel and think better. Even 15 minutes of vigorous exercise, that gets you breathing hard and your heart rate up three times a week is enough to make a change in your metabolism.

18. Sunshine makes you feel better by making vitamin D. Unfortunately, this does not work in the cold months if you live north of Atlanta or Los Angeles. That far north, the sun is not intense enough during the winter months to make vitamin D, especially if you have dark skin. If you can't be in the sun, take a vitamin D supplement. *If you were in the Caribbean having fun, your body would make about 10,000 units of vitamin D in 15 minutes of sunshine.* The 400 units in a multi-vitamin pill are not enough. Taking 4000 to 6000 units of vitamin D_3 a day, during the cold winter months in the north, helps people feel better.

19. Turn off the TV and hang out with friends, and skip the late show and get plenty of sleep at night. Sleep deficits increase the desire for sweet and fatty foods that promote obesity, and insufficient sleep at night is associated with inflammation and weight gain. Siestas are great but don't prevent the weight gain that a full night's sleep does.

20. Take time to be happy and enjoy life. A year of chronic stress can cause the equivalent of six years of normal aging while meditation and having a purpose in life can repair the effect of aging on the DNA[5]. Chronic physical or psychological stress causes hormones to be released from the brain, which cause fat to be stored as a spare tire at the waistline. This metabolically active fat produces inflammatory hormones that are involved in the development of ischemic heart disease. Communicate (listen and relate) with those you love. Forgive. Talking helps us understand what is going on inside of us. Set time aside for having fun.

21. Avoid foods that you have food sensitivity or allergic reactions to. They cause inflammation, and inflammation causes obesity.

22. Serve and eat fresh cut fruit as a part of every meal as is done in Caribbean cuisine.

Migraine Foods:

Certain foods can trigger migraine headaches, but most do it inconsistently – making it hard to determine where to place the blame. In some cases, foods trigger a migraine through interactions with other foods or with alcohol. Since there is often not a single factor triggering the headache, it is often difficult to figure out what food caused the problem.

Immune reactions to foods (food sensitivities) are a common trigger of migraines. These are individualized reactions and can occur with almost any food that an individual reacts to. IgG testing for food sensitivities can be helpful to identify these triggers.

Fermented products, including aged cheeses, may have a large variation of the amount of migraine causing bioamines present. The amount produced depends on which strains of yeast and bacteria are present in the fermentation process). Fermented foods or beverages that cause no problem most of the time might trigger migraines in a different batch. Alcohol can block the degradation of these bioamines by enzymes in the intestine, so having wine with a meal may increase the chances for a headache the next day, when the same amount of the same wine may not cause any problems when consumed with different foods.

Tropical fruits seem to be especially good triggers for migraines. With foods that trigger migraines because of bioamines, the amount consumed is important. Among the foods on the list of tropical fruits that can trigger migraines from the National Headache Foundation in Chicago are:

- Avocado
- Banana (and Plantains)
- Citrus Fruit (Oranges, Grapefruit, Lemon, Limes)
- Papaya
- Passion Fruit
- Pineapple

Coffee and cocoa (chocolate) are a couple of other tropical favorites that make the list. Dried banana chips seem to be especially potent.

A more extensive list of foods that trigger migraine headaches is available at:

www.headaches.org/pdf/Diet.pdf

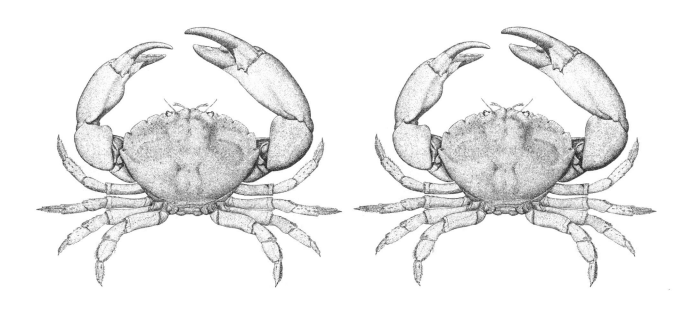

Breakfast-Desayuno

Avena Caliente

OATMEAL GRUEL DESSERT; OATMEAL ATOLE

Gruel: the name conjures squalid images of malnourished orphans in rags, or of dank rations doled out to political prisoners in dungeons. This comfort gruel, however, could be used to sweeten up little cherubs. It is high in protein and calories. It is too liquid to be considered porridge, being more similar to the Mesoamerican atole. It is just as often eaten as an evening meal or dessert as it is for breakfast in the Dominican Republic. It can be eaten with a spoon or drunk hot from a mug.

INGREDIENTS:
1 cinnamon stick (3")
1 ½ cups of water
½ cup oatmeal (quick rolled oats)
1 cup evaporated milk (or substitute whole milk)
¼ cup light brown sugar
A pinch of salt

PREPARATION: Place the water in a saucepan with the cinnamon stick, and bring it to a boil for a couple of minutes. Add the oatmeal, and allow it to return to a boil for about 4 minutes, stirring occasionally. When the oatmeal begins to thicken, add the milk, brown sugar, and salt. Continue heating the gruel, stirring frequently. Cook it for an additional five minutes after it returns to a simmer. Remove the cinnamon stick. Serve it hot, after allowing it to cool for several minutes to a safe eating temperature.

Insufficient salt will cause it to be sweet but bland; too much, and it will be salty. The correct amount is about 1/2 of an eighth of a teaspoon.

For a less calorically intense version, use low fat evaporated milk or fresh milk.

If using whole milk, a tablespoon of butter stirred in just as the gruel is removed from the heat will add richness.

Harina Negrito

Semolina Porridge; "Cream of Wheat"

"Harina el Negrito" is the brand name for semolina found in the Dominican Republic. It is made from wheat, minus the bran and some of the germ. In the U.S., semolina is sold under various trade names such as Cream of Wheat, Farina, and Malt-o-meal.

INGREDIENTS:

3 tablespoons semolina
2 cups milk
1 six-inch cinnamon stick
2 tablespoons sugar

A pinch of salt
1/4 teaspoon vanilla extract

PREPARATION: Warm the milk in a saucepan with the cinnamon over medium heat. After the milk has warmed, slowly sprinkle in the semolina while stirring continuously to avoid forming lumps of semolina. Add the sugar and salt. Stir continuously as it comes to a simmer and while it cooks for ten minutes. Turn the heat off, stir in the vanilla, and serve while warm.

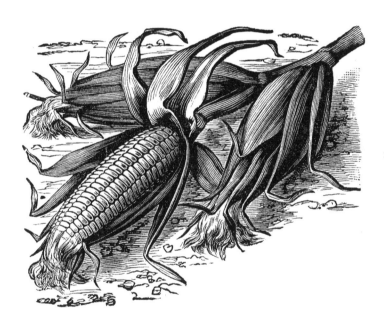

Harina de Maíz

Cornmeal Porridge

INGREDIENTS:

14 oz. can coconut cream
1 cup water
2 cups milk
1 six-inch cinnamon stick
½ cup sugar
¾ cup corn meal
1 tablespoon butter
¼ teaspoon vanilla extract

PREPARATION: In a deep saucepan add the coconut cream, water, milk, sugar and cinnamon stick. Cook over medium-low heat.

Slowly sprinkle in the cornmeal while stirring to avoid forming lumps of corn meal. Stir continuously, as it comes to a simmer, and let it cook for 20 minutes, stirring continuously. Turn the heat off, stir in the vanilla and butter. Serve while still hot.

About Eggs:

Fresh eggs have the best flavor, texture and nutritional value and are easiest to cook with. With fresh eggs, the yolk is firm and has a dome shape. As eggs get older, the membrane of the yolk thins and breaks more easily and the yolk will be flatter in the pan. This thinned membrane will make it more difficult to separate the yolk from the egg white without breaking for recipes such as flan. The egg white also thins and becomes runny and more difficult to whip. Older eggs are more likely to have the yolk turn greenish, as can occur with hard-boiled eggs.

Eggs are marked with "best by" dates or a number that indicates the day of the year that the eggs were packed so that January 1st would be one and December 31st would be 365. The expiration date for eggs kept under refrigeration is usually 44 days (6 weeks 2 days) after the packing date. Try to purchase eggs that have at least 4 weeks remaining before the "best by" date.

When buying eggs open the carton and inspect them to make sure that none of them is cracked. Even doing this, there may be cracks you cannot see. Eggs are clean when they are laid, but often get contaminated by the hen's feet or in the nest. Thus, any crack in the egg can allow *Salmonella* bacteria to grow in the egg.

Eggs have about 70,000 pores that allow for loss of water. As this occurs, the air bubble at the fatter end of the egg enlarges from being nearly invisible in a newly laid egg. Eggs that are not fresh have a large air bubble and old eggs that float in water should be discarded. These pores also allow eggs to take up air along with odors from the refrigerator or from whatever area in which they are stored, and this can give an off taste to the eggs. Eggs should be stored in their cartons to protect them from odors and from breakage. Eggs will stay fresh longest by keeping them in the coolest area of the refrigerator, usually on the lowest shelf towards the back. Store the eggs with the pointed end down and so that the air bubble is up.

Eggs turn solid when the egg proteins get denatured. This occurs in egg whites at around 150°F (66°C) and in egg yolks at about 158°F (70°C).

A temperature of 160°F (71°C) is high enough to kill the bacteria associated with contaminated eggs which can cause disease. A soft-boiled egg or an egg with a runny center has not been heated enough to denature the yolk proteins or to kill these bacteria. Pregnant women and infants and other immune compromised individuals should avoid soft-boiled eggs or eggs cooked with a runny yolk. Cracked, but otherwise good eggs should only be used for making baked foods to avoid risk from *Salmonella*.

There is not much reason to heat an egg any hotter than the temperature needed to kill salmonella. Temperatures over 180°F (82°C) will make the egg firmer, but temperatures too high overcook eggs making them tough and rubbery. Brown lacing on a cooked egg indicates that it was cooked either at too high a temperature or for too long.

You can make much better "hard boiled eggs" by not boiling them, as cooking them at boiling temperature makes them rubbery and more likely for the yolk to turn green. Instructions for hard cooked eggs are given on page 118.

Butter is about 16% water, and thus when heated to simmering temperature of about 185°F (85°C) tiny bubbles begin to form. Thus, butter is an excellent indicator to tell when the cooking pan is the perfect temperature for cooking eggs. Big bubbles in the butter indicate that the temperature is over boiling temperature, too hot to cook eggs. Smoking butter indicates that the pan is over 300°F, and much too hot for cooking eggs. Browned eggs may indicate the formation of carcinogenic heterocyclic amine compounds.

Huevos No Fritos

EGGS SUNNY INSIDE

Sadly, I rarely saw anyone cook eggs at home. Instead, they destroyed them. The usual torture technique used was to crack an egg into a pan of hot oil and let it blister there until it was bubbly, brown, rubbery and repulsive. When I returned to visit the Dominican Republic after living in the United States, my cousins begged me to make them eggs every morning, and then to leave my skillet and to leave with them the secret ingredient for cooking great eggs.

INGREDIENTS:
1 teaspoon butter per egg
2 eggs
Patience

PREPARATION: Place a cool well-seasoned cast iron skillet on the stove and turn the heat to medium-high. A sauté pan with a thick base also works. Place the butter in the pan and as it melts, spread the butter around to cover the inside of the pan evenly. As soon as tiny bubbles begin to appear in the butter turn the heat to medium-low, and crack the 2 eggs into the pan overlapping each other, and cover with a glass lid.

In about 2 minutes, the egg whites will be solid and opaque. Slide a spatula under the edges all the way around to make sure they are free, and then slide halfway under the eggs, and fold one-half over on top of the other side. Cover and wait about 45 seconds. Slide the spatula under the eggs and make sure they are free from the pan, and then gently flip the eggs over. Turn off the heat, cover, and allow the eggs to cook for another 45 seconds. Move the eggs onto a plate for serving with tostones, in a chimichurri, or as you like. Actual cooking time will depend on temperature and on how solid or runny you would like the yolks to be.

Huevos Salseros

EGGS IN SALSA

INGREDIENTS:

½ teaspoon olive oil
1 cup medium-hot salsa*
4 large eggs
½ cup shredded cheese (i.e.; jack, cheddar, etc.)

PREPARATION: Place the oil in a sauté pan, and spread the oil so that it coats the inside of the pan. Add the salsa. Place the pan over medium heat and cover. When the salsa begins to simmer, lower the heat to medium-low, and crack the eggs into each quarter of the pan, so that they float in the salsa, and then replace the cover.

Cook for about 4 minutes or until the whites have turned opaque, and the yolks are starting to get cloudy. (The goal is to have the yolks still runny when served, so that they can mix with the salsa.) Spread the shredded cheese evenly over the eggs, replace the cover and allow the cheese to melt for one minute with the heat turned off.

Use a spatula to serve onto a plate, separating the eggs between the yolks so that they remain intact until eaten.

Serve with toasted bread and quarter inch thick slices of fresh oranges with the rind left on to add color.

* Salsa Fresca may be used (see page 117).

Huevos con Arenque

EGGS WITH SMOKED HERRING

The combination of dried herring and eggs may seem an implausible combination if you didn't grow up with it, but it is a classic dish.

INGREDIENTS:

3 oz. salted, smoked herring
2 tablespoons olive oil
½ medium red onion; diced
1 clove garlic; sliced thin
¼ red or yellow bell pepper cut into ¼-inch strips
2 ají dulce (or 2 teaspoons Cuban peppers), minced
2 plum tomatoes; diced
4 eggs

PREPARATION: Pull the dried herring into small bits about ¼ inch by 1 inch long, discarding the skin and bones. Place the pieces of herring into a bowl of water. Allow the herring to soak for 10 to 15 minutes to get rid of the excess salt, stirring a couple of times. Then drain off the water.

Heat the oil over medium heat in a 10" sauté pan. Add the onion and sauté it for about 30 seconds, followed by the garlic for another 30 seconds. Next, add the peppers and tomatoes. Cover the pan and allow the vegetables to steam for about 45 seconds. The tomatoes should begin to cook into a sauce. Now, add the herring to the mix, cover and allow it all to sauté together for about 2 more minutes. Adjust the temperature so that the sauce cooks at a low simmer. Add a tablespoon of water if it starts to get dry. If it is boiling hard, lower the heat.

Now crack the eggs into the sauce and cover, allowing the eggs to steam until the egg whites are completely cooked. The yolks can be left a bit runny, or cooked until barely solid. This should take about 3 minutes.

Use a spatula to serve the eggs lying in the sauce with the herring. This recipe makes two servings.

Revoltillo de Huevos

EGGS WITH VEGGIES

INGREDIENTS:

1 tablespoon olive oil
2 tablespoons butter
1 small onion quartered and sliced
1 clove garlic, minced
1 small Cuban pepper, diced
3 plum tomatoes, sliced
2 tablespoons water
¾ teaspoon salt
4 eggs

PREPARATION: Place the oil and butter in a sauté pan over medium-low heat. Sauté the garlic until it is light golden brown. Add the onions and Cuban pepper, and sauté for 3 minutes. Add the tomatoes, salt, and water. Cover the pan, allowing the sauce to stew for 2 to 3 minutes. Stir, replace the cover, and allow it to steam for another 2 minutes.

Add the eggs and cover the pan, allowing the eggs to poach in the sauce you have made. After about 3 minutes use a fork to cut the eggs in the sauce into ¾ inch pieces and stir them into the sauce. Allow the eggs to simmer for another minute.

Serve with boiled green bananas or plantains.

This recipe makes three servings. Preparation time is about 20 minutes.

Torta de Huevo

EGG OMELET

INGREDIENTS:

1 clove garlic; finely minced
½ small onion; finely chopped
1/8 teaspoon salt
1 sweet pepper (ají dulce*); minced
4 large eggs
½ tablespoon butter

PREPARATION: Place all ingredients listed above (except the butter) in a bowl, mix together, and beat the eggs.

Heat a cast iron pan with the butter in it over medium heat. As soon as the butter has tiny bubbles, lower the heat to medium-low. When the butter is completely melted, spread it around so that it coats the pan and then pour in the eggs with the vegetables. Cover (preferably with a glass lid so that you can watch it cook.) If the temperature is right, the omelet should dry on top without toasting the bottom of the eggs. Lift an edge of the eggs to see the progress. If you see that the bottom is dry, and the top is still wet, you may need to flip the omelet over.

The trick to cooking eggs is getting the temperature correct, low enough that they do not brown on the bottom, hot enough that they cook.

* AJÍ DULCE: Throughout this book ají dulce has been substituted in most recipes with Anaheim of Cuban peppers, as ají dulce are hard to find in the U.S. For this recipe, a better substitute is one tablespoon of minced ripe red bell peppers.

Soups and Stews
Sopas y Sancochos

Asopao de Camarones

SHRIMP STEW

An "Asopao" is a thick soup with vegetables and rice. It is often served as the main dish of a meal, especially during the cooler parts of the year.

INGREDIENTS:

2 pounds fresh shrimp (heads off)
1 teaspoon salt
3 cups water
2 tablespoons olive oil
5 cloves garlic, sliced
1 small red onion; diced
2 plum tomatoes; diced
1½ teaspoons salt
½ cup rice
3 cups water
1 cup butternut squash; diced into ½ inch cubes
1 large carrot, sliced into ¼ inch thick rounds
1 cup diced celery

PREPARATION: Broth: Peel the shrimp. If the shrimp are large, cut them into bite-size pieces, and then put them in the refrigerator. Place the shrimp skins in a pot with 3 cups of water and one teaspoon of salt. Bring it to a boil, cover, and allow it to simmer for 10 minutes. This makes about 2 1/3 cups of broth.

Place the oil in a 4-quart pot. Over medium heat, sauté the garlic for 30 seconds. Add the onion and sauté for 1 minute. Add the tomatoes and cook for a few minutes until the tomatoes form a sauce. Add 1½ teaspoons of salt and the rice and sauté it for 1 minute. Using a strainer, add the broth to the saucepan with the rice. Discard the shrimp skin. Add 3 more cups of water. Bring the soup to a boil, and then lower the heat to a simmer for 6 minutes. Add the squash, carrots and celery and cook for 5 more minutes. Add the shrimp and cook for 4 more minutes, and then turn off the heat and cover. Allow the soup to sit for about 3 minutes before serving.

Garnish with grated aged cheese and/or small sprigs of watercress for extra flavor.

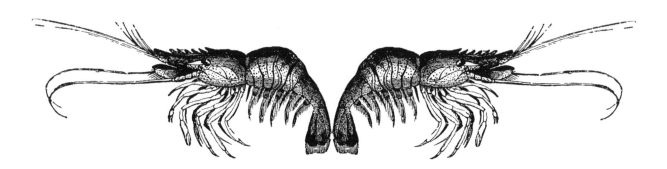

Ensalada y Sopa Jardinera

GARDEN SALAD AND SOUP

INGREDIENTS:

3 medium tomatoes
2 celery stalks
1 cucumber
3 scallions
1 jalapeño pepper
½ teaspoon fresh oregano minced
   or ¼ teaspoon dried oregano
¼ teaspoon salt
¼ cup white merlot

PREPARATION OF THE SALAD: Cut the tomatoes in half, top from bottom and then cut each half into 8 wedges. Slice the celery into ¼ inch lengths. Peel the cucumber and slice it into 8-inch slices. Cut the scallion greens into half-inch sections, and slice the white section of the root finely. Cut the jalapeño open, remove and discard the seed cluster and membranes. Mince the rest of the pepper.

Mix all the ingredients together in a glass or ceramic container with a lid that will not react with the acids of the vegetables, and that can be placed in a microwave. At this point, you have made the Garden Salad, and it is ready to eat.

SOUP: Place the Garden Salad (or leftovers) in the refrigerator overnight. The vegetables will weep overnight and form a tart broth. Place the container in the microwave (covered) for about 2 minutes. It should get hot enough to lightly steam the vegetables and heat the liquid. Serve hot as a refreshing tart soup for an appetizer.

Asopao de Pollo

CHICKEN STEW

INGREDIENTS:

1½ pounds of chicken (legs, wings, thighs, or breasts with bones)
2 tablespoons olive oil
1 tablespoon brown sugar
5 cloves garlic, thinly sliced
2 plum tomatoes, cut into chunks
½ medium red onion, quartered and sliced
1 small Cuban or Anaheim pepper
1 teaspoon salt
1 cup rice
2 vegetable bouillon cubes (5 grams each)
6 cups water
2 carrots into ½ inch wheels
½ cup sliced celery
¼ cup cilantro in small sprigs

PREPARATION: Remove the skin from the thigh, breast, and legs, and feed it to the dog, pigs or InSinkErator. Heat the oil in a large (4-6 quart) saucepan over medium heat. Add the brown sugar, when it begins to bubble add the chicken. Sauté the chicken for about 4 minutes, turning the chicken so that it browns in the sugar. Add the garlic and let it sauté until golden, add the tomatoes, onions, pepper and salt, and sauté everything together for another minute. Cover and cook for another 5 minutes. The captured steam helps form a sauce. Add the bouillon, stirring it to dissolve it, and cover the stew for another 2 minutes.

Add the dry rice and let it simmer in the sauce for one minute. Add the water and carrots. Turn up the heat, and once it begins to boil, lower the heat to medium-low, and allow the stew to simmer for about 20 minutes. The ends of the rice grains should split open.

Add the celery. Cook for another 2 minutes. Serve in a wide, shallow bowl garnished with cilantro leaves.

Makes 4-5 servings.

Asopao de Longaniza

SAUSAGE STEW

Here is another thick and hearty soup; this one made with spicy sausage.

INGREDIENTS:

1 tablespoon olive oil
½ pound sausage
1 large carrot cut into small cubes
1 tablespoon butter
3 cloves garlic sliced lengthwise
2 vegetable bouillon cubes (5 grams each)
¼ cup sliced mushrooms
½ teaspoon saffron
¾ teaspoon salt
4 cups water
½ cup rice
½ cup winter squash, in ½ inch cubes
½ cup diced celery

PREPARATION: Peel the skin from the sausage and discard the skin. Cut the sausage in half along its length and then cut it into half-inch lengths.

Place the oil in a 4-quart pot, and over medium heat sauté the sausage for about 2 minutes, add the carrots and sauté for another minute. Add the butter and the garlic and sauté for one minute. Add the bouillon, mushrooms, and saffron, and sauté them another minute until the mushrooms get dark and soft.

Add the salt and 4 cups of water. Stir in the rice. Bring the soup to a boil, lower the heat to medium-low and cover the pot. Allow the stew to cook at a simmer for 15 minutes. Add the squash and celery and cook for 5 more minutes. Allow it to sit and rest for another few minutes before serving.

Asopao de Longaniza Vegetariano

VEGETARIAN SAUSAGE STEW

The recipe above is quite tasty using vegetarian Italian Sausage (available along with veggie burgers in supermarket freezer sections). Simply substitute the carnivorous form with 8 oz. of veggie sausage.

Sopa de Petit Pois

FRESH PEA SOUP

INGREDIENTS:

2½ cups of green peas (1 pound)
¼ teaspoon dried epazote leaves (optional)
1½ cups water
1 tablespoon olive oil
1 teaspoon butter
4 large cloves of garlic
¼ small onion; finely diced
1½ teaspoons ginger, peeled and finely minced
¼ teaspoon salt
1 6 oz. can of chopped clams
Dash of cayenne
Freshly shaved or grated Parmesan or Romano cheese

PREPARATION: Fresh or frozen peas may be used for this recipe. If using frozen peas, give them a few minutes to thaw. Place the peas, epazote and water in a blender and blend for about 2 minutes until smooth and creamy. In a large saucepan add the oil and butter and heat until the butter begins to sputter. Sauté the garlic, onion, and the ginger until the garlic is golden brown. Add the blended peas, salt and clams with the juice, and raise the heat to bring the soup to a boil, and then lower the heat to a low simmer. Allow the soup to simmer for 10 - 15 minutes, stirring frequently to prevent scalding. Add the cayenne to taste.

Serve with a garnish of shaved or grated hard cheese.

Rancho

Stone Stew

When we want to take a day to relax and enjoy with friends in the Dominican Republic, we love "un día de Campo"; a day in the countryside. Many successful doctors and businessmen in the cities have a small farm just for this purpose, although they justify their farm as a place to grow plantains, mangoes, papayas and other fresh produce for their families. I grew up in a smaller town, and many people including my father and uncles had conucos. Conucos are usually small piece of land (a couple of acres) near town planted with a mix of fruit trees, coconut palms, bananas, plantains, papayas and vegetables, and were used to supplement the family table and income. In the Caribbean, small farmers traditionally live in town and in the mornings would walk to their farms. These small farms are often the site for days off in the country, although the day off may also be used planting or harvesting. These days were still fun.

On a "día de Campo" rather than picnic sandwiches, a hot meal was usually prepared. The traditional meal we prepared was a "Rancho". A rancho is made similar to the Stone Soup from folk tales. We would gather what was available and put it together. If the day was spent at the beach, lake or stream and fishing was done, fish, crab or other seafood would be added. If a chicken could be caught, then it was prepared and added.

Generally we brought along a large kettle, garlic, and salt, and grater to grate the coconut for making coconut cream (see pages 18-19), and a machete. Spoons were optional as these could be made from palm leaf stems. Plates are left at home. Sometimes we would eat out of the kettle, or more often, the contents would be poured steaming hot onto layers of banana leaves, and we would sit around and pick out the pieces we wanted. Shells from the coconuts would serve as bowls.

Typical Gathered Rancho Ingredients:
Green bananas or plantains
Young pumpkin leaves
Taro or Yautia leaves
Young yuca leaves (limited amounts)
Corn on the cob
Coconuts (green ones for drinking water)
Chicken or Fish, cut into serving sized portions.
Tubers: Sweet Potatoes, Yautia (malanga), Taro or Cassava (yuca)
Pumpkin
Pigeon peas or beans
Water
Wood for cooking over

Things Brought Along:
Salt
Garlic
Kettle
Grater
Machete
Matches
Sometimes a piece of salted cod

Directions: Fill the pot half-full with water and place it over the fire. Peel the garlic cloves. Split them in 2 and add them. Clean the meat or fish, and cut it into pieces big enough to eat out of the hand. Cut the plantains, banana, and starchy vegetables into large chunks. Add other ingredients available, and salt to taste. Cover the pot, and bring it all to a boil, stirring occasionally and checking to see when it is done, making sure that it is salted like soup. Cooking time is usually about 45 minutes. If coconut cream is used, it becomes the base for the stew, and much less water is used.

When ready, the stew is poured out onto a bed of fresh cut banana leaves where it cools enough to be eaten either with skewers or moved to another banana leaf used as a plate. Remember that a rancho is about cooperation, sharing, and good times with old friends and with the ones you meet today.

Asopao de Vegetales

VEGETABLE STEW

INGREDIENTS:

2 tablespoons olive oil (or 1 tablespoon butter and
   1 tablespoon olive oil)
½ medium onion, sliced and quartered
6 cloves garlic sliced thin
2 tomatoes, cut into chunks
½ cup rice
1½ teaspoons salt
5 cups of water
2 carrots cut into 1-inch wheels
1 cup of yautia cut into one-inch pieces
1 cup sliced celery
1 cup sweet potato cut into pieces about 1 inch in
diameter
¼ cup of cilantro in small sprigs

PREPARATION: Heat the oil in a large (4-6 quart) pot over medium heat. If using butter use lower heat to avoid burning the butter. Add the onions and sauté them until they become clear. Add the garlic and continue to sauté until the onion and garlic just begin to brown. Add the tomatoes and carrots, stirring frequently, sautéing until a sauce forms. Add the dry rice and cook for one minute. Add the water and salt, turn up the heat and allow the mix to boil for about 10 minutes until the rice starts to split open.

Add the yautia. Cook for another 5 minutes, add the sweet potato and celery and cook for about 5 more minutes until the tubers are cooked. To determine if the tubers are cooked, pass a fork through them to make sure they are soft. Before serving, mix in sprigs of cilantro.

Yautia and sweet potato can be substituted or mixed with potatoes, yuca, ñame or winter squash.

This is a variation of asopao for vegetarians. A more traditional recipe with sausage is given on page 36. Asopao can be made with shrimp, seafood, and chicken.

Asopao de Almeja

CARIBBEAN CLAM CHOWDER

INGREDIENTS:

2 tablespoons olive oil
4 cloves garlic sliced axially
1 cup celery; chopped
1 small red onion; diced
1 small orange bell pepper; diced
3 plum tomatoes; diced
1 large carrot, cut along its length and then cubed
½ cup rice (short grain preferred)
2 cans of diced clams
1 vegetable bouillon cube (5 grams)
5 radishes, sliced
1 zucchini (about ¾ cups sliced)
½ teaspoon salt
1 teaspoon fresh cilantro, chopped
3 cup water

PREPARATION: Place the oil in a large saucepan over medium heat. Add the sliced garlic and cook for about 30 seconds. Lower the heat and add the carrots. Sauté the carrots for a couple of minutes, and then add the celery, onion, bell pepper and tomatoes. Raise the heat back to medium and sauté for 4 minutes. Add the bouillon cube, clams with the juice, and rice. Sauté these ingredients together, allowing the rice to simmer in the sauce for a couple of minutes.

Add the water, salt, radishes, and zucchini, stir together and cover the pan. Once it has begun to boil, lower the heat to a simmer and cook for about 10 minutes. When cooked, the rice grains should be split open.

Allow the soup to cool for a few minutes with the lid on. Serve with a garnish of cilantro and grated hard aged cheese.

Sancocho

COUNTRY STEW

At home, we would use yuca, plantains, rulo, and yautia to make this spicy stew. Here it is adapted to use potatoes and carrots, but if you have the traditional tubers, give them a try.

INGREDIENTS:

1½ pounds of beef short ribs)
8 cloves of garlic, minced
1 small onion; diced
4 ají dulce; minced
3 ají pipí (chili pequín)
1 teaspoon dried oregano
1 teaspoon salt
1 teaspoon vinegar

2 tablespoons olive oil
2 vegetable bouillon cubes (5 grams each)
5 cups water
4 medium potatoes, cut into 1½-inch chunks
2 large carrots; sliced ½ inch thick
1 teaspoon flour
3 teaspoons water

Notes:

PREPARATION: Cut the ribs into separate pieces, and place them in a bowl with the peppers, garlic, onions, vinegar, salt and oregano, and mix it all together so that the spices are evenly distributed over the meat.

Place the oil in a large saucepan and heat over medium heat. When the oil is hot, add the meat, and any spice that remains in the bowl. Cover and allow the meat to steam in its juices for 10 minutes.

Add the vegetable bouillon. Mix the contents of the pan so that it gets covered in the bouillon. Next, add the water. Cover the pot and bring it to a boil, and then lower the heat to medium and cook for 5 minutes.

Add the carrots and potatoes, set to medium heat and cover. After a couple of minutes check the heat and set it to simmer for 15 minutes.

Mix the flour with 3 tablespoons of water in a cup. Slowly stir this into the stew to give it more body, cover and let it simmer for another 5 minutes. Serve with rice and avocado.

Sopa de Oro (Sopa de Calabaza)

Winter Squash Soup

INGREDIENTS:
4 tablespoons butter
2 tablespoons olive oil
12 cloves garlic, minced
1 can minced or chopped clams with juice
4 medium butternut squash
Fresh grated aged hard Parmesan, Romano or
   Asiago cheese
Salt to taste

PREPARATION: Cut the butternut squash at the neck as shown in the picture. Take the necks from 2 of the squash, cut off the stem and peel the necks. Dice the necks into 3/4-inch cubes.

Take the 4 squash bellies and use a paring knife to carefully cut into the seed cavity. Using a small spoon clean out the seeds and fibers, forming a hollow bowl, leaving the wall and skin of the squash intact. Cook the squash bellies with the blossom end down (the opening up). They can be steamed, boiled or heat in a microwave (see below for approximate cooking times). Expect to cook them for about 15 to 30 minutes. They need to be cooked until the flesh is tender but firm enough that the belly holds its shape. Be careful not to pierce the skin when testing to see if sufficiently cooked.

Meanwhile, place the diced squash in a saucepan with a quart of water and simmer for 10 minutes, and then allow it to cool enough to put the squash and water into a blender. Liquefy for one minute and return it to the saucepan.

In a separate pan sauté the garlic in the oil at medium to low heat only until the garlic is light golden brown. Melt in the butter and bouillon cubes, stirring to form a sauce. Add this sauce to the creamed squash, stirring it in. Heat this soup, and allow it to simmer for one minute.

When the squash bellies, are cool enough to handle, use a paring knife to make a series of V-cuts around the upper rim, forming a crown-like pattern along the top edge. Ladle the soup in to fill the belly like a bowl. Garnish with grated or shaved aged hard cheese and basil, rosemary, or sage leaves. It is ready to serve.

To prepare these in advance of a meal, cook the belly slightly less time, so that they are fully cooked, but a bit firmer. The squash, filled with soup, can be reheated in a microwave before serving. Add the garnishes just before serving. The squash belly should be cooked enough so that the flesh wall is relished as part of the meal.

Recommended approximate cooking times for the belly:

SIMMER: Bring to a boil, then turn the heat down and allow it to a simmer for 20 minutes. Then drain off the water and allow the squash to cool, so they do not continue to cook.

STEAM: 17 minutes. Uncover and turn off heat when done.

MICROWAVE: 15 minutes. Cover the squash and allow it to sit for 10 more minutes.

Caldo de Gallina Vieja

CHICKEN NOODLE SOUP

The use of chicken for medical properties was recorded by Pedacius Dioscorides, an army surgeon under Emperor Nero nearly 2000 years ago. The use of *Caldo de gallina vieja* (broth of an old hen) for respiratory infections was traditional among the Sephardic Jewish people of Spain, including the physician and philosopher Maimonides in the 12th century, who recommended its use for asthma. The Spanish inquisition began in the late 14th century and with it the traditional use of chicken soup was lost for some time in Europe, but the tradition survived with settlers in the Caribbean. Chicken vegetable soup may reduce inflammation by reducing the number of white blood cells that gather and become activated[6]. The hot soup also thins respiratory secretions, making them easier to clear and making breathing less work[7].

This recipe for chicken soup has large chunks of chicken to make a get-well meal.

INGREDIENTS:

1 – 1½ pounds of boneless, skinless chicken,
    cut into large pieces
1 tablespoon olive oil
5 cloves garlic; sliced lengthwise
½ small onion, quartered and sliced
1 chicken bouillon cube (5 grams)
4 cups water
2 medium potatoes; diced
2 oz. fine noodles (about 1 cup)
½ cup sliced celery
½ cup sliced carrots
1 sweet potato, with skin, cut into 1-inch cubes
½ teaspoon salt
½ teaspoon dry oregano
1 teaspoon red wine vinegar

PREPARATION: Add oil to a 4-quart saucepan. Sauté the garlic for about 2 minutes, and then add the onion and sauté for an additional minute. Add the chicken and sauté it for about 3 minutes. Turn down the heat to low. Add the bouillon and braise the chicken for a couple more minutes in order to coat the chicken with the bouillon.

Add 4 cups of water, oregano, and the carrots and turn up the heat and let it come to a boil. Cover and adjust the heat to a simmer for 5 minutes. Add the noodles and sweet potatoes and simmer for another 4 minutes. Add the potatoes and simmer for 8 more minutes. Add the celery and simmer for 2 to 3 minutes. Turn off the heat. To your taste, add about one teaspoon of red wine vinegar and a half teaspoon of salt if needed.

Sopa Boba

VEGETABLE NOODLE SOUP

This soup is very similar to chicken noodle soup but is vegetarian. It is also used as a remedy for colds and illness.

INGREDIENTS:

1 tablespoon olive oil
5 large cloves garlic, sliced
1 small red onion; diced
1 cup diced celery
1 cup sliced carrots
1 large sweet potato, cubed
¼ cup red bell pepper; diced
¼ cup scallions or green onions; diced
1 teaspoon salt
1 teaspoon dried oregano
3 cups water
2 –3 oz. fine egg noodles
1 cup watercress, chopped
2 teaspoons fresh chopped cilantro

PREPARATION: Prepare the vegetables. Cut out any bad spots, but do not peel the sweet potato.

Heat the oil in a large saucepan and add the garlic and lightly sauté it for about a minute until it is

Notes:

light golden brown. Add the onions, celery, carrots, sweet potatoes, bell pepper and scallions, and sauté the vegetables for 3 minutes. Add the water and stir the ingredients. Add the noodles, oregano and salt.

Cover the pot and bring it to a boil, and then lower the temperature. Allow it to simmer for 15 minutes. Taste the broth to make sure it has enough salt. Stir in ¼-teaspoon salt at a time if more is needed and allow the soup to cook at a very low simmer for five more minutes.

Serve the soup while still hot. Place the watercress and cilantro as a garnish on the soup, to retain their flavor. (See note on cruciferous vegetables page 119).

Substitution: One cup of broccoli florets diced into ½ inch pieces may be used in place of watercress. Add the broccoli to the pot of soup after it has been removed from the heat, and it has stopped simmering. Cover the pot and allow the broccoli to warm for one or two minutes before serving.

Sandwiches

About Sandwiches

Sandwiches fill a different role in the Caribbean diet than in America. We traditionally enjoy our supper at midday, followed by a nap, although as places become more urbanized, not all businesses close from 12 to 2 in the afternoon for supper, nap and a shower as they did when I was younger. In the Caribbean, sandwiches are not carried in a lunch bag, but rather purchased at small eateries, lunch counters, and cafés. Sandwiches are mostly eaten grilled and as a hot snack on the go, as a light dinner, or a late evening snack accompanied by a smoothie, fresh juice, or sometimes a cold beer.

The most famous Caribbean sandwich is the Cuban sandwich, which is also known in Cuba and on other islands as "sándwiche de jamón y queso"; a grilled ham and cheese sandwich. Cuban sandwich makers take much pride in their sandwiches, and their special ingredients and methods. Herein is offered a very generic form, and I humbly yield to the specialists in this matter.

Another famous sandwich is the chimichurri, a criollo hamburger, sold by vendors with street carts with a mobile, gas-heated grill.

BREAD: The bread typically used for sandwiches in the Hispanic Caribbean Islands is pan de agua. These are individual rolls about six to seven inches long with tapered ends. Pan de aqua (water bread) is made by preparing the bread rolls to be placed in the oven, with dough just as would be used for French or Italian bread. The difference is rather than letting the dough rise and placing the bread in a hot oven, boiling water is poured into a tray on a lower rack, in a cool oven, and the rolls are put in this steamy oven to rise. After allowing the bread to rise for about 10 minutes, the oven is turned on, and the bread baked. This gives denser bread, with a thin crisp crust.

When selecting bread for making sandwiches, I have found French bread buns make a good substitute for pan de agua. Italian bread rolls are too soft, baguettes too narrow. Hoagie rolls work okay. Gluten free bread has become more easily available and allows wheat free, gluten free sandwiches.

PANINI PRESS: Most Caribbean sandwiches are heated in a Panini sandwich press. A Panini press is used to cook sandwiches, and compacts the bread to about 1/3 of its original height, gives a crispy crust and heats the sandwich, melting the cheese and blending the flavors. The press can be lightly buttered, and should not get hot enough to burn the butter (about 300°F). If you are not fortunate enough to have a Panini press handy, a waffle griddle or electric grill may be used. If you do not have one of these conveniences, a cast iron pan, and a brick will do. Wrap a standard sized red brick in aluminum foil and use it as the press. Turn the sandwich over a few times during cooking; so that both sides get cooked.

A couple of secrets: Preheat, but be careful not to overheat the sandwich press, or the bread will toast before the cheese melts. The goal is to have the cheese just start to ooze out at the same time as the bread just starts to get golden brown and crispy. If the butter burns, the press (or the skillet) is too hot.

Also, avoid putting cold ingredients (tomatoes, cheese, meats, and condiments) in the sandwich. Allow refrigerated ingredients to warm to room temperature before assembling the sandwich. Slicing tomatoes thin (no more than about 3/16ths inch thick) also helps prevents cold areas and helps the center of the sandwich heat evenly. (Exception – do not allow mayonnaise to come to room temperature as it grows bacteria all too well, and in any case, mayonnaise does not belong in a Cuban sandwich).

Cut the sandwich at an angle to serve it. It gives more exposed area and thus better exposure to the flavors inside, as well as encouraging smaller bites and more enjoyment.

44

GREEN TOMATOES: Green tomatoes are used as much or more than ripe tomatoes in sandwiches. They are nicely crisp and mildly acid. A green tomato is a full sized tomato that has just begun to ripen and is a light-green, not a dark-green color.

Green tomatoes can be hard to find in the grocery store, and when you do, they may be nearly flavorless. I find that green tomatoes for markets in the U.S. that are already beginning to have patches of pink will give the right texture, better flavor and are prettier. Let the tomatoes warm to room temperature before using them. When they are cold, they will have almost no flavor, and they will keep the inside of the sandwich from warming and keep the cheese from melting as easily. Slice the tomato about 3/16ths of an inch thick and sprinkle a pinch of salt on them before using them on a sandwich.

Green tomatoes are also great in salads, or just sliced and served as part of a meal.

Sándwiche de Pollo

DOMINICAN CHICKEN SANDWICH

INGREDIENTS (FOR 2 SANDWICHES):

1 pound skinless chicken breast
2 teaspoons salt
1 green tomato (full ripe size, just starting to turn color), sliced 1/8th to 3/16th inch thick
2 cloves garlic, crushed
2 tablespoons mayonnaise
2 ounces sliced cheese
2 hoagie buns (8-inch) or (French bread)
Red onion; sliced thin
Ketchup

PREPARATION: Place the chicken in a saucepan with sufficient water to float along with the crushed garlic and 2 teaspoons salt. Cover and boil the chicken for 20 minutes. Drain the chicken to allow it to cool enough to handle. Pull the meat away from the bones, tearing the meat into bits about ½ inch thick and 2 inches long.

Place the chicken in a bowl and add the mayonnaise and mix them together. Slice the hoagie buns to open them and spread about half the chicken into each sandwich. Lay out slices of cheese to form a layer followed by a layer of thinly

OTHER GRILLED SANDWICHES:

Many other grilled sandwiches are made using other fillings following the general recipe as for a Ham and Cheese Sandwich.

SÁNDWICHE DE CARNE DE RES: ROAST BEEF SANDWICH: Use meat prepared as in the recipe for Carne Mechada or Ropa Vieja on pages 81 and 83.

SÁNDWICHE DE ATUN O SALMÓN: TUNA SALAD, SALMON SALAD: Use fish salad from page 62 to fill the sandwiches.

SÁNDWICHE DE PESCADO AHUMADO: SMOKED FISH SANDWICH: Use smoked fish dip as prepared in the recipes on page 63 to fill the sandwiches.

sliced red onions, and green tomato slices. Sprinkle a few grains of salt on the tomatoes. Add a bit of ketchup and close the sandwich.

Place the sandwich in a sandwich press and cook until the cheese begins to melt and run, and the bread is toasted on the outside. Cut into 2 with an angle cut and serve with a glass of mabí or passion fruit juice over ice!

(Rather than boiling chicken, leftover chicken can also be used for these sandwiches.)

Sándwiche de Pollo Limón Pimienta

LEMON PEPPER CHICKEN SANDWICH

Build the sandwich using chicken prepared as in the recipe for Lemon Pepper Chicken from page 69 to fill the sandwich.

Chimichurris

DOMINICAN BURGER

Another favorite sold by street vendors from carts with a grill and a propane tank. It's a tasty burger buried in cabbage and shredded carrots. In the Dominican Republic, this is a fast lunch or a late meal when out to see a movie.

INGREDIENTS:

1 pound ground chuck
1 medium red onion; finely diced
½ red bell pepper; finely diced
3 cloves garlic, minced
½ teaspoon dried oregano
2 teaspoons soy sauce
4 teaspoons Worcestershire sauce
1 large egg

4 French bread buns
2 cups thinly sliced cabbage
¾ cup shredded carrots
¼ teaspoon salt
1 small onion; cut into rings
1 medium tomato, in thick slices

1 tablespoon orange juice
1 tablespoon ketchup
1 tablespoon brown mustard
1/8th teaspoon Worcestershire sauce

PREPARATION: If the beef has been frozen it needs to be thawed overnight in the refrigerator. Place the ground beef, onions, pepper, egg, and condiments from the first set of ingredients into a bowl and mix them together well. Divide the meat into 4 parts and form each into a patty, about ¾ of an inch thick. Place then in a frying pan or on a griddle. The grill temperature should be about 300° F.

Flip the burgers once every minute to cook them evenly. Expect it to take about 12 minutes to cook them through. (See section About Meat on page 75 for best preparation of hamburger patties.)

While the patties are cooking, toast the inside of the buns with a small amount of butter on the griddle or in a pan.

When a burger is done, transfer it to a bun.

Mix the cabbage, shredded carrots, and a quarter teaspoon salt, and cook these vegetables on the grill until the cabbage looks wilted. Pile a quarter of these veggies on top of each burger. Grill the tomatoes and the onion rings, allowing the onions to brown slightly, and divide these on top of the cabbage.

Top this with the secret sauce made from orange juice, mustard, ketchup and Worcestershire sauce mixed together.

Enjoy with lemonade, a cold smoothie, or an ice cold pilsner beer.

Makes 4 large sandwiches.

Chimi de Huevo

EGG CHIMI

Vegetarian chimichurris are also made and sold as street food in the Dominican Republic. using a fried egg as filling in place of meat. Use the recipe on page 31 for "Egg Sunny Inside" but give the egg an extra minute cooking time to allow the yolk to solidify, so that it does not run out of the sandwich.

Sándwiche de Jamón y Queso

TOASTED HAM AND CHEESE SANDWICH

In 1978, there was an outbreak of African swine fever in the Dominican Republic. It was not a people disease, but rather a pig disease and the U.S. government did not want it to come to their shores. Thus, the American government paid for and convinced the Dominican government to do an eradication and replacement program. This was no easy feat, and it did not go over well with people in villages and towns where a family's pig was their piggy bank. It was common for families to raise a couple of small criollo pigs, and sell them for emergency cash if someone in the family fell ill, and if not, there was a Christmas feast

For several years, there were military roadblocks on every road leading in and out of every large town, and all vehicles were inspected. Any ham or pigs were confiscated. There were soldiers combing the hills. It was a dark day for my family when someone betrayed my uncle and told the soldiers where he had his pigs hidden in the mountains.

You may note a lack of pork recipes in this book. I grew up in the time between the pigs. After they had eliminated the criollo pigs, it was several years before the new American pigs were introduced. They were large, aggressive animals that needed to live in pens, have clean water and shade, and that would die easily. They were very different from the small tame Spanish pigs that had acclimated to the island over several hundred years, and would thrive on banana peels and other kitchen wastes.

Still, one dish that needs to be in a collection of Caribbean dishes is the grilled ham and cheese sandwich.

INGREDIENTS:

French bread or Hoagie bread for two 8 inch sandwiches
Butter (softened)
¾ pound thin sliced ham
¼ pound sliced cheese (pepper jack cheese is nice)
Green tomato sliced 1/8" thick
Red onion; sliced thin
Ketchup

PREPARATION: Split the sub roll into top and bottom halves. Spread a thin layer of butter on the insides of the roll. Place the sliced ham, followed by a layer of cheese, and green tomatoes, onion rings, and a drizzle of ketchup.

Place the sandwich in a heated sandwich press (Panini) and toast until the cheese melts and starts oozing out.

Sándwiche de Queso

TOASTED CHEESE SANDWICH WITH GREEN TOMATOES

INGREDIENTS:

French bread bun or roll
1 teaspoon mayonnaise or softened butter
2 oz. sliced cheese
3 green tomato slices, 3/16 inch thick
5 red onion rings; sliced thin
1 teaspoon ketchup
½ teaspoon butter

PREPARATION: Split the sub roll into top and bottom halves. Spread a thin layer of mayonnaise or butter on the insides of the roll. Place sliced cheese, and green tomatoes, onion rings, and a drizzle of ketchup.

Place the sandwich in a heated and lightly buttered sandwich press (Panini) and toast until the cheese melts and starts oozing out. Cut diagonally into two halves. The crust should be crisp. Serve with a smoothie.

Sándwiche de Almejas ó de Lambí

CONCH AND CLAM SANDWICHES

What was once my favorite sandwich is now illegal in 50 states and in much of the Caribbean, and for good reason. The queen conch is highly prized not only for its beautiful shell but also for it meat. Over-harvesting has caused the decline in conch populations throughout its range, and it is considered an endangered species. To protect the remaining populations, harvest of queen conch is restricted throughout the Caribbean and is completely prohibited in Florida and Puerto Rico.

Two substitutes are given below. Clams are farmed from Alaska to Florida in the U.S., and thus are sustainable and available. Minced clams can be found in most grocery stores. The lightning whelk, which is native to the waters of the Bay of Campeche in Mexico to the shores of North Carolina, as well as Cuba and Hispaniola, has a very similar flavor to conch. Sold as conch or scungilli, it may be found in Italian fish markets. Scungilli from the Mediterranean is also sold canned, and can be ordered on the internet.

HAPPY AS A CLAM SANDWICH

INGREDIENTS FOR THE FILLING:

2 teaspoons butter
2 cloves garlic, minced
1 scallion with greens, minced
¾ cups minced clams (6 oz. can drained)

French bread roll (Pan de Agua if available)
1 teaspoon mayonnaise
3 slices of tomato, 3/16th inch thick
3 very thin red onion slices
Butter for the sandwich press or grill

PREPARATION: Place the butter in a saucepan over low heat. When the butter is melted, add the garlic. The butter should be hot enough to form tiny bubbles but not large bubbles. Sauté the garlic for 30 seconds to a minute, and then add the scallions and sauté for another 30 seconds, until the garlic is light golden. Add the minced clams and sauté for another 30 seconds and remove from the heat.

Split the bread roll open leaving a hinge (like a clamshell), and put a thin layer of mayonnaise on each side. Fill the sandwich with the sautéed seafood, and cover with a layer of tomatoes and onions. Close the sandwich, and heat in a lightly buttered Panini press or in a grill for about 40 seconds until the bread is lightly toasted. Serve hot, along with a smoothie.

CONCH SANDWICH

Whelk (conch) usually needs to be tenderized by beating it with a wooden mallet for most dishes, but since it is minced for this recipe, the pounding is not required. Cut the whelk into pieces no larger than ¼ inch.

INGREDIENTS FOR THE FILLING:

2 teaspoons butter
2 cloves garlic, minced
1 scallion with greens, minced
½ cup minced whelk

PREPARATION: Place the butter in a saucepan over low heat. When the butter is melted, add the garlic. The butter should be hot enough to form tiny bubbles but not large bubbles. Sauté them for about a minute until the garlic is light golden brown. Add the scallions and whelk and sauté for another one minute, and remove the whelk from the heat.

Prepare the sandwich as for the clam sandwich on this page.

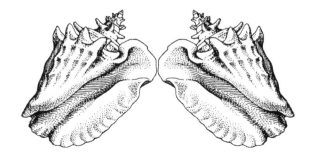

Seafood - Mariscos y Pescados

About Seafood Safety

Seafood needs to be properly cared for as it can easily grow bacteria. These bacteria can quickly ferment amino acids in the flesh of the fish into biogenic amines such as histamine that can cause food poisoning. Sometimes this will cause a peppery flavor. It may not taste so bad tasting, but the nausea and headache that comes later may keep you from ever wanting to eat it again. The same thing can happen with fish that was not frozen quickly enough or allowed to thaw and then be refrozen.

FROZEN SEAFOOD: Thaw frozen seafood in the refrigerator or in a bowl, under a trickle of cold running water. Do not try to thaw seafood at room temperature or in warm water, as this encourages bacterial growth. Frozen fish and shellfish can be cooked directly from the frozen state, but this will change the cooking times and should not be used for quick cooking methods such as flash cooking.

When preparing raw seafood at home, clean the cutting board, and wash your hands with soap and water. Do not allow any utensils used with the raw fish to come into contact with the cooked fish. After using the cutting board and utensils on raw fish clean them. Discard the paper the fish was wrapped in.

Cacerola de Mariscos

SEAFOOD CASSEROLE

This seaside dish is a fisherman's stew. It is made with conch, crab, whelk, octopus, oysters, clams or any other edible seafood that can be gathered. Here it is made with more easily accessible ingredients.

INGREDIENTS:

2 tablespoons olive oil
½ medium onion; diced
3 cloves garlic, in thin slices
1 Cuban pepper, diced
2 diced plum tomatoes, diced
1 16 oz. can of diced tomatoes
½-teaspoon salt
2 cans chopped clams
1 can (15 oz.) baby corn ears
1 pound cleaned shrimp
1 cup scallops
Optional: ¼ teaspoon ground cayenne pepper or
   paprika

PREPARATION: Prepare a sofrito (page 90), lightly toasting the onions and garlic, Cuban pepper and plum tomatoes and salt in a large saucepan over medium heat. Add the chopped clams to the pan with their juice and the canned tomatoes. Add the baby corn ears, cover and simmer for 5 minutes. Add the shrimp and the scallops, cover and simmer for another 4 minutes.

Note: Spiced canned tomatoes may be used for extra flavor. One pound of fresh ripe tomatoes can be used in place of the canned tomatoes. See note on page 9.

Serve with rice, tostones and salad.

Makes 4-6 servings

Vieira con Ajo

GARLIC SCALLOPS

INGREDIENTS:

½ pound bay scallops
½ teaspoon olive oil
½ tablespoon butter
2 cloves garlic, minced
1/8th teaspoon oregano
1 teaspoon chives or minced onion greens

PREPARATION: Heat the butter and oil in a shallow pan. Add the garlic and sauté it for 2 minutes at medium-low heat until it is light golden brown. Add the chives and oregano. Then add the scallops and sauté them for three minutes. Avoid overcooking them as they will shrink and become tough. Serve immediately. It is delicious over pasta or with rice.

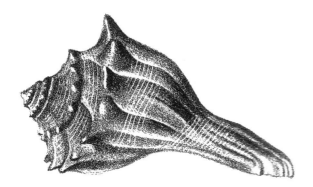

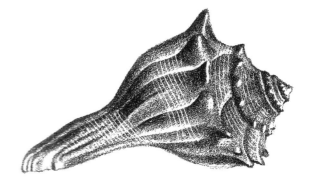

About Bacalao: Salted Cod

In the U.S., salted cod needs to be refrigerated until it is used. Where I grew up in the Dominican Republic salted cod was sold from a box on the shelf. It was salted as a preservative and sold in large slabs in colmados (small stores that sell one or two dozen items from behind a counter) where there was often no refrigeration. Now I can usually only find it frozen in one pound wooden boxes.

The salted cod needs to be "refreshed". Cover the fish you will use with about 2 inches of water and let it soak, changing the water 3 or 4 times over 24 hours. It can be left in the refrigerator in the water for about 3 days, refreshed and ready to be used if you change the water daily. It should still taste salty, but not excessively so.

Bacalao Guisado

STEWED COD

INGREDIENTS

½ pound of dry salted cod
1 small onion
2 tablespoons olive oil
1 small Cuban pepper
3 plum tomatoes
½ cup water

PREPARATION: Rinse the cod to remove the loose salt, and then soak in 2 quarts of warm water for one hour. Dice the onion, the Cuban pepper, and the tomatoes. Place the oil in a sauté pan. Add the onions, and sauté them for about 3 minutes. Add the diced peppers and cook for 2 minutes, and then add the tomatoes and sauté for another 4 minutes, until a sauce is formed.

Remove the bacalao from the water and break it into small pieces and rinse it again in cool water. Add the bacalao into the sauce with the ½ cup of water, stir in and simmer for 10 minutes, or until the sauce becomes thick again.

Serve over potatoes, plantains, rice, or moro.

Bacalao con Coco

SALTED COD IN COCONUT CREAM

Ingredients:
½ lb. salted cod
6 cups water
4 cloves garlic, minced
1 small onion; diced
1½ cups coconut cream
½ Anaheim pepper, remove the seeds, cut into narrow 1-inch strips
2 ají dulce if available, diced (with seeds)
Salt to taste
1/4 teaspoon saffron

PREPARATION: Rinse the dried cod to remove excess salt, and then place it in a saucepan with the water over heat and bring it to a boil. Lower the heat to a simmer and allow it to cook for 10 minutes.

Remove the cod from the hot water, and place it in a bowl of cold water, deep enough to cover it.

Place the coconut cream in a clean saucepan, along with the garlic, onion, peppers and saffron. Place over medium heat, and bring to a simmer stirring it to blend the flavors. Lower the heat to medium-low.

Take the cod and break it into small bite-sized chunks, and rinse it again. Add the cod to the sauce and simmer it for another 15 minutes.

Serve the cod and sauce over rice, with boiled plantains or boiled green bananas.

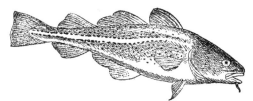

Bacalao con Papas

DRIED COD WITH POTATOES

INGREDIENTS:

4 oz. dried salted cod
1/8 cup vegetable oil
1 cup red onions, twice quartered and sliced
3 cloves of garlic, minced
¼ cup red bell peppers, quartered and sliced
¼ cup Cuban peppers, quartered and sliced
3 medium plum tomatoes; diced
6 medium red potatoes (about 1 pound), diced
¾ teaspoon salt

PREPARING BACALAO: Rinse the bacalao in cool running water to remove excess salt. Next place the bacalao in about 1 quart of water for 1 hour allowing it to rehydrate and to remove excess salt. Discard the water and briefly rinse the fish in cool running water. Place the bacalao in a small saucepan with about 3 cups of water. Bring to a boil, and then lower to a simmer. Allow to cook for 5 minutes, and remove it from the water and let it

cool. (Retain the water the fish was cooked in).

Prepare the sauce while the potatoes are boiling. Boil the diced potato in water with a half teaspoon of salt, cooking them until a fork passes through easily and splits the piece of potato. Drain the potatoes and cover with cool water to stop further cooking.

In a sauté pan, heat the oil over medium heat. Add the onions and sauté them for a couple of minutes until they begin to clear, add the garlic and sauté until the garlic begins to turn golden. Add the peppers and tomato. Sauté until the tomatoes turn into a sauce. Add ½ cup of the water in which the bacalao was boiled and ¼-teaspoon salt, and simmer. Dice the bacalao and add to the sauce, let it simmer in the sauce for 3 minutes. Drain the potatoes and gently stir them into the sauce. Allow them to simmer in the sauce for another 2 minutes. Remove from the heat and serve.

About Calamari

Spaghetti with squid sauce just does not sound as delicious as spaghetti with calamari sauce. I have served seafood salad to guests who loved it until they found out that it contained squid. Calamari by another name just does not taste the same.

CLEANING AND PREPARING CALAMARI:

Cut the tentacles just before the eyes and set them aside. Pull on the head with a little twist while holding the end of the mantle and the entrails should separate easily. Set the innards aside if you want to harvest the squid ink. At the edge of the mantle near where the eye was, feel for the clear quill or internal shell. Pull it out and be amazed by this glass clear flexible shell, and then discard it. The edible skin of the squid can usually be easily pulled away from the flesh of the mantle and discarded to give a more white and tender squid flesh. Rinse the mantle inside and out in cool water and slice it into ¼ to ½ inch wide rings.

In the center of the tentacles is the beak. It is the hard piece of cartilaginous material in the center. It can be separated and discarded. Rinse the tentacles in cool water.

In fresh squid, the ink sac is about in the middle of the entrails and is a small black bladder that looks like a dark vein. Commercially harvested squid may have had the ink squeezed out of them during netting. The ink stains so be careful where you do this, and you may want to wear gloves and an apron. Separate the ink sac from the entrails and cut it over a glass with ¼ to ½ cup of water, wine, or other fluid that you will be cooking with; squeezing out the few drops of ink. A few drops of squid ink should be enough to color the rice, spaghetti, or another dish you want to flavor and color. Discard the rest of the entrails. Often I find egg clusters in the female squid. I cannot find a reference on their edibility, but I have eaten them many times and lived to tell about it. I enjoy the flavor and texture.

HEALTH NOTE: Consumption of squid ink can cause black stools.

Squid and octopus have a type of collagen that denatures at a temperature of about 85°F (29°C), and that shrinks at a temperature of 127°F (53°C)[8]. Cooking them at a temperature that kills bacteria causes the flesh to shrink and become tough and rubbery if cooked for more than a couple of minutes. Squid and octopus can also be stewed; simmering it for an hour will hydrolyze the proteins and make the flesh tender again. Flash cooking Squid is recommended for use in salads.

FLASH COOKING SQUID AND OCTOPUS: To blanch squid, clean and cut the squid into pieces ready for cooking. Drop the squid into a large pot of boiling water deep enough to easily cover the squid for 50 seconds or until the flesh becomes opaque, and then retrieve it with a large slotted spoon. Remove the squid from the boiling water and dunk into ice water to chill, and then remove it from the cold water. Blanch small amounts of squid at a time to avoid cooling the water so much the squid does not cook in the allotted time. Avoid overcooking the squid or octopus, (more than about 90 seconds), as doing so will cause it to be tough and rubbery.

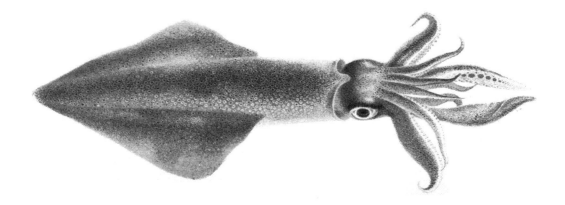

Calamar en Coco y Jalapeño

CALAMARI IN COCONUT SAUCE

INGREDIENTS:

2 lbs. squid
12 oz. coconut cream
2 tablespoons crushed garlic
1 medium onion; diced
2 green onions
1 large jalapeño pepper
½ teaspoon oregano
½ teaspoon fresh cilantro, chopped
½ teaspoon salt

PREPARATION: Clean the squid, and cut the mantles into rings ¼ inch wide, and return them to the refrigerator. Place the coconut cream in a saucepan together with the garlic, onions, jalapeño, oregano, and salt. Simmer for 10 minutes, stirring continually. Add the squid rings and stir them in, cooking for 2 minutes, and remove the pan from the heat. Stir in the chopped cilantro, and serve immediately, or transfer into a heat proof serving bowl. Allowing the squid to continue cooking will make it too chewy.

Serve over rice or with bread, and with a green salad.

Calamar en Crema de Ajo

CALAMARI IN GARLIC CREAM SAUCE

INGREDIENTS:

1½ pounds of squid
1 tablespoon finely sliced garlic
1 tablespoon butter
1 tablespoon olive oil
12 oz. evaporated milk
¼ teaspoon salt

PREPARATION: Clean and slice the calamari into rings.

Slice the garlic perpendicular to its axes to make 2 mm cross sections. In a saucepan, heat the butter and olive oil. When the butter begins to melt, add the garlic. Cook until the garlic gets golden brown. Add the evaporated milk and simmer for about 5 minutes. Add the salt. Add the calamari and simmer for another 2 minutes. Remove from the heat and serve immediately.

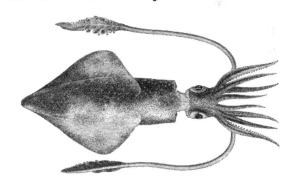

Pulpo a la Vinagreta

OCTOPUS

INGREDIENTS:

½ pound cleaned octopus
1 teaspoon olive oil
1 teaspoon vinegar
A pinch of salt

PREPARATION: Rinse the thawed octopus in water, and then dice it into ¼-inch pieces. Boil 3 cups of water, remove it from the heat and immediately pour the octopus into the hot water. Allow it to cook for 60 to 90 seconds. Drain and rinse the octopus in cool water. Place it in a bowl, blend in the olive oil to coat the octopus, and then mix in the vinegar and salt to taste.

Serve with tostones or rice.

About Shrimp

FRESH OR FROZEN: We live in a small fishing village on the Gulf coast of Florida and have shrimpers as neighbors. There are a few bay shrimp boats that go out at night and return with a fresh catch in the morning. They put the shrimp on ice, and it is possible a few times a year to buy shrimp here that have never been frozen. However, most shrimp boats go out for days or weeks and follow the shrimp in different parts of the Gulf of Mexico. They flash freeze the shrimp to ensure the best quality and prevent bacterial growth and degradation of the flesh.

Fish and shrimp should be frozen rapidly to prevent damage to the muscles fibers. This cannot be done in a home refrigerator, especially one that is nearly filled. Every time shrimp are thawed and refrozen; ice crystals form in them, breaking up the muscle fibers. This especially occurs if the freezing is done slowly. This causes mealy textured shrimp.

When you buy shrimp, it has almost certainly been frozen in the past. Each time it is frozen and thawed, the quality is lowered, and even on ice bacteria are actively growing[9]. The only benefit of buying thawed shrimp is that they look nice on display. If you want fresh tasting shrimp with a good texture, buy shrimp that was flash frozen on the boat and thawed only once - at home when they are being prepared to be cooked.

THAWING SHRIMP: To retain freshness and the best texture, taste, and lowest bacterial count, thaw shrimp in the refrigerator at a temperature under 40°F. Place the frozen shrimp in a colander, cover it, and place the colander in a bowl or on a plate to catch any water that may drip. Allow the shrimp to thaw overnight in a refrigerator for about 18 hours before you plan to use it[10][11].

Shrimp can also be thawed quickly by placing it in a bowl of cold water, under a faucet with just a trickle of slowly running water into the bowl, with the overflow running down the drain. This method is fast, and a pound of shrimp can be ready in as little as a few minutes.

DEGRADATION AND BACTERIA: Raw shrimp come with bacteria and are a great growth medium for bacteria that break down the shrimp, and ruin the flavor. Shrimp that smell like bleach have bacterial degradation. Or they can just smell bad. These shrimp can also make you and your family ill. To keep your seafood fresh and with a low bacterial load, keep them frozen during storage, and very cool during preparation. Do not thaw shrimp at room temperature. Before preparing seafood, wash your hands, cutting board and utensils. When you are done handling seafood, wash your hands, cutting board and utensils. As you clean the shrimp, place the cleaned shrimp in a bowl of water with ice to keep the shrimp cold, as this will greatly slow bacterial growth.

SHRIMP COOKING TIMES

When shrimp are overcooked, they get tough and shrink. If they are undercooked, they can have bacteria and parasites that are best avoided. To minimize shrinkage and to ensure death to the body invaders the internal temperature needs to get to 145°F (62. 8°C) for 15 seconds. Here are some recommended cooking times for *thawed* shrimp.

VERY SMALL SHRIMP: For 100 count shrimp (headless, 100 shrimp per pound) boil the shrimp for 55 seconds, or simmering at 195°F (90.6°C) for 60 seconds.

LARGE SHRIMP: For 45 count shrimp (headless, 45 shrimp per pound) boil the shrimp for 90 seconds, or simmering at 195°F (90.6°C) for 108 seconds. The larger the shrimp, the more time it takes to get the internal temperature up to 145°F.

LARGE BUTTERFLY CUT SHRIMP: Forty-five count butterfly cut shrimp, have been cut open and thus cook more quickly. Boiling time: Boil for 70 seconds or simmer at 195°F (90.6°C) for 90 seconds.

JUMBO SHRIMP: For 25 count shrimp: boil for 90 seconds when butterfly cut. It is better to simmer intact jumbo shrimp than to boil them to give more time for heat transfer to the interior. It takes 2 to 3 minutes to cook jumbo shrimp adequately.

Add 2 seconds for every 1000 feet elevation above sea level.

Use sufficient hot water so that adding the shrimp to it does not cause the water to cool below the desired cooking temperature.

A second method is to boil the water, turn off the heat, quickly stir in the room temperature shrimp, and cover. Allow the shrimp to cook for 5 minutes. Use one quart of water for each pound of shrimp. (Place the water into a saucepan and bring it to a boil. Turn the heat off, immediately add the shrimp, cover and allow it to sit for 2 minutes. Drain the water and allow the shrimp to cool.)

SHRIMP AMOUNTS:
These are rough estimates but can help with planning:

- About 1/3 the weight of the shrimp is the head.

- About 1/5 the weight of a headless shrimp is shell and tail.

- 16 oz. of whole shrimp with heads on:
  = about 11 oz. of headless shrimp

- 16 oz. of whole shrimp with heads on
  = about 9 oz. of peeled shrimp

- 16 oz. of headless shrimp
  = about 13 oz. of peeled shrimp.

PEELING AND DEVEINING SHRIMP

Start with thawed shrimp. If the shrimp are whole, first remove the head. Then make a shallow slit along the back of the shrimp with a paring knife, just deep enough to go through the shell. Peel away the shell and legs. Depending on how you plan to use the shrimp, the tail can either be left on or removed.

Now with the peeled shrimp, make a shallow cut down along the center of the back of the shrimp from the tail to end where the head was, about an eighth of an inch deep. If you started with whole shrimp, you might have already made this cut. Under running water, grab the vein between the tip of your knife and your thumb to remove the vein. If it breaks, just pick out the remaining parts.

As you prepare the batch of shrimp, place the cleaned shrimp into a bowl of water with ice to keep them fresh.

BUTTERFLY SHRIMP:

Butterfly cut shrimp not only is more attractive, it also gives it a larger surface area to be coated with flavorings and allows the shrimp to cook more evenly and more quickly. Thus for larger shrimp, it allows quicker cooking time and less shrinkage. Butterfly cutting the shrimp also allows for more complete deveining the shrimp.

To butterfly shrimp use the same technique as for deveining, but slice deeper, about 2/3rds the way through along the back, when removing the vein. Place the cleaned shrimp in a bowl of water with ice as you butterfly the other shrimp being prepared.

SHRIMP SHELL BROTH:

Rather than just discarding the tails and shells of the shrimp, it can be used to make a broth as a basis for soup or for cooking rice, locrio, or other dishes. Note: The broth is only worth making if the shrimp it is made from are very fresh.

INGREDIENTS:
Shells and tails from 1 pound of shrimp
   (about 3 oz. of shells and tails)
1 clove of garlic, minced
¼ cup onion; diced
1 quart of water
¼ teaspoon salt

PREPARATION: Place the shells and tails from the shrimp in a bowl and rinse them off, and then drain the water. Add a quart of water, shrimp shells and tails, garlic, onion and the salt to a saucepan and cook at a low simmer (85℃) for 30 minutes. Strain the broth, and discard the shells. This broth can be frozen and used later.

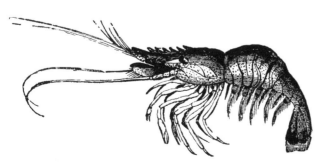

Camarones en Salsa de Tamarindo

SHRIMP IN TAMARIND SAUCE

INGREDIENTS:

1½ pounds of shrimp without heads
2 oz. tamarind paste (1/4 cup)
¼ cup warm water
2 cloves of garlic, minced
1 tablespoon coconut oil
1 tablespoon butter

PREPARATION: Thin the tamarind paste by placing it in a bowl with ¼ cup of warm water. After the tamarind has softened, mash it with the water, and then strain out any pulp and seeds from the paste. Peel, devein, and butterfly the shrimp as described on the previous page.

Place the oil in a sauté pan over medium-low heat. Add the garlic and toast it to a golden brown color. Melt in the butter and add the shrimp, then raise the temperature to medium. Sauté the shrimp for one to 2 minutes. Cooking time depends on the size of the shrimp; larger shrimp require more time. Add the thinned tamarind paste and sauté the shrimp in the sauce for one minute. For best flavor serve immediately, while still hot.

Serving ideas: Serve with coconut rice or fried plantain. When serving with spaghetti, use small shrimp.

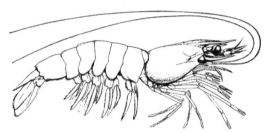 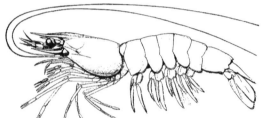

Camarones con Vegetales

STIR FRIED SHRIMP WITH PORCINI MUSHROOMS

INGREDIENTS:

1½ pounds headless shrimp
2 tablespoons olive oil
2 cloves garlic, sliced along their long axis
1 tablespoon brown sugar
1 vegetable bouillon cube (5 grams)
1 cup carrots; diced into 1 cm cubes
½ cup diced red onions
¼ cup diced dry porcini mushrooms
1 cup celery; diced
½ cup diced red bell peppers

PREPARATION: Peel and clean and butterfly the shrimp (see directions on page 55). Set them in the refrigerator in ice water. Cut the vegetables and place them into separate containers. Rinse the dry mushrooms and drain them.

Heat the olive oil in a medium-sized saucepan over medium heat and sauté the garlic for about 30 seconds. Add the brown sugar and stir together for one minute with a wooden spoon. Add the bouillon, followed by the carrots. Sauté for 30 seconds, then add the onions. Sauté for 30 seconds and then add the mushrooms. Sauté for 30 seconds and add the celery and red bell peppers. Cover and steam for 2 minutes. Add the shrimp and sauté them for one minute to make sure that they are covered with the sauce. Cover and allow everything to steam for 2 minutes and then turn off the heat and let it steam for one more minute. The steam helps to form a sauce.

Serve with or over jasmine rice.

Camarones Mariposa para Ensalada

FLASH COOKED BUTTERFLY SHRIMP FOR SALAD

This is a method of quickly cooking shrimp that may be eaten cold as for salads, or used in making ceviche. This method prevents the shrimp from getting hard and chewy and retains the fresh shrimp flavor but kills bacteria and parasites. The longer the shrimp are cooked, the tougher and smaller they get.

Fish and shrimp are great growth media for bacteria. Most of the bacteria are on the outside of the flesh, although the parasites are inside. Flash boiling is designed to raise the internal temperature of the flesh to 145°F for 15 seconds, hot and long enough to kill the bacteria of concern. The surface, where most of the bacteria are, gets much hotter.

INGREDIENTS:

1 pound cleaned shrimp
3 quarts water
1 quart of ice water (with ice)

PREPARATION: First, defrost the shrimp as described in the section on shrimp. Peel the shrimp if they were purchased with the shell. If preferred, the tail can be left on for its decorative effect. To butterfly the shrimp, use a small paring knife. Cut along the back curve of the shrimp, cutting about 2/3 the way through; remove the vein. As you prepare the shrimp, place them in a bowl of ice water to keep the shrimp fresh.

Place 2 quarts of water in a large pot over high heat. Place one quart of ice with a quart of water in a large bowl or pot. When the water is boiling hard, put a couple shrimp into the boiling water and let them boil for the amount of time specified on page 54, according to the sized of the shrimp. Be ready to retrieve them using a slotted spoon or strainer, immediately immerse them in the ice water.

Taste the shrimp. It should be delicately cooked with a great flavor, and not slippery inside; but not hard either. If not right, try adjusting the cooking time; adding or subtracting 10 seconds.

If the time is correct, cook about ¼ to 1/3 of a pound of shrimp at a time. Cooking too many at once will cool the water too much. As soon as the shrimp have been immersed for the right amount of time, get them out of the boiling water and into the ice water.

(When you are finished, the water used for boiling the shrimp can be used with the shrimp shells and tails to prepare shrimp broth; see page 55)

Camarones Ajote

GARLIC BRAISED SHRIMP

INGREDIENTS

1 pound shrimp (about 10 oz. cleaned)
5 large cloves garlic; diced
1 tablespoon olive oil
1 tablespoon butter

PREPARATION: Place the oil and butter in a sauté pan over medium heat. As soon as the butter is completely melted, add the garlic and sauté it for one minute. Add the cleaned shrimp, and sauté it for 2 minutes, remove it from the heat, and serve hot.

Camarones Mariposa en Leche de Coco

BUTTERFLY SHRIMP IN COCONUT CREAM

INGREDIENTS

2 pounds of peeled shrimp
  (or about 3 pounds shrimp with heads)
1 can of coconut cream
1 tablespoon crushed garlic
2 green onions, sliced
½ teaspoon salt
A pinch of crushed red pepper, according to taste
Sprigs of fresh cilantro

PREPARATION: Peal the shrimp, removing the heads and tails. Slice lengthwise about 2/3rds the way through along the back, and remove the vein. Rinse the shrimp in cold water and set aside in ice water.

Combine the garlic, onion, coconut cream and salt in a sauté pan and bring it to a boil over low heat. Allow it to simmer for about 2 minutes, being careful not to allow it to foam over. Add the shrimp, salt, and red pepper. Allow to cook at a low simmer for about 5 minutes spooning the coconut sauce over the shrimp to keep the sauce from curdling. Garnish with sprigs of fresh cilantro. Serve with rice.

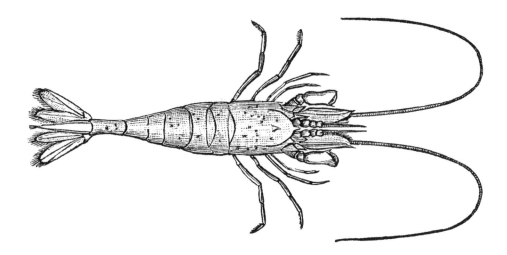

Camarones en Salsa de Mani

PEANUT BUTTER SHRIMP

INGREDIENTS

1 teaspoon vegetable oil
1 small onion chopped
1 tablespoon crushed garlic
2 tablespoons natural peanut butter
1 small tomato, diced
¼ cup water
½ teaspoon curry powder
1/8 teaspoon salt
1 pound shrimp peeled and deveined
1 small red bell pepper, diced
1 small yellow bell pepper, diced

PREPARATION: Heat the oil in a sauté pan over medium heat. Add the onion and sauté them until the onions become clear. Add the garlic and cook until the onion and garlic are light brown. Add the peanut butter, tomatoes, water, curry, and salt. Mix in, cover the pan and let it cook for 4 minutes. Add the shrimp, cover, and cook at a low simmer for 5 more minutes. Add the peppers, and cook for 2 more minutes on low to medium heat. Serve.

Camarones en Salsa de Guayaba

SHRIMP IN GUAVA SAUCE

This is a sweet, savory dish, where the shrimp are cooked to be a bit denser than in most recipes.

INGREDIENTS:

1 pound shrimp without heads
1 tablespoon olive oil
2 cloves garlic
Pinch of salt
¼ ripe bell pepper (yellow, orange or red)
4 oz. (by weight) guava paste
½ cup snow peas

PREPARATION: Peel and butterfly the shrimp as described on page 55. Cut the bell pepper into long strips, removing the seeds and white membrane. Peel the garlic, and cut it into thin lengthwise slices. Remove any stems from the snow peas.

Place the olive oil in a sauté pan over medium heat.

Once hot, sauté the garlic for about 30 seconds until it is just turning light golden brown. Cut the guava paste into several small pieces so that it will be easier to dissolve. Add the guava paste and a pinch of salt to the pan with the garlic and stir it with a wooden spoon until it melts. If it forms large bubbles, turn the heat down to medium low.

Add the shrimp, and sauté them in the guava sauce for one minute. The shrimp should be evenly coated with the sauce. Add the bell pepper strips and cover the pan. Let the shrimp steam for about 90 seconds. Next, add the snow peas, and gently sauté them in for about 15 seconds, just long enough to get them warm. Remove from the heat and serve.

Serve with rice, pasta, tostones or potatoes, with a salad.

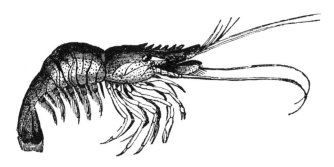

Ensalada de Camarones

SHRIMP SALAD

INGREDIENTS

1 lb. medium cleaned shrimp (weight after cleaning)
1-quart water
2 medium tomatoes; diced
¼ cup diced celery
½ cup finely diced red onion
1 small carrot, grated
6 mint leaves, chopped
2 tablespoons olive oil
½ teaspoon salt
1 teaspoon red wine vinegar or of white merlot

PREPARATION: Place the water in a saucepan and bring it to a boil. Turn the heat off, and immediately add the shrimp, cover and allow it to sit for 2 minutes. Drain the water and allow the shrimp to cool.

Place all the other ingredients in a salad serving-bowl, and gently mix them together. Add the shrimp and mix again. Place the dish in the refrigerator to chill before serving.

About Ceviche

Ceviche most likely originated in Peru but spread with the Spanish traders to other countries in the Americas. We did not make it at home, but it was prepared in restaurants and sometimes sold by street vendors in large coastal towns.

Ceviche is made by "cooking" in fruit juice acid. When heated, proteins denature – meaning that they unfold or clump up or break up into pieces, causing the nature of the protein to change. In eggs, denaturing causes the clear albumin to turn white and solid and for the yolk to solidify. Cooking fish causes the muscle layers to separate easily, and then with more cooking the flesh becomes firmer. Acid can also denature certain proteins, which is what occurs in the preparation of ceviche.

Heating also kills bacteria, viruses and parasites. Fruit acids impair the growth of bacteria but do not kill them. The acids do not eliminate parasites or viruses.

The outbreaks of cholera in Peru in the 1990's have been attributed to consumption of ceviche and other raw seafood, with cholera then spreading and killing thousands of people.

Anisakis is a parasitic worm that infects fish and squid. It is estimated that over 75% of wild caught salmon has this parasite, and it is common among many other species. Eating sashimi and ceviche, is a great way to get this parasite, because the preparation of these dishes does not kill the worms. Humans get infected by eating the fish or squid, but usually can mount an immune defense and clear it from their bodies. But this creates a new problem for many people; they can become allergic, and sometimes severely allergic to the parasite. This means that even if the parasites are cooked and dead, the body still can have a severe allergic reaction to them. Many people who are allergic to fish or squid are not allergic to fish but rather to fish parasite.

Anisakis worms can be killed by cooking fish at a sufficiently high temperature or by freezing it at a sufficiently cold temperature. Since ceviche is not cooked (or in this recipe cooked at a high enough temperature) to kill the worms, fish for ceviche needs to be frozen before using it.

The FDA recommends freezing fish at a temperature below -4°F (-20°C) for 7 days or at minus 31°F (-35°C) for 15 h to kill fish parasites of concern. Most home refrigerator freezers are not set to temperatures below -4°F, and thus are not cold enough to kill the parasites. If you fish, or have friends that give you fish they caught, cook it, but don't eat it uncooked and don't use it for making ceviche unless your are certain it has been frozen at sufficiently cold temperatures. Heating the fish to an internal temperature of 140°F (60°C) for 1 min will also kill Anisakis larvae.

The muscles in healthy living animals are bacteria free zones. The guts and skin are massively colonized with bacteria. If a fish is cleaned properly, the muscle should have very little bacteria. Some contamination with bacteria occurs from the knife cutting through the skin. But when fish are cleaned, if the knife cuts the intestines, or the cutting board is contaminated by the guts or skin, heavy contamination of muscles occurs and bacteria grow quickly. A nice fish filet should not have many bacteria, and food born disease from fish is no more common in the U.S. than it is for chicken. If bacteria have colonized the fish, cooking the fish will kill the bacteria. But for ceviche, you don't want to heat-denature the protein, you want to denature it with fruit acids.

Fish (muscle) can be pasteurized at about 62.8°C, (145°F), and this will kill most of the dangerous bacteria. This temperature will not heat denature the protein. Typical temperatures for heat denaturing fish flesh proteins are about 180°F.

Smoking fish usually does not heat fish sufficiently to kill bacteria, but dehydration impairs the growth of bacteria. It may be desirable to pasteurize fish before smoking it.

Thus, to make safer ceviche use high quality commercially frozen fish, and then prepare the fish as in the following recipe.

1. Thaw the fish or other seafood in water or inside of a refrigerator. Never thaw fish at room temperature, as it allows bacteria to grow.

2. Place thawed fish in Pyrex bowl with lime juice in a pot with water. Place a cooking thermometer

probe in the center of the thickest piece of fish being pasteurized. Heat the juice to 148°F (65° C) long enough for the internal temperature to get to 145°F (63° C) for at least 15 seconds.

3. Turn off the heat and place in the refrigerator for at least 2 hours.

4. Enjoy.

An alternative is to pasteurize seafood in 148° F water for sufficient time for the interior of the seafood to come up to 145° F and then to place it in chilled ceviche juice.

Included in this section is a recipe adapted to making shrimp ceviche at home, without special equipment, by flash boiling the shrimp. Using this very quick cooking preserves the tenderness expected with ceviche. Immunocompromised individuals, those with diabetes, liver disease, or other diseases in which the immune system is not working well, should avoid uncooked seafood altogether.

Escabeche

Escabeche is similar to ceviche, but in escabeche the fish (or meat) is cooked prior to marinating it in acidic fruit juice or vinegar. Escabeche is then chilled in the refrigerator in the marinade for several hours before serving it cold. Here too, the acids prevent bacterial growth. Since the bacteria and parasites have already been killed, there is much less safety concern with the preparation of escabeche.

If you enjoy the flavor of ceviche but are not confident that the fish or other seafood is pathogen free and don't want to fiddle with a pasteurization process as described above, Escabeche is an alternative. First cook the seafood by poaching it, or steaming it until it is cooked; then place it in a marinade as a pickling broth as described in the recipe for shrimp ceviche. Allow it to sit for at least an hour, preferably a few hours in the refrigerator before serving it.

Ceviche de Camarones

Shrimp Ceviche

Ceviche is seafood pickled in an acid, usually citrus juice or pineapple juice. Contrary to a widely held belief, the acid does not kill the bacteria or parasites although it does slow bacterial growth. This recipe is designed to making a safer ceviche. Please read the sections on fish and on shrimp. It is important to prepare the shrimp correctly, not only for safety but also to have the very best flavor and presentation.

Ingredients

1 pound flash cooked butterfly shrimp

Pickling Broth:

½ cup fresh lime juice
½ teaspoon salt
1 large clove of garlic, minced
¼ teaspoon crushed red pepper
2 ají dulce, minced (or 2 tablespoons minced Anaheim pepper)
1 tablespoon cilantro leaves, chopped
¼ cup red onions; diced

½ cup tomatoes; diced
1 tablespoon olive oil
Preparation: Prepare the shrimp as described in the recipe for Flash Cooked Butterfly Shrimp.

Mix the ingredients for the pickling broth (except the olive oil) together, and place in a glass bowl that will be large enough to accommodate the broth and the shrimp. Flash cook and cool the shrimp, and then move the shrimp from the ice water bath after it has cooled into the pickling juice. Turn the shrimp in the juice a few times to ensure that the shrimp has been covered in the juice. Cover the bowl, and chill in the refrigerator for an hour. Add the olive oil and again turn the contents so that the oil gets mixed in. Chill for another hour and serve.

Traditional ceviche is kept overnight in the refrigerator before serving, but with this recipe, it is best to serve it within a few hours, as the shrimp get tough if held too long.

Ensalada de Tuna

TROPICAL TUNA SALAD

INGREDIENTS

1 6 oz. foil pack or one can of tuna; drained
1 tablespoon mayonnaise
¼ cup red sweet onion; finely diced
3 tablespoons canned crushed pineapple (drained)
1 tablespoon minced fresh cilantro

PREPARATION: This tuna salad is slightly sweet. The canned pineapple is cooked, which inactivates the proteolytic enzymes. If fresh pineapple is used, it should be heated or microwaved for a couple of minutes (heated to over 85° C (185° F) to inactivate the enzymes in the pineapple.

Gently mix the ingredients together, adding the tuna last to avoid mashing it too much so that it retains some chunks. Chill in the refrigerator. Serve as a side dish or as a dip with crackers or as a sandwich filling.

The pineapple should be sweet and tart. Note that some brands of canned pineapple are bland, and will not work well for this recipe. You may need to sample a few brands to find one that works well.

Ensalada de Salmón

SALMON SALAD

Follow the Tropical Tuna Salad recipe, replacing the tuna with about 6 ounces of cooked salmon.

Steam a salmon filet, with the skin side down with a couple of teaspoons of olive oil and 2 tablespoons of water in a covered sauté pan over medium heat. Cook the salmon until the flesh separates easily with a fork and the color changes inside. Remove the skin and any visible fat. Prepare the salad as for the tuna salad in the recipe above.

Foil pack salmon can be used as an alternative.

Pescado con Coco

FISH POACHED IN COCONUT CREAM

INGREDIENTS

8 large cloves of garlic; sliced thinly
1 medium red onion; diced
4 cups coconut cream made with a medium coconut
   (or 2 cans of coconut cream)
½ teaspoon dried oregano leaves
½ teaspoon coriander seeds
1 teaspoon curry powder
½ teaspoon salt
3 pounds freshwater fish filets

PREPARATION: Combine the garlic, onion, coconut cream, spices and salt in a sauté pan and bring it to a boil over low heat. Allow it to simmer for about 2 minutes, being careful not to allow it to foam over. Place the fish in the pan, and poach the fish at a low simmer for about 10 minutes, spooning the coconut sauce over the fish to keep the sauce from curdling. Serve with tostones, green boiled bananas or plantains.

Pasta de Pescado Ahumado

SMOKED FISH DIP

INGREDIENTS:

½ pound of smoked mackerel
2 tablespoons mayonnaise
1 small onion; finely diced
2 tablespoons olive oil
4 oz. cream cheese; warmed to soften it.
2 tablespoons finely diced pickles (sweet cucumber
    salad cubes)

PREPARATION: Clean the smoked mackerel, by removing any bones and skin, and break into small pieces. Place the mackerel in a bowl, add the olive oil and mayonnaise and mix it with the fish. Add the other ingredients and mix well. Chill before serving.

Serving ideas: serve with crackers, chips or cucumber slices.

Tilapia en Salsa de Tomate

BRAZED TILAPIA IN TOMATO SAUCE

INGREDIENTS

FISH:

2 fresh tilapia, about ½ pound each
4 cloves garlic
½ teaspoon dried oregano
½ teaspoon coriander seed
½ teaspoon salt
½ whole lime

SAUCE:

3 tablespoons olive oil
½ small onion diced
3 cloves garlic, minced
1 Cuban pepper, diced
½ medium red bell pepper, diced
1 vegetable bouillon cube (5 grams)
¼ teaspoon salt
1½ cups of diced plum tomatoes

¼ cup olive oil for frying the fish.

PREPARATION: Prepare the fish: Place the oregano and coriander in a mortar and grind them together. Add 4 cloves of garlic and grind them with the spices to make a paste.

The fish should be cleaned with the scales removed. Make two 2-inch long diagonal slits to expose the flesh on each side of the fish and squeeze the lime juice over and inside of the abdominal cavity of the fish. Sprinkle the salt on and in the fish. Then spread the garlic/spice paste

on and inside of the fish. Cover and set aside while preparing the sauce.

Prepare the sauce: Make a sofrito (page 90); sautéing the onion in the olive oil until golden, followed by the garlic. Next add the peppers and bouillon and salt and sauté them together. Then add the tomatoes and sauté them for 4 minutes.

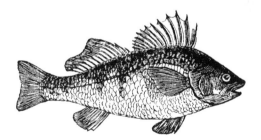

In a sauté pan place ¼ cup of olive oil over medium heat. Add the fish and cook for about 7 minutes on each side moving them occasionally with a spatula so that they do not stick to the ban. The pan should be hot enough to hear the fish cooking, but not so hot that the oil is smoking.

Serving: Pour about half the tomato sauce into a serving plate, and then lay the fish into the sauce. Pour the remainder of the sauce over the fish

Serve with tostones, rice, or boiled green plantains. Serves 2.

Alternative to fried tilapia: Bake the fish for 20 minutes at 400°F.

Tilapia Guisada con Coco

TILAPIA IN COCONUT SAUCE

INGREDIENTS

2 pounds whole cleaned tilapia (4 small fish)
1 teaspoon dried oregano
1 teaspoon coriander seeds
8 cloves garlic
1 lime
28 oz. coconut cream (two cans)
2 vegetable bouillon cubes (5 grams each)
1 teaspoon salt
¼ teaspoon paprika or
    1/8th teaspoon cayenne pepper
Pinch of saffron
2 teaspoons fresh chopped cilantro leaves

PREPARATION: The tilapia should be cleaned, and the scales removed. Make 2 two inch diagonal slits into each side of each fish an inch or more apart. Take a slice of the lime and squeeze lime juice over the fishes and into the body cavities.

Grind the oregano and coriander seed and then the garlic to make a paste.

After letting the lime sit on the fish for about 5 minutes, rinse the fish.

In a wide sauté pan place the coconut cream, garlic paste, pepper and bouillon, and salt, and blend them together over medium heat for about 2 minutes. Bring to a simmer, and add the fish and the saffron.

After a minute, lower the heat to medium-low. Cover the pan and allow the fish to cook at a low simmer for 15 minutes. Check every few minutes and ladle the sauce over the fish. This helps keep the coconut cream from curdling.

Place the fish on a serving tray or on individual plates, and ladle on the coconut sauce. Garnish with fresh cilantro leaves and sprinkle with paprika or cayenne to taste.

Serving suggestions: Serve with tostones, boiled plantains, rulos, or with moro. (Rulos are a short, thick banana usually used green for cooking.) Serves 4.

Ensalada de Calamar

CALAMARI SALAD

INGREDIENTS

3 or 4 pounds of squid
1 medium red bell pepper
1 small yellow bell pepper
1 small red onion
2 plum tomatoes
2 green onion tops
2 teaspoons finely chopped cilantro
1 teaspoon fresh finely chopped jalapeno
2 tablespoons mayonnaise
1 tablespoon olive oil
½ teaspoon red wine vinegar
Salt (less than ¼ teaspoon)

PREPARATION OF CALAMARI: Clean the calamari as instructed on page 52, but do not slice the squid yet. Flash boil the calamari and egg clusters for 1 minute, remove the squid from the boiling water and then place in warm water bath for 10 minutes. The quill (the hard clear spine) may be removed before, but is easier to remove after boiling. Allow to cool, and then slice into rings or bite sized pieces.

Chop the peppers, onions, tomatoes into ¼ inch pieces. Chop the jalapeno and cilantro finely.

In a bowl mix the mayonnaise, olive oil and vinegar, followed by the calamari and the egg clusters. Add salt to taste if needed. Mix these, and then add the rest of the ingredients, and allow the salad to chill in the refrigerator. Serve with crackers as an appetizer or with rice as a main dish.

Birds ~ Aves

Pato Asado

ROAST DUCK

INGREDIENTS:

1 small duck, about 4 pounds
1 small onion, peeled and quartered
8 cloves garlic, peeled
1 tablespoon olive oil
1 small Anaheim pepper
½ cup white merlot

PREPARATION: Preparation of duck, like turkey, takes advanced planning. A frozen bird needs to thaw, and then a day for marinating. Thawing in the refrigerator takes about 2 days, but a fast thaw can be achieved by submerging the bird (still sealed in waterproof packaging) in cool water that is changed every 30 minutes, allowing 45 minutes of thaw time per pound of bird. Microwave thawing is not recommended for birds that are to be marinated.

Remove any contents from the abdominal cavity of the duck that may have been placed there by the processor. Starting from the neck, introduce your fingers between the skin and the breast of the bird, carefully separating them without tearing the skin. The objective is to keep the skin intact. Continue separating the skin away from the meat by separating your fingers as you introduce them, continuing to loosen the skin at the thighs and the back of the bird.

Prepare the marinade by combining the marinade ingredients in a blender until they are liquefied. Place the duck in a bowl large enough for the bird. Using a small cup, pour some marinade into the abdominal cavity of the bird. Turn the bird over in the bowl so that the neck is up. Now pour more marinade between the skin and the muscle where you have dissected it, around the bird. Lay the

duck in the bowl with the breast down and pour the rest of the marinade over the bird, making sure to moisten the wings and thighs. Let the duck soak in the bowl in the refrigerator at least overnight (but not for more than 2 days) before cooking it.

BAKING: Remove the duck from the marinade and place it in a baking pan. Take about ¼ cup of the marinade and pour it over the duck, and then discard the rest of the marinade. Fill the bird's cavity with stuffing, and place the bird in the oven at 275°F, breast down. After 2½ hours turn the bird over so that the breast is up and increase the temperature to 350°F, and cook for another 30 minutes. The safe cooking temperature for fowl is achieved when the breast meat reaches 180°F. Adding stuffing increases the cooking time by about 20 to 30 minutes. The juice in the baking pan at the end of baking may be used to make gravy.

Allow 15 minutes for the duck to cool a little before serving.

Pato Borracho

DRUNKEN DUCK

Duck is all moist, dark meat with a rich flavor. Perhaps because of its higher fat content, it has been considered a special treat for Christmas or other holidays. This recipe is simple to prepare.

INGREDIENTS:

A duck, about 5 pounds
2 tablespoons olive oil
6 cloves garlic; sliced thin
2 vegetable bouillon cubes (5 grams each)
2 plum tomatoes; diced
1 cup white merlot*

PREPARATION: Remove any contents of the abdominal cavity**. Separate the thighs and wings from the body of the duck and separate the limbs at the joints. Then cut the rest of the duck into pieces about 2 inches wide.

Place the oil in a saucepan over medium heat. The goal is to brown the meat at a temperature below the boiling point, at about 190° F, and cook the duck meat to an internal temperature of at least 165° F.

Begin by sautéing the pieces of duck in the oil for about 5 minutes. Next, add the sliced garlic and the bouillon cube and sauté them in with the duck pieces. Lower the heat to medium-low, cover, and cook for another 15 minutes. Next, add the tomatoes and sauté for 5 minutes. Turn the heat down to low, add the wine, cover the pan and steam the duck in the wine for an additional 7 minutes.

*Red wine will darken the meat too much. A mix of half red and half white wine also works well.

** Thawing a frozen duck: It takes 24 hours to thaw a 5-pound bird in the refrigerator (with the temperature below 40°F to prevent bacterial growth). A bird can be thawed more rapidly by submerging it in water with a tiny, steady stream of flowing water or changing the water every 30 minutes, but the duck must be in a sealed package or bacteria can enter and water can soak the bird, ruining the flavor. In water, it takes about 45 minutes per pound, or nearly 4 hours to thaw a 5-pound bird.

Pollo en Melaza con Ají Pipí

CHICKEN IN MOLASSES CHILI TEPIN

For this recipe, chicken thighs are the perfect size. Drumsticks may also be used.

INGREDIENTS:

2 to 2½ lbs chicken pieces (with bones)
2 tablespoons olive oil
3 tablespoons molasses
5 large cloves of garlic; diced
½ teaspoon salt
6 dried tepín chili peppers*

PREPARATION: Using kitchen scissors, remove the skin from the chicken. Place the skinned chicken in a large bowl and add the molasses, garlic, crushed peppers and salt. Mix together to coat the chicken in the flavorings.

Warm the oil in a sauté pan over medium heat. Add the chicken with the spices to the pan and sauté them, turning the chicken a few times for about 2 minutes. Lower the heat to medium-low and cover, so that steam will condense and form a bit of sauce. Turn the chicken about every 5 minutes and then replace the cover on the pan. The chicken should slowly brown over a total of about 20 minutes. Turn off the heat and cover for 2 minutes.

Serving suggestions: Serve along with rice, moro, tostones or potatoes, and a salad.

*Ají pipí (chili tepín) can be substituted with cayenne peppers or with ají pequín. See the section on peppers on pages 12-13 for more information.

Coliflor Cacarear

CAULIFLOWER AND CHICKEN

INGREDIENTS:

1 tablespoon vegetable oil
3 cloves of garlic, minced
½ cup white onion, finely chopped
2 cups cauliflower florets, 1 – 1½ inch
2 cups napa cabbage, cut into 1 inch squares
½ pound boneless skinless chicken breast
1 teaspoon soy sauce
A pinch of salt to taste
A pinch of freshly ground of black pepper
¼ teaspoon salsa picante (or Tabasco sauce)

PREPARATION: Cut the chicken into thin strips about 2 inches long and half inch wide.

Place the oil in a sauté pan over medium-low heat. Sauté the garlic for about one minute, and then add the chopped onions and sauté them for an additional 30 seconds. Add the chicken strips and sauté them for one minute and then cover the pan to cook the chicken in its steam. Stir the chicken around every couple of minutes until the chicken is cooked through. Thinner strips will cook more quickly.

Add the cauliflower and sauté it for one minute, and then add the napa, soy sauce, salt and black pepper, sauté everything together for 2 minutes, and cover until the napa appears lightly steamed. The goal is to have the cauliflower and napa hot, but not cooked through. (See note on page 119). Add the salsa picante, and serve.

Serving ideas: Serve with rice, tostones or pasta.

Pollo Ajícoco

COCONUT GARLIC CHICKEN

INGREDIENTS:

1 14 oz. can coconut cream
2 heads of garlic peeled (about 15 large cloves)
1 jalapeño pepper; diced
¼ teaspoon salt
1½ lbs. skinless, boneless chicken breast
1 vegetable bouillon cube (5 grams)
¼ teaspoon saffron

PREPARATION: Place the coconut cream, whole garlic cloves, jalapeno and salt in a 2-quart saucepan, and heat over medium heat. Cut the chicken into strips along the fiber of the flesh, half-inch by half-inch wide and about 3 inches long. When the coconut cream comes to a simmer, add the chicken. Cover and turn the heat to medium-low, so that the chicken continues to cook at a low simmer for about 25 minutes. Add the saffron and bouillon, stir them in, and cook for another 5 minutes. Turn off the heat; it is ready to serve.

Serve garnished with fresh cilantro.

Pollo Guisado

DOMINICAN CHICKEN

INGREDIENTS:

2 pounds of chicken
2 plum tomatoes (Romano), diced
1 small onion
2 tablespoons crushed garlic
½ cup chopped Cuban peppers
½ teaspoon oregano leaves
2 tablespoons vinegar
1 teaspoon vegetable oil
½ teaspoon salt
1 teaspoon brown sugar

PREPARATION: Prepare the chicken by separating it into pieces (drumsticks, wings, etc.). Cut the breast into 1 to 2-inch chunks. Remove the skin to lower fat content. Wash the chicken in a large bowl with water and lemon juice, and then drain it. Add the crushed garlic, chopped onion, peppers, oregano leaves, vinegar, and salt into the bowl. Next, add the tomatoes and mix all these ingredients together, and spread them over the meat. Cover the chicken and let marinate in the refrigerator for at least 20 minutes.

Place one tablespoon of oil in a frying pan over medium heat. When the oil is hot, spread the brown sugar over the bottom of the pan. When the sugar begins to melt, place individual pieces of chicken in the pan, and mix the chicken around so that the sugar coats as much of the chicken as is easily done. Allow it to cook for a couple of minutes before placing the remaining vegetables and spices from the bowl into the frying pan. Cover the pan to retain moisture and cook over medium-low heat stirring frequently. Add a couple of tablespoons of water as needed to maintain the sauce and to keep the chicken from drying and sticking to the pan.

Cooking time is about 45 minutes to an hour. There should be a small amount of sauce in the pan that is served with the chicken. Typically, pollo guisado is served with rice or boiled plantain.

Pollo Relleno

SAUSAGE STUFFED CHICKEN

This meal has an appearance somewhat like a hotdog sandwich where the bun is formed by the chicken breast.

INGREDIENTS:

2 large skinless split chicken breasts,
    about 1 pound each
2 Italian sausages or bratwursts,
    about 1 to 1½ inch in diameter
Lemon pepper seasoning

PREPARATION: Remove the skin from the sausage, and then slice the sausage in half lengthwise so that there are two long thinner pieces.

Cut a slit into the chicken breast along the longest axis most of the way through to the ribs, leaving the ends intact. This should form a pocket on each side of the first slit. If needed, cut laterally to form a larger pocket. Cut the sausage pieces so that they are just shorter than the length of the pocket,

and stuff one piece into each side of the chicken breast. Gently close the breast pocket avoiding tearing the chicken breast.

Sprinkle the outside of the chicken with lemon pepper seasoning.

Wrap the two chicken breasts in a piece of aluminum foil with the breast pocket opening face up so that while cooking, the spices in the sausage cook into the chicken. Fold the foil to seal at the top and ends to retain the juices as it cooks. Place in a baking pan and bake at 400°F for 35 minutes. Each breast can be cut in half and served.

Serves four.

Serving ideas Serve with vegetable rice (Arroz con Vegetales) and salad or with potato salad (Ensalada Rusa).

Pollo con Limón y Pimienta

SPICY LEMON CHICKEN

INGREDIENTS:

1 pound boneless chicken breast, cut into 1 inch
    cubes.
1 tablespoon olive oil
1 tablespoon butter
1 teaspoon lemon pepper

PREPARATION: Warm the oil in a sauté pan over medium heat, and then add the butter. Add the chicken and braise the chicken, turning about once a minute for 5 minutes. Add the lemon pepper seasoning, and turn the chicken to distribute the spices. Lower the temperature to medium-low and cover. Cook for another 30 minutes, stirring occasionally.

It is ready to be served hot, used in other dishes, or cooled and used in salads.

Guanaho Asado, Pavo Horneado

TAÍNO TURKEY

NOTE: This recipe requires marinating a turkey overnight, and the turkey needs to be either fresh or thawed.

INGREDIENTS:

Turkey (about 12 to 16 pounds)
Turkey Marinade (see next 2 recipes)

Take a fresh or thawed turkey that has been cleaned and the cavity cleared. Beginning at the neck, carefully work your hand between the muscles and the skin of the bird; separate without tearing the skin. First, separate the skin from around the breast; then around the thighs and then along the back of the bird.

Place the turkey in a large bowl, and use your hands to spoon and spread the marinade under the skin, being careful not to tear the skin. Also spread the marinade over the skin, including the thighs and wings. Reserve some marinade, and place it in the cavity of the bird. Refrigerate the turkey overnight with the breast down in the bowl so that it is soaking in the marinade sauce.

Look at the temperature and time instructions from the package as a guide. Preheat the oven to 400° F. Place the turkey in a baking pan breast down to get moister breast meat. Take the marinade sauce from the bowl and pour it over the turkey and into the cavity. Tie the legs together if they are not held together with a clip. Cover the bird with aluminum foil, folding the edges over the edges of the baking pan to form a tent and seal as tightly as possible to help retain moisture.

Place in the oven at 400° F. After 30 minutes decrease the temperature to 350° F and cook for 2 hours. Then, turn the temperature down to 250° F for the remainder or the cooking time, unless you want to brown the breast. Typical total baking time will be about 15 minutes for every pound of turkey. Thus, total cooking time for a 14-pound bird will be about 3½ hours.

If you want to place the turkey on the table with a nicely browned skin, you will need to turn it over and let it bake with the breast up for the last 20 – 25 minutes of cooking at 275° F. Browning requires an oven temperature of over 250° F, so do this step when 20 minutes cooking time are left.

The turkey is done when the temperature of the meat is at 175° F, or when the little popper thermometer pops out. Remove the turkey from the oven and let it rest for 15 minutes before carving it.

Mojo para Guanaho (Adobo)

MARINADES FOR ROAST TURKEY OR OTHER MEATS

Marinades are used to add moisture, and flavor to meat. Acidic marinades also help to tenderize the meat, important especially when a wild or an older bird is used. Two recipes for "mojo" are below. The first is more acidic and traditional; the second milder with more Spanish influence.

Juice from bitter oranges (Naranja agria)* would traditionally be used for the marinade, but they are not usually found in markets in North America. Here grapefruit juice is used to add acidity. If you want to avoid grapefruit juice, it can be replaced with orange juice. Seedless oranges are easier to use but usually have a milder flavor.

INGREDIENTS FOR TAÍNO MARINADE:

2 medium oranges
1 cup grapefruit juice
20 cloves of garlic, peeled
½ of a medium red onion
1/2 red bell pepper; seeds removed
12 fresh mint leaves
1/3 cup fresh lime juice
2 tablespoons coconut oil (or butter)
½ teaspoon salt

PREPARATION: Peel the oranges, and cut them in half across the sections, so that the center area with most of the seeds is exposed. Remove the seeds, and discard them. Add the rest of the orange to the blender, along with the other ingredients. Blend for 3 minutes until the mix is liquefied.

*Bitter oranges are very acidic. They are too acidic to eat as a fruit but are used for flavoring and beverages. The skin is used to make marmalade.

INGREDIENTS FOR CRIOLLO MARINADE:

20 cloves of garlic, peeled
½ small onion
1 tablespoon dry oregano
½ tablespoon dry thyme
½ teaspoon coriander seed
¼ cup olive oil
1 teaspoon salt
½ cup of orange juice
½ cup wine (white zinfandel or other white wine)

PREPARATION: Place the marinade ingredients into a blender and liquefy for 3-5 minutes at high speed.

Pollo Enjugado

CHICKEN BRAISED IN FRUIT JUICE

Chicken can be cooked in fruit juice to give it sweetness and to help with browning. Trim the fat from boneless skinless chicken, and dice into ¾ inch pieces. Braise the chicken in a sauté pan with a fruit sauce, fruit juice, or honey. Reducing sugars such as fructose and glucose in the fruit help with the browning, but table sugar (sucrose) does not.

Most fruits are acidic and may need to be neutralized slightly to get the pH above the ideal pH of 4.7. This pH gives the best flavor while still allowing browning. A small amount of baking soda can be added to reduce acidity.

SCIENCE ALERT: Braising meat in fruit juice or honey, supplies reducing sugars that help promote the Maillard browning reaction that gives color and flavor to the meat. A bit of baking soda is used to raise the pH level slightly and lower the acidity or the orange juice. If the juice is too acid, browning will not occur; the chicken flesh will stay white, and not give the stewed flavor sought here. An ideal pH is about 4.7 to 5. If you add too much bicarbonate, the juice looses its tangy fruit flavor. The baking soda is dissolved in water to make it easy to measure small amounts. Most fruit juices are too acid to allow the Maillard reaction and need to be buffered. If you use fresh orange juice from a sour orange, it may prevent the browning unless enough baking soda is added.

Commercial orange juice is blended to give a fairly consistent pH, so the amounts used given for the following recipe should be close. Simmering just below the boiling temperature helps support the desired browning reaction. Adding more acid fruit juice after browning, allows a fruit-like tang to the dish.

SUGGESTED FRUIT JUICES:

FRUIT	pH	FRUIT	pH
Apple juice	3.4 – 4.0	Jams/Jellies	3.1 – 3.5
Apricot juice	3.3 – 4.0	Mango sauce	3.9 – 4.6
Figs	4.6	Peaches	3.4 – 3.6
Guava Juice	5	Pineapple Juice	3.3 – 3.6
Grape juice	3.4 – 4.5	Prune Juice	4.0
Honey	3.9	Tomato	4.1 – 4.2

Pollo Enjugado - Naranja

CHICKEN BRAISED IN ORANGE JUICE

INGREDIENTS:

2 pounds of boneless chicken
1/2 cup orange juice
1/8th teaspoon salt
2 tablespoons extra virgin olive oil
¼ teaspoon baking soda
¼ cup warm water
4 cloves garlic, sliced
1 vegetable bouillon cube (5 grams)

PREPARATION: If the chicken came with skin, remove it using kitchen shears, and discard the skin and visible fat. Cut the chicken into ¾ inch cubes, discarding the bones, and place the meat in a bowl with ¼ cup of orange juice and 1/8th teaspoon of salt. Stir these ingredients together and cover and place in the refrigerator for a few minutes to marinade.

Dissolve a level ¼ teaspoon of baking soda in ¼ cup of warm tap water. You will only need a small amount of this mixture, and will discard the rest.

Place the olive oil in a sauté pan over medium heat, and add the chicken with the juice it was marinated in. Add 2½ teaspoons of the baking soda water solution to the sauté pan. Braise the chicken at a simmering temperature for about 2 minutes, and then add the sliced garlic. If you do not see any browning, add another ¼ teaspoon of baking soda water. Braise the chicken for another 5 minutes, turning the chicken with a wooden spoon.

Add the vegetable bouillon, and the other ¼-cup of orange juice, and mix it all together. Turn the heat to low, and cover the pan, allow it to simmer for another five minutes.

Serves one 13-year-old boy, or 4 adults.
Serving ideas: with rice, potatoes, in burritos, in a Caesar salad.

VARIATIONS: Try other juices, honey, or fruit pastes, such as guava paste.

Guinea fowl are commonly raised in the Caribbean for food. They are excellent watch hens as they make a huge racket when anything unusual happens. They can fly and are hard to catch!

Paloma Asada

GRILLED SQUAB OR DOVE

INGREDIENTS:

1 bird (about 12 oz)
¼ teaspoon salt
½ teaspoon dry oregano
3 large cloves of garlic
1 lime
2 tablespoons butter

PREPARATION: Make 2 diagonal slits into each side of the bird's breast. Take half of the lime and squeeze the juice on the bird, making sure to cover the surface. Allow it to sit for a minute or two and then rinse the bird in running water.

Place the dove in a bowl and squeeze the other half of the lime to cover the bird again, concentrating the juice on to the breast. Crush 2 peeled garlic cloves in a mortar along with the oregano and salt and blend them together to make a paste. If a mortar and pestle are not handy, mince the garlic and make a paste with the oregano and salt. Use this paste to spread over the breast and into the slits cut into the breast. Cover and place in the refrigerator for an hour.

Crush the remaining clove of garlic and blend it with softened or melted butter. Spread a thin layer of this garlic butter over the bird, and place the bird on the grill over hot coals.

Turn the breasts every 2 minutes and using a basting brush, apply more garlic butter to keep the skin from drying excessively. Generally, it takes about 7 minutes to cook. The skin should be golden brown when done.

Hoofed Beasts ~ Carne

About Meat

Protein is made up of amino acids that are connected together like a long chain, with each amino acid welded to the next by a strong covalent bond. Two out of the 21 amino acids that make up protein contain sulfur, and these sulfur atoms link together with somewhat weaker sulfur-to-sulfur bonds between amino acids that form loops in the chain of amino acids. Additionally there are weak hydrogen bonds that make the string of amino acids stick to itself. The sulfur and hydrogen bonds cause the protein to fold into specific shapes that give the proteins their various functions.

The protein we eat gets broken down by enzymes in our digestive systems, into individual amino acids that are absorbed into our bodies and reused to form new proteins. Cooking food helps make most proteins more digestible.

The weak hydrogen bonds in proteins can be broken during cooking by heat, and by acid, such as stomach acid, or by the acid in fruit as is done in the making of ceviche. This causes the protein to become denatured; it looses its original structure and reforms new hydrogen bonds.

When cooking fish, it will make the flesh more tender and break apart more easily. When cooking egg white, the proteins unwind and reattach to each other forming cross-links and becoming solid. If the egg continues to cook or is cooked at a higher temperature, more cross-linking of the proteins occurs. This forces water out of the matrix and the egg becomes rubbery. The same happens in cooking meat, overcooking, or cooking at too high a temperature can result in tough, dry meat.

Proteins are depicted in the cartoon below. The bows (A) represent proteins in uncooked egg white and in B proteins are arranged into strings to represent protein fibers in meat. In C, the proteins have been denatured and unraveled and form some random cross-linking. With higher temperature or longer cooking, there is further cross-linking, shrinkage, and water loss as illustrated in figure D.

Thus cooking an egg will cause it to become solid. Cooking meat may make it more friable and tender, but overcooking can make it rubbery or tough.

Collagen is a tough structural protein in animals that is made up of chains of amino acids twisted together like a rope. Collagen is found in tendons and ligaments, which are not usually eaten, but it is also distributed in muscle tissue; especially weight-bearing muscle where it keeps the muscle from stretching too far. Older animals have more collagen in their muscles, which explains why we get less flexible as we get older.

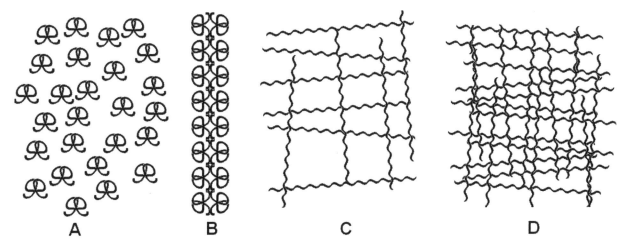

A   B   C   D

Heating the collagen allows the weak bonds to break, but rather than making the meat tender, the fibers cross-link more and just get tougher as the strands form into tighter masses. Since most of the meat sold in grocery stores comes from young animals, it is the cut of the meat that makes the difference.

The strong covalent bonds in proteins are broken during digestion by digestive enzymes, or by meat tenderizer that also uses enzymes to break some of the covalent bonds in proteins. Papain from papaya is one such enzyme used as a meat tenderizer. Cooking in water or steam for long periods can also break some of the covalent bonds in collagen in a process called hydrolysis. This extended cooking turns the collagen into gelatin. After slow cooking meat and storing it in the refrigerator you may notice that gel forms in the bottom of the container. The gelatinized protein gives the meat a better flavor and better mouthfeel because the gelatin retains moisture so that the meat is not dry. This is what occurs during the stewing of meat, and it is the reason that old hens and range animals were traditionally stewed or used to make soup. Stewing is also used for cuts of meat that contain more collagen.

When stewing meat, the fat separates out and is mostly discarded. This results in a lower fat, but dryer meat. The moisture, however, is replaced by gelatin formed from hydrolyzed collagen. Cooking the meat requires moist heat (steaming with a cover or simmering) for three to four hours. The shanks and shoulders are highest in collagen and are best for stewing. Meats low in collagen only become dryer with extended cooking.

To kill bacteria that may be in meat, the USDA makes the following recommendations for the internal cooking temperature to kill bacteria:

- Fish: 145°F (63°C)
- Steaks and Roasts: 145°F (63°C)
- Ground Beef: 160°F (71°C)
- Pork: 160°F (71°C)
- Poultry   165°F (74°C)

One principal muscle protein (actin) denatures at about 151°–163°F (66–73°C). Collagen in most meat denatures at about 154°F (68°C) and then becomes rubbery. For beef steaks and roasts an internal temperature of 145°F (63°C) can be used if the surface temperature reaches 160°F (71°C) to kill surface bacteria; there should be few bacteria in the interior if the meat has been properly stored. Cooking beef to 170°F (77°C) causes shrinkage and toughness.

STEAKS AND ROASTS: Beef can be braised to an internal temperature of over 145°F (63°C) for fifteen seconds to kill bacteria, while reaching an external temperature of over 160°F (71°C). This medium to done meat should not lose much moisture and can be cooked quickly and has a tender texture. Keeping the temperature below 170°F (77°C) allows for a moister, more flavorful meat while avoiding shrinkage and toughness.

Ground meat requires a higher temperature for safe preparation than steaks and roasts. Since the meat has been ground, there are bacteria in the center of the meatball or hamburger patty. While it may be safe to eat steak medium rare, this is not true for ground meat. Ground beef should be heated to an internal temperature of 160°F, or to 155°F for at least 15 seconds to kill the bacteria Since the meat has been ground up, denaturing the collagen is not a concern as it is for a steak where overcooking will cause the steak to get tough or rubbery. With ground beef, however, overcooking will cause shrinkage, dryness, and crumbling and loss of flavor, and overheating can cause the formation of carcinogenic compounds. (See below.)

Cooking Temperatures for Red Meat

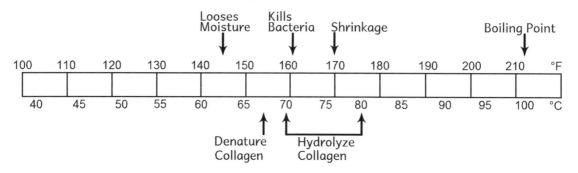

The interior of a piece of meat, a meatball or hamburger patty is heated by conduction from the outside. It takes time for this to occur. The higher the temperature of the grill or skillet, the faster the outside will cook, but a hotter cooking temperature has little effect on the time it takes to cook the center of the meat. Using too high a temperature overcooks the outside but may leave the inside raw. This is especially true if the meat is still frozen at the center.

STEWED BEEF: Stewed meat should be cooked in moist heat for several hours to hydrolyze the collagen. The preferred temperature for hydrolyzing collagen is between 158°F and 176°F (70°C to 80°C); a very low simmer, with temperatures at the lower end of this range giving the most desirable results. Poultry is more forgiving because, except in older birds, there is little collagen in the muscles. These older birds are traditionally used for soup or for stewing.

In comparison, fish live in water at a cooler temperature, and the bacteria that live in them tend to live and die at lower temperatures. Thus, lower cooking temperatures are required to kill the bacteria in fish that can cause disease. Additionally, since fish are not weight bearing they have little collagen to worry about.

Squid and octopus, however, do have a large amount of collagen in their flesh. This collagen is of a different variety than found in beef, and it denatures at a temperature of about 85°F (29°C). It also has a shrinkage temperature of about 127°F (53°C)[12]. Therefore, squid and octopus shrink and become rubbery when heated to a safe cooking temperature. The trick to cooking squid and octopus is to cook them very quickly, usually for about one minute, which is not enough time for the collagen to do much cross-linking, and then to cool it. The other alternative is to stew them for an hour.

AVOIDING CANCER RISK FROM MEAT:

Heterocyclic amines (HCA) are the most significant carcinogens in the American diet, causing breast, colon and prostate cancers. The formation of HCA requires five things; heat, moisture, and a reaction between creatine (or creatinine) and amino acids and a reducing sugar. Cooking meat provides all these components. Creatine is used as an energy source for muscles and is found in high concentration in the muscles of mammals, birds, and fish. Invertebrates such as shrimp, oysters, clams, and squid, do not have significant creatine,

and so do not form HCA during cooking. It is not found in milk or cheese. Egg yolk contains creatine, so eggs can form HCA if overcooked[13].

Little HCA formation occurs at or below boiling temperature, but the amounts rise quickly as cooking temperatures exceed 300°F (150°C)[14]. Cooking in water usually does not create a significant amount of carcinogens. When grilled, braised, pan-fried or deep-fried, the formation of HCA increases with temperature. Browning of egg yolk indicates excessive cooking temperature and HCA formation.

In addition to preventing HCA formation by controlling the cooking temperature, it has been demonstrated that using traditional Caribbean style marinades can decrease HCA formation during cooking of a steak by 88%[15]. A traditional Caribbean type marinade (Criollo Marinade) is given on page 71.

Creatine, amino acids, and glucose are released from muscle cells when meat is cut. Thus after slicing meat, it is a good idea to rinse it, which is another tradition in Dominican cooking. Adding the lemon juice adds an additional step that removes creatine and free amino acids. One reason that marinades and washing work is at least in part the result of removing creatine and free amino acids from the surface of the meat, and the marinade also contains antioxidants. Even if you prefer not to use lemon juice, meat can be rinsed off and patted dry before cooking to remove the juices that contain creatine.

DIRECTIONS: Coat all the surfaces of the meat with the lemon or lime juice. For one or two pounds of meat, use the juice from half of a large lemon (about ¼ cup). Cover the meat, and let it sit for a couple of minutes, and then rinse the meat with fresh water. Drain the water before cooking it

If meat is cut into smaller pieces, a larger surface area is exposed, and more cells are cut open, releasing more creatine and amino acids. Thus, ground beef has a huge surface area exposed and has large amounts of exposed creatine and free amino acids. Mechanically tenderizing meat in a roller press or with a mallet also serves to disrupt muscle cells and release creatinine and amino acids. Fortunately, it is usually only the surface that is cooked at a high enough temperature to form large amounts of HCA. Much of the free creatinine can be removed from a hamburger patty by gently heating the patty in a microwave at low power for 1 to 2 minutes and draining off the liquid that is released, before grilling the hamburger[16], but excess heating in the microwave will dry out the patty. Adding vitamin C to the hamburger also decreases HCA formation. Cooking ground beef properly (below) prevents almost all HCA formation. This advice can be applied to other meats and fish as well.

COOKING GROUND BEEF: Ground beef needs to reach a higher center temperature to kill bacteria than steak, and needs more cooking time to allow heat to transfer into the center of the patty or meatball. The grill or skillet temperature should be set to 320°F (160°C)[17] and no higher than 356°F (180°C). A higher temperature has little effect on how long it takes to heat the center but increases carcinogen formation. A grill temperature over 212°F (100°C) gives the hamburger its outer crust.

- Meat needs to be completely thawed before cooking to cook properly
- Patties should ideally be about 6/10th to ¾ inch thick, to be juicy, but no thicker to cook well
- Do not use the spatula to press the juice out of a hamburger; it dries out the patty and creates more carcinogens. (See below)
- Flip the patty once a minute to cook it more quickly and evenly and avoid HCA formation.
- Expect it to take 9 to 12 minutes to cook, the hamburger, depending on its thickness.
- A brown center does not guarantee that the temperature got to a safe temperature.
- Cook hamburger meat to an internal temperature of 160°F (71°C), or to 155°F (68°C) for at least 15 seconds.

Fish or meat that has been incompletely thawed is much more like to be overcooked on the outside and raw in the center; resulting in HCA on the outside and live bacteria on inside

SCIENCE FACT: It takes one calorie of energy to heat one gram of water by 1 C. It however takes 80 calories to overcome the enthalpy of fusion of ice and heat one gram of ice one degree from minus 0.5 C to 0.5 C water. Chilled water from the refrigerator at 38 F (3 C) could be heated to 181 F (83 C) with the same amount of energy required to melt the same amount of ice. It thus takes about the same amount of heat energy to thaw a piece of meat as it does to cook it.

Digital thermometers that can test internal meat temperatures are inexpensive and should be considered a basic tool in every kitchen.

Pan residues from cooking meat are very high in HCA and should be discarded. They should not be used for making gravy.

HCA cause cancer by attaching to DNA in the cell's nucleus that code for proteins that regulate cell growth. This damage can be partially avoided or even reversed by eating a couple of serving of cruciferous vegetables every week. Cruciferous vegetables include broccoli, cabbage, cauliflower, mustard, and watercress. These vegetables provide the most benefit when lightly steamed just before serving. The beneficial effects are lost if these vegetables are boiled[18]. See page 119 for proper preparation of these vegetables to provide the most protection from cancer.

Carne de Res en dos Vinos

BEEF IN TWO WINES

INGREDIENTS:

¼ pound beef; cut into ¾ inch cubes
1 teaspoon oil
2 cloves garlic; finely diced
1 tablespoon butter
½ of a 5-gram bouillon cube
3 plum tomatoes; diced
A pinch of salt
2 tablespoons red wine
¼ cup white wine

PREPARATION: Warm the oil and butter over medium heat. When hot, add the beef to the pan and brown it for 5 minutes. If the butter browns or smokes, you have the pan too hot. Add the garlic and cook for 2 minutes. Add the bouillon and tomatoes and cook for another 2 minutes. Add 2 tablespoons of red wine and a pinch of salt. Lower the heat and cover the pan with the lid slightly ajar to allow the steam to escape, until the liquid has evaporated. Add 1/4 cup of white wine, and stir it in. As soon as it simmers, it is ready to serve.

Serve with rice, potatoes, mangú or mofongo. Makes a single serving.

Carne Guisada

SAUTÉED GOAT, LAMB, VENISON, BEEF OR FOWL

Goat and lamb are cooked more for special occasions, such as weddings and holidays. It is on these occasions that Carne Guisada is cooked with wine. More commonly, carne guisada is prepared with beef and without the wine, but why limit good food to holidays? Venison or other meats may also be used.

INGREDIENTS:

2 pounds meat; cubed into ¾ inch chunks
1 cup red onion, finely chopped
2 medium Anaheim or Cuban peppers, diced;
    (about 1 cup), or use red or yellow bell peppers
2 medium tomatoes cut into chunks
5 cloves garlic, minced
¼ teaspoon dry oregano
1 cayenne pepper chopped
    or ¼ teaspoon ground cayenne powder
½ teaspoon salt
2 tablespoons olive oil
1 teaspoon brown sugar
½ cup water
¼ cup red wine

PREPARATION: Seasoning the meat: place the meat in a bowl with the chopped onions, garlic, salt, oregano, cayenne pepper, half of the peppers and half of the cut tomatoes. Mix together, cover and allow them to sit for 10 minutes.

Place the oil in a saucepan over medium heat. When it warms, add the brown sugar and stir it in with a wooden spoon. When the sugar melts and begins to caramelize, place the seasoned meat and vegetables in the pan. Gently stir the meat in so that it is coated with the caramelized sugar/oil mixture. Cover the pan, letting the contents steam until all the liquid is reduced (about 10 minutes), and the meat begins to braise in oil. About every 2 minutes add a tablespoon of water and stir the meat to keep the pan moist. This keeps the meat from sticking to the pan and helps give a brown caramelized surface to the meat. Next add the wine and the rest of the peppers, and cook for 2 minutes. Add the rest of the tomatoes, cover the pan and turn off the heat, allowing the tomatoes to warm for a minute. Serve immediately.

Cooking time: Half hour. Serve with rice, Moros or Mangú.

Albóndigas

MEATBALLS

MEATBALL SAUCE INGREDIENTS:

2 tablespoons olive oil
1 small onion quartered and sliced
3 large cloves garlic; sliced lengthwise
1 beef or vegetable bouillon cube (5 grams)
¼ teaspoon salt
5 plum tomatoes; diced
¼ cup wine

PREPARATION: Place the olive oil in a sauté pan over medium heat. Add the onions and sauté them until they are clear. Add the garlic and sauté it until it begins to turn golden. Add the bouillon, salt, and tomatoes and sauté these ingredients together until a thick sauce forms. Last, add the wine. A red wine will give a darker color than white wine. I prefer a white merlot. Pour onto a deep plate and cover to keep warm until the meatballs are ready.

MEATBALL INGREDIENTS:

2 pounds of ground chuck
1 head of garlic (12 – 15 cloves) peeled
1 Anaheim or Cuban pepper, diced
1 small onion; finely diced
2 eggs

½ teaspoon salt
1 beef bouillon cube (5 grams)
1/3 cup vegetable oil

PREPARATION: Meatballs: Place the meat in a large bowl. Crush the garlic and the pepper in a mortal, or otherwise blend them. Add these to the ground chuck with the diced onion, eggs, and salt, blending them together using your hands to mix thoroughly. Take a pinch of the dough large enough to roll into balls about 1¼ inch (3 centimeters) in diameter.

Heat a sauté pan with about 1/3 cup of vegetable oil over medium heat, preferably to about 320°F. Be careful to keep the pan temperature below the smoke point temperature. (See Cooking Ground Beef on page 78. Place the balls into the oil and cook them, moving them around so that all surfaces are cooked, and so that the inside of the balls are cooked as well. Remove the meatballs from the pan, and into the deep plate filled with the meatball sauce.

SERVE: With spaghetti, rice, or tostones.

Carne Picada con Hongos

BEEF WITH MUSHROOMS

INGREDIENTS:

1 pound chuck or round beef; cut into ¾ inch cubes
1 tablespoon olive oil
1 teaspoon brown sugar
¼ teaspoon salt
5 cloves garlic; sliced thin
¼ cup green onions; diced
½ cup mushrooms; diced
½ cup celery; diced
1 teaspoon (low sodium) soy sauce

PREPARATION: Heat the olive oil in a skillet over medium heat. Add the brown sugar and mix it in with a wooden spoon. When the sugar starts to bubble, add the beef and salt. Sauté the beef for about 3 minutes, turning it frequently. It should be hot enough to sizzle, but not to smoke. Turn the heat back down to medium add the garlic and sauté for a few seconds. Add the green onions, mushrooms, celery and soy sauce and cover. Lower the heat to medium-low, allowing the contents to cook in the steam for fifteen minutes. Serve with rice, yuca or other starch tuber, and sliced ripe tomatoes. Serves two.

Carne Mechada

STUFFED POT ROAST

This recipe is for slow cooked beef that is tender and full of flavor. Growing up, this entree was served on holidays, as it was not often that a piece of meat this large was purchased. It can be served with rice and veggies, or can be used in sandwiches.

INGREDIENTS:

2 lbs. chuck or round beef, at least 2 inches thick
8 cloves garlic
3 sweet peppers
1 teaspoon salt
1 teaspoon oregano
1 cup water*
¼ teaspoon whole coriander seeds

PREPARATION: Use a steak knife to poke holes through the meat to form channels about 1 inch apart.

Mash the garlic and sweet peppers in a mortar and then place the paste in a small dish. Add the salt and the oregano, mixing them all together. Stuff the channels that were made in the roast with this paste.

Place the roast in a saucepan and add the water and the coriander seed. Heat the water to a simmer, cover with a well sealing lid and lower the heat to medium-low to maintain it at a low simmer. About every 20 to 30 minutes ladle some of the juices from the meat over the top. It takes about 2 hours of cooking, and the meat should be very tender and easy to tear apart when ready. The liquid in the pot can be used as gravy or to make gravy.

* NOTE: As holiday fare, half cup of water can be replaced with a half cup of white merlot or white zinfandel wine. White wine is used as red wine darkens the meat too much.

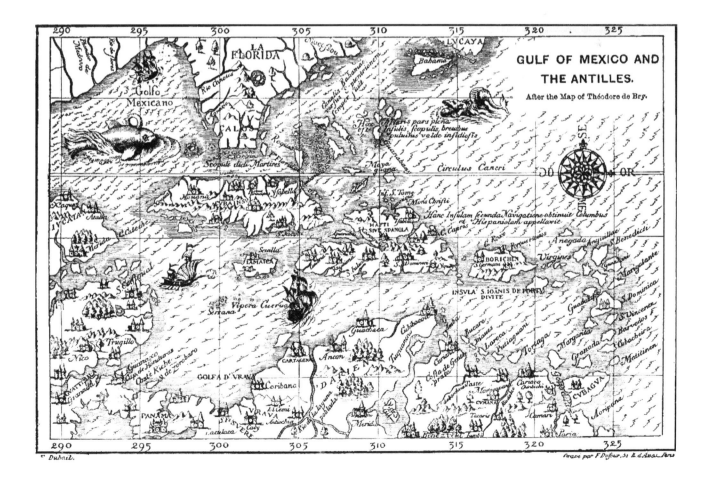

Chivo Cimarrón

VENISON STEWED IN WINE

Once, traveling with friends in the countryside in the south of the Dominican Republic, we stopped at an open-air restaurant with a view of the sea. My companion ordered chivo guisado (stewed goat). Two hours later, famished, we asked about the delay. The server explained that the meal was nearly ready and apologized for the wait; it had taken longer than expected to catch a goat.

Venison (venado) is not a dish often seen in the Caribbean, but goat certainly is. And even though goats may not be truly cimarrones (feral), most goats in the Dominican Republic are free ranging, and have a gamey flavor. Venison has a flavor similar to our free-range goats. Venison, goat, lamb or other meat can be used with this recipe.

INGREDIENTS:

2 pounds of venison (or other red meat) cut into 2 cm cubes.
1 cup red onion, finely chopped
2 medium Anaheim peppers; diced
2 medium tomatoes, cut into chunks
5 cloves garlic, minced
¼ teaspoon dry oregano
1 cayenne pepper, chopped
    or ¼ teaspoon ground cayenne powder
½ teaspoon salt
2 tablespoons olive oil
1 teaspoon brown sugar
½ cup water
¼ cup red wine

PREPARATION: Seasoning the meat: Place the meat in a bowl with the chopped onions, garlic, salt, oregano, cayenne pepper, half of the Anaheim peppers and half of the cut tomatoes. Mix together, cover and allow them to sit for 10 minutes.

Place the oil in a saucepan over medium heat. When it warms, add the brown sugar. Stir it in with a wooden spoon. When the sugar melts and begins to caramelize, place the seasoned meat and vegetables in the pan. Gently stir the meat in, so that it is coated with the caramelized sugar/oil. Cover the pan and allow the contents to steam until all the liquid is reduced (about 10 minutes), leaving the meat to cook in the oil that remains. About every 2 minutes add a tablespoon of water and stir the meat to keep the pan moist. This keeps the meat from sticking to the pan and helps give a brown caramelized surface to the meat. Next add the wine and the rest of the Anaheim pepper, and cook for 2 minutes. Add the rest of the tomatoes, cover the pan and turn off the heat, allowing the tomatoes to warm for a minute and then serve immediately.

Cooking time: Half hour. Serve with rice, moro or mangú.

Ropa Vieja

PULLED BEEF

Ropa Vieja means "old clothes", an allusion to tattered rags. This method of preparation was originally used for meat that was too tough for other dishes. The meat may have come from older or range fed animals. The cooking times can be as long as 10 hours to get to the point that the muscle fibers separate easily. Here the cooking time is reduced, as most beef is no longer grass fed and herded long distances to market.

INGREDIENTS:

1½ cups water
2 cloves garlic; halved
½ teaspoon dry oregano
¼ teaspoon salt
1 lb. beef cut into 2 or 3 pieces

PREPARATION: Place the water, garlic, oregano, and salt in a medium saucepan, and bring to a boil. Add the meat (the boiling water kills surface bacteria) and immediately lower the temperature, cover and cook at a low simmer (160°-175°F) for about 40 – 60 minutes with a vented lid or one slightly ajar to allow a bit of evaporation. Cook the meat until the meat is very tender, and a fork passes into the meat easily. Remove the pan from the heat and allow the beef to cool in the broth so that it reabsorbs moisture and flavor. When cool enough to handle, tear the meat into small bits, about the size of a small olive. Reserve the broth that has been made.

INGREDIENTS FOR SOFRITO SAUCE:

3 cloves garlic; sliced thin
2 tablespoons olive oil
1 small red onion; finely diced
4 plum tomatoes; diced
1 vegetable bouillon cube (5 grams)
1 Anaheim pepper; diced
Pinch of salt
Pinch of ground cayenne pepper

Place the oil in a sauté pan over medium heat, and sauté the onion for about 1 minute until it begins to get transparent and then add the garlic. When the garlic turns golden, add the tomatoes and cook for about 3 more minutes and then add the Anaheim pepper, the salt and the bouillon and cayenne, and stir together for another minute.

Add the pulled meat to the sofrito sauce, gently stirring the meat in for one minute. Add ½ cup of the broth and cook for a couple of minutes at a low simmer.

Serving ideas: Ropa vieja is usually served with rice or boiled plantains. It is also used in sandwiches.

Vaca Verde

Stuffed Cabbage

Ingredients: Meat

1 pound ground chuck
2 plum tomatoes finely diced
3 cloves garlic, minced
½ small onion; finely diced
1 small Cuban pepper; finely diced
½ teaspoon dried oregano, rubbed
½ teaspoon salt
2 tablespoons olive oil
1/8th teaspoon cayenne pepper

Ingredients: Cabbage and Sauce:

A medium sized head of cabbage
  (loose better than tight)
6 plum tomatoes; diced
1 Cuban pepper, diced
½ small red bell pepper; diced
½ small red onion; diced
5 cloves garlic, minced
3 tablespoons olive oil
1 teaspoon brown sugar
1 vegetable bouillon cube (5 grams)
½ teaspoon salt
1 tablespoon fresh cilantro leaves

Preparation:

1. Place the ground chuck in a large mixing bowl and add the tomatoes, garlic, onion, Cuban pepper, oregano, and salt. Mix the ingredients together thoroughly.

Place 2 tablespoons of olive oil in a large saucepan over medium-low heat and add the ground beef. Use a wooden spoon to break the meat into small pieces. Cover and allow the meat to cook in its juices for 20 minutes, stirring occasionally, making sure that the meat is in small grains. Do not allow it to dry out. Mix in the cayenne pepper. Turn the heat off and set to the side to let the meat cool.

2. While the meat is cooking, take the cabbage head and cut it in half through the center of the stem so that the leaves will hold together. Cut out the center 2-inch ball of leaves. Starting with the outside leaves, carefully loosen the layers of leaves from each other without breaking them.

3. Sauce: Place the olive oil in a large saucepan over medium heat, and sauté the onions until they become clear. Mix in the brown sugar. Add the garlic, and sauté it until it is golden brown. Add the tomatoes and bouillon and sauté it all together until the tomatoes form a sauce. Add the peppers and the salt, cover, and set the heat to low.

4. The meat should now be cool enough to handle. Using a teaspoon, work ½ of the cooked beef into each half of the cabbage between layers of leaves and fill the center. When done, take the 2 halves and put the cabbage back together, and tie the 2 halves together with cotton string. Place the cabbage head in the pot with the sauce, cover it and allow it to steam over medium heat for 15 minutes. Turn off the heat and allow it to rest for another 10 minutes before serving. Place it on a serving tray, cut the string so that the 2 halves are open and ladle the sauce over the halves and garnish the dish with fresh cilantro leaves.

Serve with rice, or boiled red potatoes.

Preparation time: about 2 hours. Serves six.

Rice Dishes – Arroz

About Rice:

When I was in high school, I lived with an aunt who owned a small rice mill patronized by rice farmers from my town. The farmers would bring their harvest to the large shed behind her house, and the rice would be fed into the mill that would spit out the husks and the rice would go into a pile to be bagged. The pigs would get the husks, and my aunt kept a percentage of the rice as payment. We would put the rice out on a large concrete slab to dry in the sun.

Pigeons would come and steal the rice. I would steal it back by putting out a metal wash pan with one side held up with a stick tied to a string. I would snatch the string when the pigeons strolled under the pan capturing them. I would clean the birds, and hang them on the clothesline to dry in the sun for a couple of hours before grilling them and enjoying them with my accomplice. A recipe for grilled poached squab is given on page 74.

We had many different varieties of rice. Most were long grain suited to our dry climate. Some were red, some brown, some white. Sadly, most of these varieties are disappearing as the economy of scale drives out smaller farmers in favor of larger ones serving more uniform markets.

Brown rice and other unpolished and unrefined rices, have more nutrients, but this makes them more susceptible to becoming rancid. Rice should be stored in a sealed container and out of the sunlight to keep it fresh and dry. Purchase only the amount of rice you expect to use in the next few months, leaving the professionals to warehouse the food.

When I was little, cleaning rice to remove twigs, dirt and pebbles was an ordinarily part of its preparation. Nowadays rice is sold clean and does not need picking through. Rice still should be rinsed in tap water and drained to remove excess starch.

Cook rice in a saucepan with a base made to disperse the heat, (either a thick aluminum or copper bottom). The pan needs to have a lid that fits well enough to trap the steam.

Generally, the longer the variety of rice grain, the more water is required for cooking. Long grain rice absorbs about 1.4 cups of water per cup of rice during cooking while short grain varieties may only absorb about 4/5th of a cup of water per cup of rice. Since some water is lost in steam, more water than this is required. A general rule for long grain rice is 1¾ cups of water to every cup of rice. Short-grain rice varieties tend to be stickier while long grain gives more individual loose grains. Cooking with more water will also make the rice softer and clump more. The goal is to have all the water soaked up by the rice at the end of cooking. Short-grain rice varieties need less cooking water, but brown rice requires more water (and more cooking time).

Most of the recipes in this book call for long grain rice, as these are the ones preferred in the Dominican Republic. I enjoy the flavors of different rice varieties, such as jasmine and basmati rice as well as the ordinary long grain rice. These flavors are volatile and will be lost if the rice cooked with too much water. To preserve even more flavor, the rice can be soaked before cooking for 20 to 30 minutes. Even soaking for 10 minutes will help, but it can be soaked for up to about 2 hours to help shorten cooking time and decrease the loss of aroma. Longer soaking times should be avoided to prevent the growth of spores that can cause sickness. Place the rice in the amount of water that you intend to cook the rice in, and just delay cooking.

When the rice is done simmering, and the heat is removed, it is not yet done cooking. Use a wooden spoon or other large spoon and gently lift the rice from below to fluff it. The rice then needs to "rest" with the lid on to retain the steam for 5 to 30 minutes. This will make the rice texture more uniform and bring out the flavor.

RESCUING RICE:

If after cooking rice it is a bit undercooked, a couple of tablespoons of water can be added and reheated to allow the rice to steam longer. If the rice turns out too wet, you can try a trick my mother used: place a clean cotton towel on top of the rice and let it steam on low heat for a couple of minutes. The towel will absorb the extra moisture. Or just leave the lid ajar for a few minutes and then replace it.

Rice cookers are convenient and great time and attention savers. The ingredients can be added to the cooker, and the timer set, giving consistent, worry-free, never-burned rice. Rice cookers, however, will not make concón.

Rice should not be left out at room temperature for long periods. Spores that resist cooking can grow, and cause gastrointestinal sickness.

Leftover rice can be kept in the refrigerator for a few days or frozen, but will get hard. Heating to over 160°F will soften it again. I like to heat rice in the microwave just long enough that I can hear it sing (the steam noise) when I take it out.

Arroz Blanco y Concón

WHITE RICE WITH CONCÓN

When rice is made in the traditional manner over wood, the rice at the bottom of the pan gets toasted and crisp. This toasted rice is called concón. The concón is a prized treat, especially among Dominican women.

INGREDIENTS:

2 cups white rice (jasmine rice is preferred)
1 tablespoon olive oil
3 cups water
1 teaspoon salt

PREPARATION: Place 3 cups of water into a pot with oil and salt, bring it to a boil, and add the rice. Boil the rice at medium heat for about 3 minutes, and then lower the heat to medium-low, and cover. Allow to cook until all the water has been consumed. Turn to low heat letting the rice cook until it splits open, typically about 15 minutes. Gently fluff the rice, lifting it from below and away from the inside edges of the pot with a wooden spoon. Turn the heat off and let the rice rest for another 10 minutes before serving.

Arroz con Coco

COCONUT RICE

INGREDIENTS:

14 oz. coconut cream
2 cups water
1¼ teaspoons salt
2½ cups (jasmine) rice

PREPARATION: Place the coconut cream, water, and salt in a saucepan and heat it. As soon as it begins to boil, stir in the rice. Cover the pan and lower the temperature to maintain the rice at a simmer. Cook until the liquid is gone. Place on low heat for another 15 minutes. The rice should be split open when it is cooked, and the rice at the bottom should be lightly toasted.

The toasted coconut rice concón is my favorite.

Arroz con Hongos

MUSHROOM RICE

INGREDIENTS:

½ cup sliced mushrooms
2 tablespoons butter
3 cloves garlic, minced
14 oz. coconut cream
1½ cups water
1 vegetable bouillon cube (5 grams)
½ teaspoon salt
2 cups long grain rice

PREPARATION: Place the butter in a saucepan over medium-low heat and allow it to melt. Gently sauté the garlic and the mushrooms. The garlic does not need to brown. When the mushrooms have darkened, add the other ingredients, except the rice. Turn the heat up to medium and stir to mix the ingredients together. When the liquid is warm, stir in the rice. Cover, and lower the heat if boiling hard. Allow the rice to simmer until all the liquid is consumed, and turn the heat to low. Cook for another 15 minutes at low heat, or until the rice splits open.

Arroz con Fideos

RICE WITH NOODLES

INGREDIENTS:

1/8th teaspoon saffron
2 tablespoons olive oil
4 cloves garlic; sliced into thin rounds
¼ cup diced onions
2 oz. fine egg noodles
3 vegetable bouillon cube (5 grams each)
1½ cups rice
2 cups hot water (total)
½ teaspoon fresh basil, minced

PREPARATION: Crumble the saffron into ½ cup of warm water and set aside. Warm the oil in a deep sauté pan over medium heat. Add the garlic and sauté it for one minute; add the onions and cook for 3 more minutes. Add the bouillon and stir it in to form a sauce. Break the noodles into pieces about ½ to ¾ inches long, and add them to the pan. Stir the noodles into the sauce and cook for 2 minutes. Next, stir in the rice and sauté it for 2 more minutes. Stir in 1½ cups of hot water, followed by the ½ cup of water with the saffron. Turn up the heat to bring it to a boil, and then lower the heat to medium, cover and simmer it until the broth is consumed. Cook over low heat for another 15 minutes. Serve garnished with basil.

Arroz con Pollo

RICE WITH CHICKEN

This is a moist rice dish, between a stew and a locrio. This recipe uses broth made while preparing the chicken, and uses more liquid than for a typical rice.

INGREDIENTS:

2 pounds of chicken leg quarters
1 teaspoon salt
1 tablespoon olive oil
1 medium onion; diced
4 cloves garlic, minced
3 ripe plum tomatoes; diced
¼ cup stuffed olives
½ cup diced celery
3 cups chicken broth (made while preparing the chicken)
2 cups long grain rice

PREPARATION: Simmer the chicken leg quarters in a large sauté pan with sufficient water to make sure that the chicken floats. Add a teaspoon of salt. Cover, and cook at a simmer for 20 minutes. Remove the chicken pieces from the pot and place them on a plate to cool, setting the broth aside.

Allow the chicken to cool until it can be handled. Separate the meat from the skin and bones, that can be discarded. If not already small enough, tear the meat into large bite-sized pieces.

The pot with the broth will have fat floating on the surface. Spoon off this fat and discard it. Set aside 3 cups of this broth for later use with this recipe.

Place the olive oil in a medium sauté pan and heat over medium heat, add the onions and sauté them for about 30 seconds, followed by the garlic for another minute, until the garlic is just beginning to turn light golden. Add the tomatoes and sauté them for about 2 minutes, until they form a paste. Stir in the olives, followed by the celery and boiled chicken meat, gently sauté together for another minute avoiding breaking the chicken. Add the rice and 3 cups of the chicken broth that had been set aside. Bring it to a boil, cover it, and lower the heat to medium-low. Cook it at a simmer for about 8 minutes, adjusting the heat if needed to prevent boiling over. When the water is almost consumed, turn heat to low and allow it to steam for another 15 minutes. The rice should be split open when it is done. Fluff the rice, lifting it from below with a large spoon, and allow it to sit covered for 5 minutes before serving or transferring to a serving plate. Serve with a salad.

Arroz con Maíz

RICE WITH CORN

Bright yellow corn kernels add color to the plate.

INGREDIENTS:

2 tablespoons olive oil
4 cloves garlic, minced
1 teaspoon fresh ginger root, minced
2 cups cut corn (frozen or fresh)
1½ cups rice
1½ cups water
¾ teaspoon salt
1 carrot; diced (optional)

PREPARATION: Warm the oil in a medium-sized saucepan over medium heat. Add the garlic and ginger and sauté them for about a minute until the garlic is golden. Add the corn and carrot (optional) and sauté for about 2 minutes. Add the rice and salt and sauté together for about 30 seconds. Add the water and bring it to a boil. Cover the rice and turn the heat to medium-low; high enough to maintain the rice at a simmer. Cook it until the liquid is consumed, about 10 minutes. When the water has been depleted, turn the heat to low, allow the rice to steam in its own vapor for about 10 minutes. Remove the rice from the heat, and fluff the rice by lifting it with a large spoon from below. Cover the rice again and allow it to sit for about 5 minutes.

Arroz con Almendras y Pasas

RICE WITH ALMONDS AND RAISINS

This is rice for a special occasion, for guests or just a bit of indulgence. Pine nuts, chopped walnuts, or pecans may be used in place of the almonds; golden raisins, dried cranberries or other dried fruit may be used in the place of raisins.

INGREDIENTS:

2 cups white rice (jasmine rice is preferred)
1 tablespoon olive oil
3 cups water
1 teaspoon salt
¼ cup sliced almonds or other nuts
¼ cup raisins or dried cranberries

PREPARATION: Place 3 cups of water into a pot with oil and salt, bring it to a boil, and add the rice. Boil the rice at medium heat for about 3 minutes, and then lower the heat to medium-low, add the raisins and almonds and cover. Allow the rice to cook until all the water has been consumed. Turn the heat down to low to allow the rice to steam until it splits open, typically about 15 minutes. Gently fluff the rice, lifting it from below and away from the inside edges of the pot with a wooden spoon. Turn the heat off and let the rice rest for another 10 minutes before serving.

Arroz con Ostrones Ahumada

SMOKED OYSTER RICE

INGREDIENTS:

1 tablespoon vegetable oil
1 small onion, chopped
4 large cloves of garlic, chopped
1 Cuban pepper, chopped
3 plum tomatoes; diced
Two 3.75 oz. cans of smoked oysters
1 teaspoon salt
1 cup long grain white rice
2 cups warm water

PREPARATION: Place the oil in a pan over medium heat. When hot, add the onions and sauté them until they are golden-brown, and add the garlic. Add the Cuban pepper and cook for about one minute. Mix in the tomatoes and salt. Cover for about one minute until the tomatoes are soft and begin to form a sauce. Add the smoked oysters along with the oil from the cans. Gently stir the sauce to avoid breaking up the oysters. Next, gently mix in the rice and sauté it at low heat for about a minute. Add 2 cups of warm water and mix in gently. Warm water keeps the ingredients from cooling as much and avoids the need for reheating. Bring the water to a boil, turn the heat down to medium, and cover the pot. Cook for about 8 minutes until the water is almost gone. Lower the heat to low and steam the rice for about 15 minutes until the rice water is gone and the rice is split open and fluffy. The rice should not be sticky.

SERVING SUGGESTIONS:
Serve with:

- Black or red beans with sauce
- Ripe avocado
- Ripe uncooked banana
- Fried sweet ripe plantain

90

Locrio

Locrio is a quintessential Dominican dish as it is the perfect embodiment of a single pot dish. The name is a contraction of locro-criollo": Spanish *locro* (stew) and Portuguese *crioulo* (originally meaning a descendant of Europe born in the colonies, but more often used to mean native). The Locrio is similar to the Spanish paella, (from the Latin *patella*, meaning pan, indicating that the meal is cooked in a single pot). Like paella, locrio is an adaptation of a Moorish rice casserole, which likely made its arrival to the island of Hispaniola with Columbus's sailors.

Locrio, however, is not a stew, as there is no gravy or sauce when it is done cooking. Like paella, the dish is cooked until the water has evaporated, and the rice on bottom of the pan has toasted. This caramelized rice is called concón, and it is highly regarded. The trick to cooking a locrio is to put in the right amount of water so that it is consumed by evaporation just as the cooking is done. When a toasted aroma is emitted, the locrio is ready.

Locrios are started by preparing a sofrito, a sauce used as a base for many Caribbean dishes. Each country seems to have its own distinctive flavorings and ingredients. Generally, it is prepared by sautéing onions, garlic, sweet peppers, and herbs in oil. In the following column is a typical recipe for sofrito for use in locrio as well as in many other dishes.

Once the sofrito is prepared, the following step in preparing a locrio is to braise the uncooked rice in the sofrito and get it completely coated with the flavoring. Cook the rice for about 2 minutes, stirring it into the sofrito. Add the water that is called for in the recipe, and other ingredients. Bring to a slow boil and allow it to simmer for a few minutes. Taste the broth. It should have a good flavor like soup, with enough, but not too much, salt. Carefully add a small amount of salt at a time, stirring it in until it has enough salt. Cover the pot and allow it to simmer over a low flame for about 20 minutes until the liquid is consumed. For locrio, the ends of the grains of rice should be split open when it is done. Cover with a banana leaf or a moist cloth and allow it to sit for at least 5 minutes.

Sofrito

INGREDIENTS:

3 tablespoons olive oil
2 tablespoons butter
½ cup onions; diced
6 large cloves garlic; sliced thin
6 sweet peppers, seeds removed, and minced
2 – 3 plum tomatoes; diced
½ teaspoon Salt

PREPARATION: Since sweet peppers (Ají Dulce) are hard to find, ¼ cup of diced Anaheim peppers can be used in place of the sweet peppers.
Heat a sauté pan with the oil and the butter on medium to medium-low heat. Do not overheat or it will burn (about 300°F). When the butter just begins to sputter, add the onions. Sauté the onions, turning them with a wooden spoon until they just begin to soften and clear. Next add the garlic and sauté then with the onions until the garlic turns golden brown. Add tomatoes, peppers, and salt and sauté for 2 to 3 minutes until the tomatoes have formed a sauce with the other ingredients.

NOTE ON BOUILLON: Bouillon, dehydrated broth, often sold in cubes or blocks is often used in Dominican cooking to flavor savory foods. The forms sold in the Caribbean such as Maggi brand often come in 10-gram blocks, wrapped in foil. These are twice the size of the smaller bouillon cubes most commonly found in the United States which are about ½ inch on a side. The recipes in this book call for 5-gram cubes, but may be substituted for other forms of bouillon, including one teaspoon of bouillon paste or powder to replace one cube, or an half of a 10-gram block.

Locrio de Chorizo

RICE WITH SAUSAGE

INGREDIENTS:

1 tablespoon olive oil
1 small onion, chopped
1 tablespoon chopped, garlic
2 plum tomatoes; diced
1 pound bratwurst; sliced into 2 cm lengths
½ teaspoon salt
2 cups water
1½ cups long grain rice
1 tablespoon capers

PREPARATION: Heat the oil in a 2-quart saucepan. Add the onions and the bratwurst pieces and braise them for about 5 minutes. Add the garlic and braise it until it starts to brown. Add the tomatoes and the salt, stirring them, and cook until the tomatoes form a sauce. Add the rice, braising the rice in the "sofrito" (sauce) for about 2 minutes. Add the water, stirring in the ingredients. Taste the broth to make sure it is adequately salted. Bring the broth to a boil. Add the capers, cover and cook for 8 minutes over medium heat adjusting the heat down if needed to prevent boiling over. Turn heat to low and allow steaming for another 20 minutes. The rice should be split open when it is done. Allow to sit covered for 5 minutes, before serving or transferring to a serving plate.

Serving suggestion: Serve with a green salad, with avocados, ripe banana, or tostones.

Locrio de Arenque

YELLOW RICE WITH SMOKED HERRING

Locrio de Arenque is the essence of Dominican soul food cuisine. This was made with broken rice and a few cents of dried herring, which was an inexpensive way to get flavor. This was the first dish I learned to cook as a child.

INGREDIENTS:

½ lb. smoked, salted dry herring
5 large cloves garlic, minced
½ small to medium red onion; diced
½ red bell pepper; diced
½ green bell pepper; diced
2 tablespoons olive oil
2 large plum tomatoes; diced
3½ cups water
2 cups long grain rice (jasmine rice preferred)
½ teaspoon salt
1 teaspoon small capers

PREPARATION: Prepare the herring by soaking it in a large bowl of water for about 10 minutes. Split the herring in the abdominal cavity to separate into halves so that the spine and most of the fine bones can be removed. Also, peel off the skin and discard it. Tear the flesh into strips about 1/3 inch wide and into pieces one to 2 inches long.

Warm the oil over medium heat in a medium saucepan. Add the onion and sauté for about 2 minutes until the onions turn clear. Then add the garlic and sauté them until they just start to turn golden. Add the bell peppers and sauté them for 2 minutes, and then add the diced plum tomato and stir everything together to form a sofrito sauce. Add the herring. Sauté the ingredients for another 2 minutes. If the sauce starts to get too dry, lower the heat and add 1 -2 tablespoons of water.

Add the capers and water, and bring it to a boil for 2 minutes. This will help bring the salt and flavor out of the fish. Taste the broth and add salt if needed.

Stir in the rice and let it come back to a boil. Then lower the heat to medium-low and cover to maintain the rice at a low simmer. Allow the locrio to simmer until all the liquid has been consumed (usually about 10 minutes). Lower the heat to low, and allow the rice to cook in its own steam until the rice splits open, about 15 more minutes. Gently fluff the locrio in the saucepan lifting it from below with a wooden spoon, turn off the heat, leave it covered, and allow it to rest for another 10 minutes before serving.

Locrio de Arenque con Coco

COCONUT RICE WITH SMOKED HERRING

INGREDIENTS:

½ lb. smoked salted dry herring (4 oz. cleaned)
14 oz. can of coconut cream
5 large cloves of garlic; diced
¼ cup chopped green onions
2 cups water
¼ teaspoon salt
2 large plum tomatoes; diced
2 cups long grain rice (jasmine rice preferred)

PREPARATION: Prepare the herring by soaking it in a large bowl of water for about 10 minutes. Split the herring in the abdominal cavity to separate into halves so that the spine and most of the fine bones can be removed. Also, peel off the skin and discard it. Tear the flesh into strips about 1/3 inch wide and into pieces one to 2 inches long.

Add the coconut cream, water, garlic, tomatoes, onion, and salt to a medium saucepan, over medium heat. Cover and allow the ingredients to simmer for about 5 minutes to give time for the

flavors to blend and for the salt to come out of the fish. Taste the coconut broth to make sure it has enough salt. Add 1/8th teaspoon at a time if it needs more.

Stir in the rice and let it come back to a boil. Then lower the heat to medium-low and cover to maintain the rice at a low simmer. Allow the locrio to simmer until all the liquid has been consumed (usually about 10 minutes). Lower the heat to low, and allow the rice to cook in its own steam until the rice splits open, about 15 more minutes. Gently fluff the locrio in the saucepan lifting it from below with a wooden spoon, turn off the heat. Leave it covered, and allow it to rest for another 10 minutes before serving.

Locrio de Pescado Ahumado

RICE WITH SMOKED FISH

As an alternative to using smoked herring to make locrio this recipe uses smoked fish that are not heavily salted, and the recipe has to be adapted to the difference in salt content. Smoked king mackerel, mullet or other smoked fish may be used.

INGREDIENTS:

4 tablespoons olive oil
1 small red onion; diced
6 cloves garlic, sliced
3 large plum tomatoes; diced
8 oz. smoked fish, broken into ½ inch pieces
3 teaspoons salt
1 tablespoon capers
1 tablespoon "juice" from the capers bottle
Pinch of cayenne pepper
1/8 teaspoon saffron
3 cups water
1½ cups jasmine or basmati rice:

PREPARATION: Place the oil in a saucepan over medium heat. Briefly sauté the onions (about a minute) and then add garlic and sauté for another minute. Add the tomatoes, cover and let it cook for about 4 more minutes over medium-low heat until it forms a sauce. Add the fish, salt, capers, caper juice, cayenne pepper, saffron, and mix. Add the rice and water.

Cover and raise the heat to medium and cook at a simmer for about 10 minutes, until the liquid has been consumed. Lower the heat to low and cook for another 15 minutes until the rice grains have split open.

Serving ideas: Serve with avocado or a ripe banana. Also good with a green salad, pea soup, beans, and with fried sweet plantains.

Locrio de Bacalao

YELLOW RICE WITH SALTED COD

How did dry salted cod from the cold waters of the North Atlantic become a staple ingredient in traditional Caribbean cuisine? Salted cod was likely part of a shipping trade pattern that dates to before the American Revolution. Salted cod was shipped to West Africa as part of the slave trade and to the Caribbean to feed slaves and planters. Sugar, rum and coffee shipped to Europe and North America, where it was traded for manufactured goods. Salted cod (bacalao) was an important commodity as it can keep for several years without refrigeration. For the same reason it survived as a twentieth century ingredient because of the lack of refrigeration and electrical power in many area of the Caribbean, perhaps especially in desert areas where it is still found as slabs of fish sold in open boxes in little shops called colmados.

NOTE: If you purchase bacalao refrigerated, keep it refrigerated to keep it from going bad.

INGREDIENTS:

8 oz. of bacalao
4 tablespoons olive oil
5 large cloves of garlic, minced
½ of a green bell pepper; diced
¼ of a red bell pepper; diced

1 small red onion, quartered and sliced
3 small plum tomatoes; diced
2 cups long grain rice
3 cups water

PREPARATION: Place the oil in a sauté pan and heat it over medium heat. Add the onions and sauté them until they begin to turn clear. Add the garlic, and sauté them until they begin to turn golden. Next, add the peppers and tomatoes and sauté them for about 3 minutes until a sauce begins to form. Lower the heat to medium-low, and add the bacalao and one cup of water and allow the mixture to simmer for about 4 minutes. This will help to release more salt from the fish.

Add the rice, and 2 cups more water, and stir together and raise the heat until it begins to boil. Lower the heat to medium-low and cover the pot. Cook over medium-low heat until the liquid is consumed. Lower the temperature to low, and cook for about 15 minutes with the lid in place so that the rice cooks in its own steam, until the rice grains split open. Turn off the heat and allow the rice to rest with the lid in place for another 5 minutes before serving.

Locrio de Bacalao con Coco

COCONUT RICE WITH COD

INGREDIENTS:

8 oz. dry salted cod (bacalao)
22 oz. coconut cream
1 cup water
6 cloves garlic; diced
½ of a medium onion; diced
½ of a Cuban pepper; seeds removed and diced
2 ají dulce (if available), seeds removed, minced
1 vegetable bouillon cube (5 grams)
2 cups long grain rice
1 tablespoon annatto seeds (bija)(optional)

PREPARATION: Place the salted cod in a large bowl with cool water, and allow it to soak for about an hour. Drain the water and rinse with cool water. Tear the fish into pieces, about ½" by 1", and rinse again to remove excess salt.

Pour the coconut cream and water into a 2-quart saucepan. Add the onions, garlic, peppers, bouillon and cod. Bring to a simmer.

As the liquid simmers, prepare the bija. Place the bija in a small bowl with 2 tablespoons of water. Mix together until the water turns deep red. Strain the seeds out and add the reddened water to the simmering liquid. After the liquid has simmered for about 5 minutes stir in the rice. Turn up the heat and stir frequently. When it comes to a boil, turn the heat to low, cover and cook. When no more water is visible, cook on low heat, for another 15 minutes. When it is done, the rice should be split open. You may smell the rice toasting in the bottom of the pot.

Serve with avocado or ripe bananas.

Locrio de Camarones

YELLOW RICE WITH SHRIMP

INGREDIENTS:

4 tablespoons olive oil
1 small red onion; diced
5 cloves garlic, sliced
3 large plum tomatoes; diced
½ cup diced carrots
½ cup diced celery
1½ to 2 teaspoons salt
2½ cups water
1½ cups (jasmine or basmati) long grain rice
1½ pounds of shrimp (headless)
    (or 1 pound of peeled small shrimp)

Optional: 1 tablespoon capers
          2 tablespoons sundried tomatoes,
              cut into ¼ inch strips

PREPARATION: Prepare the shrimp by peeling and deveining them, and then return them to the refrigerator. If the shrimp are large, cut them into ½-inch sections.

Place the oil in a saucepan over medium heat. Briefly sauté the onions (about a minute) and then add garlic and sauté for another minute. Add the celery and carrots and sauté for 2 minutes. Add the tomatoes, cover and let it cook for about 3 more minutes over medium-low heat until it form a sauce. Add the one teaspoon of salt (and the capers) and mix them in. Add the (sun dried tomatoes), rice and water, and mix things together. Taste the broth, to make sure that it has sufficient salt, adding about ½ to 1 teaspoon salt as needed to give it a savory soup saltiness.

Increase the heat and bring it to a boil, and then lower the heat to medium-low, add the shrimp and place a lid on the pan. Allow it to simmer until all the liquid has been consumed, usually about 10 minutes. Lower the heat to low, and allow the rice to cook in its own steam until the rice splits open, about 15 more minutes. Turn off the heat; leave it covered, and allow it to rest for another 10 minutes before serving.

For richer flavor: If starting with shrimp with skin, use the skin to make a broth as explained on page 55, and use 2½ cups of broth in place of the water used in the recipe above to give a fuller flavor.

Locrio de Picantina

RICE WITH SPICY SARDINES

Like many Dominican dishes, this one came out of the necessity for low-cost ingredients, lots of flavor, and lack of electrical power for refrigeration. This seafood from a tin could be purchased even in the smallest and most remote hamlet in a "colmado" – a shop consisting of a small room in someone's house that had a room with a Dutch door with a counter facing the street. Standard provisions that could be found at a colmados were rice, sugar, and dry beans sold by the cup; cigarettes matches and bouillon sold by the each; and cans of sardines, coffee, yuca plantains, and coconuts were sometimes available.

Locrios can use meat or seafood, this traditional one uses hot spiced sardines.

INGREDIENTS:

3 tablespoons olive oil
¼ cup garlic, minced
½ cup onions; diced
3 plum tomatoes; diced
1 tablespoon fresh finely chopped ginger
1/3 cup diced Cuban pepper
¼ teaspoon saffron
2 tablespoons green olives stuffed with pimentos
One 15 oz. can of hot-spiced sardines (in tomato sauce)

1½ cups long grain rice
¾ teaspoon salt
1½ cups warm water

PREPARATION: Heat the oil in a 2-quart saucepan. Add the onions, and cook them until they just get clear. Add the garlic either crushed or finely chopped. When the garlic starts to brown, add the saffron, tomato, ginger and Cuban peppers and cook until the tomatoes form a sauce. Mix in the sardines. Add the rice, stirring gently to avoid breaking the sardines, and cook for a couple of minutes. Add the water, olives and salt to taste. Bring to a boil. Cover and cook for 8 minutes over medium heat adjusting the heat down if needed to prevent boiling over. Turn heat to low and allow steaming for another 15 to 20 minutes until the water is gone. The rice should be split open when it is done.

Note: When cooking rice in the Dominican style, expect a brown crust of rice on the bottom of the pot. This toasted rice is known as concón and is a treat often reserved for women and children. The best concón is from coconut rice.

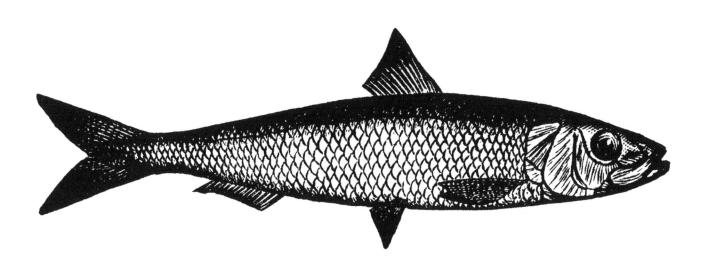

Locrio de Pollo

YELLOW RICE WITH CHICKEN

The name "rice with chicken" does little to convey the pivotal role of this dish in the social structure of the Caribbean. Locrio de Pollo is as Dominican as apple pie is American. This is the dish of friendship and sharing. Served at informal gatherings and meals with cousins and neighbors, this typifies the relaxed ease of unrushed life where there is time to sit in the shade and share gossip and other stories.

INGREDIENTS:

2 tablespoons olive oil
2 tablespoons light brown sugar
1 medium onion; diced
1½ tablespoons garlic, minced
¼ teaspoon coriander seed
½ teaspoon dry oregano
1 medium carrot; diced
¼ cup stuffed Spanish olives
1 teaspoon small capers
2 plum tomatoes; diced
2 five gram chicken or vegetable bouillon cubes
1½ pounds of chicken thighs
1 teaspoon salt
2 cups water
2 cups long grain rice

PREPARATION: Cut the chicken thighs in half lengthwise, along the direction of the bone. Heat the oil in a 2-quart saucepan over medium heat. When the oil is warm, add the brown sugar. When the sugar begins to bubble, add the chicken. Braise it for a couple of minutes, turning it so that it gets coated with the brown sugar. Add the onion, garlic, sauté together for another 3 minutes.

Mill the coriander seed and dry oregano together into a powder (traditionally in a mortar and pestle). Add these spices, the carrots, tomatoes, and salt, to the chicken and sauté together for 5 minutes, until the tomatoes melt into a sauce.

Add the bouillon and the rice, braising the rice in the "sofrito" (sauce) for about 2 minutes. Add the water, stirring in the ingredients. Taste the broth to make sure it is adequately salted. Bring the broth to a boil. Add the capers and olives. Cover and cook at a simmer for 8 minutes over medium heat, adjusting the heat down if needed to prevent boiling over. Turn heat to low and allow the rice to steam for another 15 to 20 minutes. The rice should be split open when it is done. Let the locrio rest; cover it for 5 minutes before serving or transferring it to a serving plate.

Serving suggestion: Serve with a green salad with avocados or ripe bananas.

Locrio de Cerdo

RICE WITH PORK

This is another traditional form of Locrio.

INGREDIENTS:

½ pound boneless, center cut pork chop
½ lemon or lime or 1-2 tablespoons lime juice

1 tablespoon olive oil
¼ cup diced onions
2 tablespoons minced garlic
2 plum tomatoes; diced
¼ teaspoon dry oregano
½ teaspoon small capers
¼ cup stuffed Spanish olives
¼ teaspoon saffron
¾ teaspoon salt
1 cup long grain rice
1½ cups water

PREPARATION: Cut the meat into one-inch cubes and wash the meat with lime or lemon juice. Rinse the meat under running tap water and allow the water to drain off before adding the meat to the sauté pan.

Heat the oil in a 2-quart saucepan over medium heat. When the oil is warm, add the onions and the garlic and sauté them for about 2 minutes until the garlic is just beginning to turn light golden brown. Add the pork and sauté it for about 3 minutes. Add the tomato, oregano, olives, saffron, capers and salt. Cook these together, stirring with a wooden spoon for one minute. Add the rice and sauté it in the sauce that has been formed for another minute, making sure that the rice is coated with sauce.

Add the water and stir it in. Taste the broth to make sure it has adequate salt, and add ¼ teaspoon of salt at a time if needed, and stir it in. Turn up the heat and bring the soup to a boil. As soon as it boils, lower the heat to medium-low, and cover the pan. Allow it to simmer for 10 minutes. When the sauce has been consumed, reduce the heat further to low, and allow the rice to steam for 15 minutes. The rice should be split open when it is done. Turn off the heat, and let the locrio rest, covered for 5 minutes before serving or transferring to a serving plate.

Serving suggestion: Serve with Habichuelas Guisadas, fried ripe plantains and a green salad with avocados.

Locrio de Trigo con Picantina

CRACKED WHEAT WITH SPICY SARDINES

Many Dominicans were introduced to this dish as a school lunch meal. The schools were supplied cracked wheat from the United States Agency for International Development (USAID) Food for Peace program. The stated purpose of this program was to combat hunger and malnutrition and to create an export market for U.S. commodities. It also helped to support less than democratic governments and to stabilize commodity prices in the U.S. by getting rid of surplus agricultural production. These commodity/surplus foods became Locrio de Trigo, the wheat flour Yaniqueques, and Queso Frito (Fried Cheese). Locrio de Trigo is one of the better commodity inventions and cracked wheat was a sought after gray market item.

INGREDIENTS:

1¼ cups of cracked wheat
2 cups water

2 tablespoons olive oil
5 cloves garlic; sliced thin
½ small onion; diced
3 diced plum tomatoes, diced
½ Cuban pepper, diced
1 vegetable bouillon cube (5 grams)
1 15 oz. can sardines (in hot spiced tomato sauce)
½ teaspoon salt
1 cup warm water

PREPARATION: Presoak the wheat in 2 cups of water for about 20-30 minutes to soften it, and then strain the water from the wheat.

Prepare a sofrito: Place the oil in a 2-quart saucepan, adding the onions, and cook them until they just become clear. Add the sliced garlic. When the garlic starts to brown, add the tomato and Cuban peppers and cook until the tomatoes form a sauce. Add the sardines with the sauce from the can, and the bouillon. Add the wheat, stirring gently to avoid breaking the sardines into small pieces, and cook for a couple of minutes. Add one cup of water and salt to taste. Bring to a boil. Cover and lower the heat to a simmer for 8 minutes, adjusting the heat down if needed to prevent boiling over.

In contrast to locrio with rice, when making the dish with wheat, it is important to stir the wheat while is cooking every couple of minutes to avoid having it sticking to the bottom while it is simmering. When all the water is consumed turn heat to low, cover the pan and allow the locrio to cook in the retained steam for another 15 to 20 minutes using a lid that fits well and retains the moisture.

Serving recommendations: Serve with white beans, avocado, and salad.

Locrio de Pica Pica con Coco

COCONUT RICE WITH SARDINES

INGREDIENTS:

14 oz. of coconut cream
1 cup of water
4 large cloves of garlic, minced
½ of a small onion, quartered and sliced
½ of a medium Cuban pepper, quartered and sliced
1 tablespoon fresh cilantro; diced
1¼ teaspoons salt
¼ teaspoon saffron
15 oz. can sardines in spiced tomato sauce
2 cups rice

PREPARATION: Combine the coconut cream, water, garlic, onion, Cuban pepper, cilantro, saffron and salt in a saucepan. Add the sardines, including the sauce. Stir together gently, to avoid breaking the sardines into small pieces. Heat until it begins to boil and then add 2 cups of rice. Turn the heat down to a simmer and cook until all the liquid has been consumed. Cover and place on low heat for another 15 minutes.

Serve with frijoles or with a salad.

Moro con Coco

COCONUT RICE AND BLACK BEANS

This is a Dominican variation, one of the most traditional and favored island dishes of the Caribbean. The name "moro" is the shortened form of the original name "Moros y Cristianos"; Moors and Christians, referring to the white rice and black beans eaten together in perfect harmony. Moro is also commonly made with red beans. Here moro is cooked with coconut cream.

INGREDIENTS:

1 can of black beans (2½ cups), drained
1 can coconut cream (14 oz.)
4 cloves garlic, minced
¼ teaspoon epazote
1 cup water
1 teaspoon salt
1 tablespoon chopped fresh cilantro (or culantro)

2 cups long grain rice

PREPARATION: Place all the ingredients in a medium saucepan except for the rice, and place over medium heat. After the liquid is warm, add the rice, and bring it to a boil. Cover and lower the heat to medium-low, allowing the moro to simmer until the liquid is consumed. Lower the heat to low, and cook for another 15 minutes. The rice grains should be split open when the moro is done, and the rice on the bottom just lightly toasted to a golden brown.

Serving ideas: Serve hot with a light sprinkle of cilantro leaves as a garnish. Serve with seafood or poultry.

Moro de Haba

RICE WITH BUTTER BEANS

INGREDIENTS:

1 small onion; diced
1 tablespoon crushed garlic
1 tablespoon crushed ginger
2 teaspoons olive oil

1 can butter beans, drained
1 medium tomato; diced into large chunks
2 cups water
1½ cups rice
1½ teaspoons salt

PREPARATION: Add onion, garlic, ginger and olive oil together in a saucepan, and sauté them until the onions begin to get clear. Add the beans and tomato and sauté them for about 2 minutes. Add the water, rice and salt. Bring to a boil for one minute, turn down the heat to a simmer, and cover. Adjust the heat so that it does not boil over. When no water is visible, turn to very low heat and cook until the rice splits open.

Eat with ripe banana or avocado on the side. May replace butter beans with other flat beans such as fava beans, or lima beans.

Moro de Habichuelas

RICE AND RED BEANS

This is a recipe for traditional rice and beans with Caribbean flavors.

INGREDIENTS:

½ teaspoon cilantro seeds
½ teaspoon dry oregano
6 cloves garlic, peeled
3 tablespoons olive oil
½ small onion; diced
½ small bell pepper; finely diced
2 plum tomatoes; diced
1¼ teaspoons salt
2 cups cooked red beans
¼ teaspoon dry epazote
2½ cups water
2 cups long grain rice

PREPARATION: Place the cilantro oregano and epazote in a mortar and grind them together. Next, add the garlic and mash the ingredients together to make a paste.

Warm the oil in a medium sauce over medium heat. Add the paste from the mortar, sautéing it for one minute. Add the onion and bell pepper, and sauté for another minute. Then add the tomatoes and sauté until it forms a sauce. Add the salt, the beans, and the water. Bring the liquid to a boil, and then stir in the rice, cover the pot and turn the heat to medium-low. Let the moro simmer until the water has been consumed.

Use a wooden spoon to gently lift the moro from below to fluff it. Lower the heat to low, and cook for another 15 minutes. If available, cover the moro with banana leaves for the last fifteen minutes. The rice grains should be split open when the moro is done, and the rice on the bottom is just lightly toasted to a golden brown.

Serving ideas: Serve with Pollo guisado or carne guisado, and a salad.

Alternate: For a truly authentic flavor, use 8 ají dulce in place of the bell pepper. Remove the stem and seed from the ají dulce and mash them together with the spices and garlic to make the paste for the sofrito.

Moro con Coco

Prepare as above, but replace 14 oz. of the water with a 14 oz. can of coconut cream and leave out the olive oil and tomatoes.

Moro de Guandules con Coco

COCONUT RICE WITH PIGEON PEAS

INGREDIENTS:

2 cans (about 14 oz each) coconut cream
2 cans (about 15 oz each) pigeon peas drained
5 large cloves garlic, crushed
1 small onion; diced
1/8 teaspoon dry oregano leaves
1 tablespoon chopped fresh cilantro
1¼ teaspoons salt
1½ cups white rice

PREPARATION: Place all ingredients, other than the rice, in a large saucepan, and bring it to a boil. Stir in the rice, cover it and lower the heat to medium-low to cook at a simmer. Give it a stir it after a couple of minutes to prevent sticking and replace the lid. When liquid is gone, turn heat to low and cover. Allow the moro to steam until rice splits open.

Moro de Yonyon con Coco

Djon-Djon Coconut Rice

Mushrooms are typically not a part of traditional Dominican cuisine. There is a traditional cultural avoidance of mushrooms as a food, perhaps because Spaniards who settled the Dominican Republic came mostly from Andalucía, an area where mushrooms were considered by the Christians to be associated with the devil. This is not the case in Haiti, perhaps because the French collected and ate mushrooms, or it may be that the slaves brought by the French came from areas further north in Africa than those brought by the Spaniards. The manner in which the mushroom stalk and cap are separated is similar to that used in an African recipe for elephant soup.

In Haiti, Riz Djon-djon (Mushroom Rice) also called Riz Noire (Black Rice) and is considered a delicacy. I grew up in the southern part of the Dominican Republic, in the Provence of Independencia; that was controlled for a time in the early 1800's by Haiti. Perhaps this is where we learned to make our own version of black rice. When the weather was right, about 3 days after heavy rains, we collected a djon-djon mushroom on my uncle's farm and used them to make this special dish.

Ingredients:

1 cup (2/3 oz) dried djon-djon mushrooms
1 can coconut cream (14 oz., high fat)
3 cloves garlic, minced
1½ cups water
1 tablespoon fresh cilantro leaves
2 vegetable bouillon cubes (5 grams each)
½ teaspoon salt
2 cups long grain rice

Preparation: Clean the mushrooms removing any dirt or foreign material. Separate the stems from the caps. The stems are not eaten as they are like straw, but they are used to add color and flavor. Soak the mushroom caps in 1 cup of warm water. Remove any dirt from the stems and soak the stems in a ½ cup of hot water for 30 minutes.

Add the mushrooms caps with the water from the caps and the "tea" from the stems to a saucepan, discarding the mushroom stems. Add the coconut cream, garlic, salt and the bouillon and let them sit for a few minutes before turning on the heat. Bring the mixture to a boil and then stir in the rice. Lower the heat to medium and cover. Set the heat to maintain a simmer for about 10 minutes or until the liquid is consumed. Turn the heat to low and cook for another 15 minutes. The rice grains should be split open. Serve garnished with cilantro.

Serve with avocado, alongside with fish or meat.

In the U.S. djon-djon mushrooms can be difficult to find. You can try Haitian markets or markets in areas that serve Haitian immigrants. For online purchases, you can try the Kreyol Kitchen: (kreyolkitchen.com). Store dried mushrooms in sealed containers in your freezer to keep them freshest. Djon-djon mushrooms are members of the *Psathyrella* family, likely either *Psathyrella coprinoceps* or *P. Hymenocephala*.

Alternatives:

If you cannot find the djon-djon mushrooms, you can try substituting other mushrooms. Among several different types of mushroom we have tested, dried porcini mushrooms give the best results. The flavor is similar but milder than djon-djon. Porcini mushrooms will tint the rice some, but will not give the traditional black rice color. Black trumpet mushrooms (chanterelle mushrooms) are another good choice.

Beans ~ Habichuelas

About Legumes:

Beans are an essential dietary and nutritional component in Latin America, being an important source of dietary protein. Many varieties of legumes are used in Caribbean cuisine. When prepared correctly, beans should be creamy and just a bit sweet.

If you are not from the Caribbean and speak Spanish, the naming for beans can be confusing. In the Caribbean, *habichuelas* is the most commonly used word for beans. It refers specifically to red or kidney beans but is commonly used for most beans. The word fríjol is sometimes used, especially for white or black beans. The uncooked dry beans are sometimes called fríjol, but they are frijoles when cooked. Guandules, also called gandules, are pigeon peas and sometimes are called guandul when uncooked and dry. The word for green peas comes from the French for little pea; petit pois. Haba refers to broad beans such as lima beans. In South America beans are usually called portotos, and in Spain they are called judía, fabes, or alubia.

It's quick and convenient to used canned beans, so many of the recipes that call for beans are adjusted to 1 2/3 cups of beans - the amount found in a standard 15 oz. can. Unless you are cooking for a crowd, it is a lot of work to cook a half cup of dry beans for a meal for a few people. For larger quantities, dry beans may be preferred, or when available, fresh beans are a treat. Here's an approximation of how to substitute dry beans in a recipe.

1 15 oz. can of beans = 1 2/3 cups of cooked beans (drained)
1 cups dry beans = ½ pound dry beans
1 cup dry beans = 2½ cups soaked beans
1 cup dry beans = 3 cups cooked beans; drained

It takes 4.4 oz., just over a half cup of dry beans, to make the equivalent of one can of beans.
Canned beans are precooked and only need to be heated to be eaten. Drain them and add them to the recipe. Additional cooking will soften them more.

When cooking with dry beans it takes time. If you are at high elevations - it can take a long time. Generally it is best to cook beans in plain water. Cooking beans in an acidic liquid, (with tomatoes, vinegar, and wine) or cooking in hard water with calcium or magnesium prolongs the cooking time. Adding sugar will keep the beans hard. In fact, using molasses, as done for baked beans, allows them to cook for a long time without falling apart. Adding salt to beans helps them cook faster - but makes them gritty.

To speed up cooking, presoak the beans for 12 hours (overnight) if possible. For faster soaking, boil the beans for 90 seconds to soften the skins, and then soak for 3 hours. After soaking, drain the water (see toxin note below), rinse the beans and cook in new water. When soaking, make sure that the water is 3 times deeper than the dry beans. Lentils do not need to be presoaked.

Herbs, onion and garlic do not slow cooking of beans, and thus can be cooked with the beans, and doing so will help to infuse them with extra flavor. To tell when the beans are ready check a few beans, as some may be soft while others still need a bit more time.

When the beans are cooked to the desired texture, add salt and the other components of the dish. Allowing time for the beans to soak in the salt will give more flavor and swell the beans a bit more.

Cooking beans in a pressure cooker greatly decreases their cooking time. They only take a few to cook if the beans have been presoaked. Cover the pre-soaked beans with two inches of water. With pressure uses less water as less vapor is lost as steam, and less energy is wasted.

When using a pressure cooker to cook beans never fill the pot more than half-full to avoid spewing and possible plugging of the vent and over pressuring. Adding a tablespoon of oil also helps prevent foaming and spewing. Once up to pressure, use the lowest heat possible that maintains a small venting of steam.

When cooking beans in a regular pot, boil the beans for 10 minutes, and then decrease the heat and simmer the beans until cooked to keep the skins intact. If the beans are cooked too fast or in vigorously boiling water, the skins will tend to burst, and the bean disintegrate. Use a lid that fits well so that the beans are steamed, and keep enough water so that the bottom of the pot has water to keep the beans from scorching. The cooked beans should be creamy, not grainy when done.

SILENCING THE MUSICAL FRUIT:

A notable quality of beans is their effect on digestion, which causes many people to avoid eating them. There are several tricks to silencing beans.

Epazote: Use about an eighth teaspoon of dry epazote (Mexican Tea) for each cup of cooked beans. Epazote at this amount does not change the flavor of the beans. More can be added to impart flavor.

Bay leaves, coriander or cumin help to silence beans. These spices impart flavor.

Soak the beans and discard the water prior to cooking. Make sure the beans are cooked until they are tender. In general, smaller beans seem to have less effect on digestion, perhaps because they cook more quickly and completely. Slow cooking will give better flavor as it helps the tough starch granules to hydrate, gelatinize and become more digestible. Black (turtle) beans have small starch granules and thus are more easily cooked and digested.

BUYING DRIED BEANS AND LENTILS:

When beans and lentils get old, they dry out and get hard. They then will take longer to cook, sometimes much longer. They may also cook unevenly and thus some will be too hard while others turn to sauce. Beans will have their best flavor texture and nutrition when used within a year of their harvest. Try to buy dried legumes that are not old looking. If the package is dusty or faded, it may not be the best. Avoid packages of beans that have many shriveled, cracked, chipped or faded seeds, as such seeds should be discarded. It is best to buy from stores where there is a quick turn over of stock.

Keep legumes in a sealed container to help retain their moisture level, and store them out of direct sunlight. Try to use any legumes you buy within six months. Avoid mixing new and old beans, as the newer and older ones are likely to cook at different rates.

When using dried beans, it is best to inspect and eliminate foreign matter. Small clumps of dirt won't hurt after they are cooked, but who needs it? Pebbles can break teeth. Pieces of straw and other stray matter are not uncommon in bags of dry beans.

TOXIN WARNING: Kidney beans and many other varieties of beans contain a toxin: phytohemagglutinin (Latin for "plant substance that makes red blood cells stick to each other"). Kidney beans have especially high levels of this toxin. Cooking the beans by boiling (100°C) for ten minutes almost completely denatures the toxin, eliminating its toxicity. Since the beans are usually boiled for nearly an hour, the toxin is usually not a concern.

But... sometimes people take a notion to slow cook beans in a crock pot, or even to make a salad using uncooked or lightly cooked beans. Cooking beans at 80°C (176°F; a low simmer) actually increases the availability of this toxin by about five times. Another poorly conceived idea is the use of solar ovens for cooking beans in the tropics. Most solar ovens cannot get hot enough to destroy the toxins in beans. Beans can be slow cooked, but only after soaking them for at least five hours, discarding the water and then boiling them briskly in fresh water for at least ten minutes. Never eat soaked raw beans. Even sprouted, these beans contain the toxins and should not be eaten raw.

How bad is it? The U.S. FDA website on foodborne illness indicates that five undercooked kidney beans are enough to make an adult sick, with severe nausea, vomiting, abdominal pain and diarrhea that begins about one to 3 hours after eating the beans and that last for a several hours.

Habichuelas Bobas

BACHELOR BEANS

This recipe is a family favorite, as it is quick, easy, and delicious. This makes it a perfect bachelor food.

INGREDIENTS:

1 No. 2 can of black beans (about 20 oz.)
1 No. 1 can (about 14.5 oz) diced tomatoes, preferably spiced, e.g.; roasted garlic flavor
1 tablespoon olive oil
2 to 3 cloves of garlic, diced, (optional, especially if the diced tomatoes are not spiced)
¼ teaspoon dry epazote (Mexican tea) optional
Salt to taste if needed

PREPARATION: Open the cans and dump their contents into a pot. Add the oil, garlic and epazote and give it a stir. The epazote helps avoid the "winds". Put the burner on high, and turn down to medium-low as soon as it boils. Let it simmer for 10 minutes. Serve over rice.

In place of black beans, pinto beans may also be used, especially if cooking these beans for use in tortillas. If using canned kidney beans or other red bean, drain and discard the liquid from the can, and add a half cup of water.

Guandules Guisado con Coco

PIGEON PEAS IN COCONUT SAUCE

INGREDIENTS:

1 tablespoon vegetable oil
½ small onion; diced
5 large cloves of garlic, chopped
1 2/3 cups cooked pigeon peas (guandules)
  or 1 can, drained
14 oz. coconut cream
½ cup water
¾ teaspoon salt
1 tablespoon chopped fresh cilantro
1 cup butternut squash; diced into ½ inch cubes.

PREPARATION: Place the oil in a 2-quart saucepan over medium heat. Sauté the onions until they begin to clarify and then add the chopped garlic. Sauté until the garlic begin to get toasted golden brown. Add the pigeon peas, the coconut cream, water, and salt. Stir together and bring to a boil. Reduce the heat to a simmer, cover and allow the peas to cook for 20 minutes. Watch to make sure that it does not overflow.

Add the squash and cook for another 10 minutes until the squash is tender. Turn off the heat and mix in the cilantro.

Serve with rice and sliced avocado.

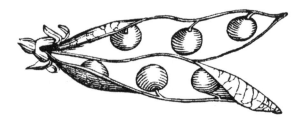

Chapea (Habichuelas con Longaniza)

BEANS WITH ITALIAN SAUSAGE

This recipe is usually made with either white (Navy) beans or black beans. In this example, it is prepared with black beans.

INGREDIENTS:

1 teaspoon vegetable oil
2 cloves garlic; sliced thin
1 pound Italian sausage
1 plum tomato; diced
2½ cup cooked black beans
  or a 20 oz. can, with the liquid

PREPARATION: Cut the Italian sausage into ½-inch lengths. Place the oil in a saucepan over medium heat. Add the garlic and sauté for 30 seconds; add the sausage pieces and tomato, and sauté for 2 minutes. Add the beans. Bring it to a boil, and lower the heat to a simmer. Cook for 10 to 15 minutes. Serve with rice.

Habichuelas Blancas Guisada

NAVY BEANS WITH COCONUT CREAM

This recipe uses dried white beans and creates a cream sauce using coconut cream.

INGREDIENTS:

2 cups dry great northern (navy) beans
14 oz. coconut cream
4 cloves garlic; finely sliced
1 small onion; diced
1 vegetable bouillon cubes (5 grams)
1 green jalapeño; diced
1 cup winter squash; cut into ¾ inch cubes
½ cup water
1 teaspoon salt
1 teaspoon epazote
¼ teaspoon saffron

PREPARATION: Clean the beans of any foreign matter, and then soak them in at least 2 quarts of water overnight. Boil the beans until they split open, and the skins begin to loosen and detach. Turn off the heat and stir to dislodge the skins, which should float to the top. Drain off the water trying to get rid of as much of the loose bean skin as possible. Add about 2 cups of water, stir the beans with a spoon to loosen more skins, add 2 quarts of water and again pour off the water and the skins.

Add 8 cups of new water and cook at a low boil for 30 minutes. Shorter cooking times can be used with a pressure cooker. The beans should be soft enough to turn into a smooth paste between your thumb and index finger.

Drain the beans again. Now add the coconut cream, ½-cup water, winter squash, garlic, bouillon, jalapeño, onion, salt, saffron, and epazote. Place over medium heat. Cover and adjust the heat to a low simmer. Cook for about twenty minutes, stirring occasionally.

Serve with rice or boiled green plantains.

Habichuelas Guisada

STEWED BEANS

INGREDIENTS:

2 cups dry red kidney beans
1 teaspoon coriander seed
¼ teaspoon epazote
1 teaspoon dried oregano leaves
8 medium cloves garlic
4 tablespoons olive oil
1 Anaheim pepper
1 medium onion
½ tablespoon salt
2 plum tomatoes or 1 medium tomato, diced
1 tablespoon fresh chopped cilantro

PREPARATION: Soak beans in water overnight. Drain the water off, add one-quart water and the epazote, cover and boil over medium heat until the beans split open. If they begin to get dry, add enough water to keep the beans just covered. Grind the cilantro seed in a mortar, then add the garlic and crush it, mixing in the cilantro seed. Finely mince the Anaheim peppers.

Place 3 tablespoons of olive oil in a frying pan over medium heat. When the oil is hot, add the chopped onions, and sauté them until they are soft and clear. Next, add the garlic/cilantro seed mix, followed by the minced Anaheim pepper. Add crushed dry oregano leaves, chopped tomatoes, and salt. Cook these together until they form a sauce. Add one more tablespoon of olive oil and turn the heat to low.

Add this sauce to the pot with the boiled beans. Add the cilantro. Cook for about 10 more minutes, until the beans become a creamy thick sauce, stirring regularly to keep from sticking to the bottom of the pot, adding a tablespoon of water at a time if needed.

Serve with rice or locrio.

Petit Pois

STEWED GREEN PEAS

INGREDIENTS:

2 cups fresh or frozen peas
2 cups water
2 tablespoons olive oil
1 small red onion, quartered and sliced
4 cloves garlic; sliced along the long axis
1 teaspoon butter
½ teaspoon salt
½ jalapeño pepper; diced
¼ teaspoon saffron
2 teaspoons fresh cilantro leaves

PREPARATION: Allow the frozen peas to partially thaw at room temperature for several minutes. Place the peas and water in a blender and blend until it becomes a paste, about 3 minutes.

In a saucepan over medium heat, add the olive oil. Lightly sauté the onions until they begin to clear. Then add the garlic, and lightly sauté them until

they get light golden brown. Lower the heat, add the salt, butter and jalapeño pepper, and sauté for another minute.

Add the blended peas to the saucepan with the onions and garlic, add the saffron, cover and cook over medium heat to maintain a simmer. Cook for about 15 to 20 minutes, stirring occasionally. Before serving, garnish with fresh cilantro.

Serve over rice, or over buttered toasted bread.

Habichuelas Guisada con Coco

BEANS STEWED IN COCONUT CREAM

INGREDIENTS:

8 oz. dry kidney beans
6 cups water
1 teaspoon epazote
1 14oz. can coconut cream
3 cloves garlic
½ small onion; diced
½ Anaheim pepper; diced
1 cup butternut squash, ¾ inch cubes
1 vegetable bouillon cube (5 grams)
1 teaspoon salt

PREPARATION: Clean the beans, removing any pebbles or other dirt, then rinse the beans with water. Place the beans on the stove in a large pot with 6 cups of water and the epazote, cover, and bring them to a boil for 2 minutes. Turn off the heat and let them soak for at least one hour.

After an hour, bring the beans to a boil again and turn the heat to medium-low; cook them for another hour. When ready, the beans should be soft and splitting open.

Add the coconut cream, garlic, onion, Anaheim pepper, butternut squash, bouillon and salt and stir the ingredients together. Cook at a high simmer for another hour.

SHORTCUT RECIPE: Add 2 cans of kidney beans and one cup of water to the other ingredients in a large pot. Bring to a boil, and then simmer for an hour.

Serves eight. Serve with rice.

Habichuelas Negras

BLACK BEANS WITH PUMPKIN

In the South of the Dominican Republic where I grew up, we often add pumpkin to our beans. Most orange-fleshed winter squashes will work (other than spaghetti squash, which falls apart). I favor butternut squash for its convenient size, and superior flavor and texture. Cut the onions vertically into quarters, and then slice them about ¼ inch wide. This will form little strips of onion.

INGREDIENTS:

2 tablespoons olive oil
1 small onion, quartered and sliced
2 cloves garlic, finely sliced
2 plum tomatoes; diced
15 oz. black beans (1 can drained)
1 cup pumpkin or butternut squash; cut into 2-cm cubes (3/4 inch).
½ cup water

½ teaspoon epazote (optional)
¼ teaspoon salt

PREPARATION: Add the olive oil to a medium-sized saucepan over medium heat. Sauté the onions until they become clear and then add the garlic. Sauté the garlic until it just turns golden. Add the diced tomatoes, and sauté them until they soften and form a sauce. Add the black beans, pumpkin or squash, water and epazote to the pot, cover it, and raise the heat and bring it to a boil. As soon at it begins to boil, turn the heat down to a simmer, and let the beans cook for 5 minutes. Add the salt according to taste, give it a stir and then let it simmer for another 5 minutes.

Ensalada de Frijoles Negros

BLACK BEAN SALAD

INGREDIENTS:

1 can of black beans (15 oz.)
¼ teaspoon very finely ground epazote leaves
1 cup sweet corn
½ medium red bell pepper; diced
½ medium yellow bell pepper; diced
½ medium red onion; diced
1 tablespoon olive oil
3 tablespoons honey
1/8th teaspoon salt
¼ cup red wine
1 tablespoon fresh cilantro leaves, chopped
1 medium tomato; diced

PREPARATION: Place the corn, beans and epazote in a saucepan with enough liquid to cover and heat to a strong simmer, just enough to heat them and then remove from the heat and drain off the water. Place the black beans and corn in a large mixing bowl and allow them to cool to room temperature.

Dice the peppers into ¼ to ½-inch pieces. Add the diced peppers, onion, tomatoes, salt, cilantro, olive oil and honey, and mix. Add the wine and chill in the refrigerator before serving.

VARIATIONS: Add diced roasted chicken breast or salad shrimp.

Lentejas con Mariscos

LENTILS WITH SEAFOOD

INGREDIENTS:

2 cups dry brown lentils
8 cups water
3 tablespoons olive oil
1 large onion, quartered and sliced into thin strips
5 large cloves garlic, minced
2 teaspoons fresh ginger root; grated
¼ teaspoon ground cumin
1 can (6 oz) chopped clams
1 lb. frozen peeled shrimp (about 120-count)
1 tablespoon salt
¼ teaspoon curry powder
2 medium tomatoes; diced into large pieces
2 tablespoons fresh chopped cilantro

PREPARATION: Place the lentils in a large saucepan, and rinse the lentils in water. Discard the water and any shriveled lentils or foreign matter. Add 8 cups of water and place the pan over high heat. When the water comes to a boil, lower the heat to medium-low, and place a lid on the pan. It may help to keep the lid slightly ajar to keep them from foaming too much. Maintain the lentils at a simmer until they begin to split open, about 30 minutes.

Check the lentils every couple of minutes to make sure they do not overcook; they should be intact and soft, but not disintegrating.

In a separate pan, heat the oil; add onion, garlic, and ginger, and sauté at medium heat until the garlic and onion are light brown. Next, add salt and about ¾ of the chopped tomatoes. Sauté the tomatoes for another minute, so that they form a sauce.

Stir this sauce into the cooked lentils. Add cumin, clams with juice, all but ¾ cups of the shrimp, and curry powder, into the lentils and sauce. Allow it to cook over medium-low heat for about 15 minutes or until thickened. Place in serving bowl. Steam the remaining ¾ cup of shrimp for about 2 minutes; long enough for them to heat, but not to over cook. Drain any water.

Use the remaining fresh tomatoes, shrimp, and fresh cilantro as decorative and flavorful garnishes when serving. This dish is usually served along with rice, toasted bread or pita bread.

VARIATIONS: If you prefer not to use shrimp, a second can of clams may be used in place of the shrimp.

Pasta

About Pasta:

The two most common problems that occur when cooking pasta are having it stick to itself and allowing it to overcook. The traditional way to cook pasta is to add the pasta to boiling water, using four to six quarts of water for every pound of pasta. Using 2 quarts of water per pound of pasta is sufficient; however, more care is needed to prevent the pasta from sticking together.

It is important to stir the pasta immediately after immersing it so that it can quickly get coated with water; otherwise the pieces of pasta are likely stick to each other. Adding a small amount of butter or oil to the pot, and lifting the pasta through the layer of oil on the water will help prevent the pasta from sticking to itself. The small amount of butter or oil also helps keep the pasta from foaming over during cooking. Adding a half teaspoon of salt to the cooking water also helps to keep pasta from getting as sticky.

Pasta needs to be near boiling water temperature for the pasta starch to absorb water, so cook it at a quick simmer to a low boil. A full boil is fine, but more likely to foam over than with a low boil.

Cooking time for pasta depends on its size and thickness. Check the recommended cooking time on the pasta package, and use the lower number of minutes. Thus, if it says 9-11 minutes; cook it for nine minutes, and then check the pasta every minute until its is cooked through. Test to see if it is done by removing a piece and testing it. Pasta should be soft on the outside, but inside should remain firm.

Pasta is best cooked "al dente", meaning that it is cooked, but still firm enough to bite. Halt the cooking of the pasta, by straining it through a colander to remove it from the hot water.

Overcooked pasta will be a sticky mass. If you overcook pasta, you can try to revive it: Immediately rinse it with cool tap water to remove excess starch. Add olive oil or butter to the pan (first letting the butter melt over medium-low heat), then add the pasta back to the pot and gently turn it to get it coated with the oil or butter, so that it does not stick to itself. The sauce that you have prepared for the pasta can also be used to coat and to reheat the washed pasta. Rewarm the pasta to blend in the sauce. Cool pasta will poorly absorb the flavors of the sauce.

GLUTEN INTOLERANCE:

For most of its history, very little wheat was used traditional Caribbean dishes. Thus, most recipes use no wheat. In the last half century, bread and pasta have become more common especially in the cities where people eat outside of the home more frequently and sandwiches, and pizza are enjoyed.

Wheat contains the protein gluten This protein has the nice ability to form a glue-like stickiness that can capture bubbles of gas, thus allowing bread to rise. Gluten also holds starch in a gel-like matrix, giving the nice doughy texture to pastries and to pasta.

Gluten includes a protein called gliadin, and many people have immune reactions to this protein. Celiac disease is the best known of these reactions, and it can have severe consequences, with malabsorption syndrome, weight loss, and lead to osteoporosis and multiple other disease conditions.

Wheat intolerance is associated with many autoimmune diseases including chronic dermatitis, rheumatic diseases, and thyroid disease. An immune reaction to gliadin can be an inherited susceptibility to an immune response. Other people are just allergic to wheat.

Wheat pasta can be substituted using corn or rice or other non-wheat pasta. Corn pasta can be found at many grocery stores, sometimes in the health food section, and rice pasta can be found at Asian markets. Corn pasta can be prepared pretty much like wheat pasta, but cooking rice pasta requires extra care. Directions for preparation of rice pasta are given below.

RICE PASTA

Rice pasta is milder in flavor than wheat pasta, and more delicate. When cooking rice pasta, it is important to be careful not to overcook it, as it can easily turn into a disappointing, gooey, sticky mass that will not soak up flavor from the sauce you have prepared for it.

INGREDIENTS:

2 quarts water
1 tablespoon olive oil
½ teaspoon salt
8 oz. rice pasta

PREPARATION: Add the water, olive oil, and salt to a pot large enough to leave at least 2 inches of space above the water. Bring the water to a boil over high heat. Add the rice pasta, stirring it in so that it does not clump, lifting the pasta so that it can be coated with the oil floating on the top of the water. Continue stirring at least until the water boils again, turn the heat to low, and cover. The motion of the actively boiling water will help keep the pasta from sticking to itself. In about 2 minutes, it's time to stir again and check the progress. The cooking time will depend on how thick the pasta is; the packaging may tell how much cooking time to expect. Check the texture of the pasta every minute, as one extra minute can easily ruin rice pasta. As soon as the pasta is at the right texture, (cooked through, but still firm in the center) remove it from the heat and drain it into a colander.

If the pasta is to be mixed into a sauce, do this right away, gently coating and lubricating the pasta with the sauce. Cover to keep warm and serve still hot.

If you realize that you have overcooked the pasta, rinse it right away with cool tap water, to rinse off some of the excess starch. Then mix it with your spaghetti sauce and reheat it.

Pastamenta

PASTA WITH MINT

This is a summertime favorite pasta dish that has a cooling mint accent.

INGREDIENTS:

4 oz. spaghetti (or other pasta)
Water
2 tablespoons olive oil
2 cloves garlic, finely sliced
1 vegetable bouillon cubes (5 grams)
2 tablespoons fresh mint leaves, chopped
2 tablespoons white zinfandel

PREPARATION: Place the pasta in a pot of boiling water, and cook according to the instructions on the package for al dente pasta. Drain the pasta in a colander, and rinse for a few seconds in cool running water. This will halt the cooking process so that the pasta does not over soften. Gently shake out excess water.

In a separate saucepan heat the olive oil over medium-low heat until it warms. Add the garlic, sautéing it for about thirty seconds until it just begins to turn golden. Add the bouillon and mint and sauté them together for about one minute. Add the wine and mix it in to form a sauce, and then add the pasta, and gently turn it in the sauce to coat the pasta. Turn the heat to low, and cover the sauté pan, allowing it to simmer for about thirty seconds. Remove the pan from the heat.

Garnish with freshly grated hard cheese, and a small sprig of mint leaves.

Serve with salad, and perhaps with baked fish.
Makes 2 servings.

Ensalada de Pasta

ROTINI SALAD

Tricolor rotini gives this dish eye appeal. It can also be made with other forms of macaroni. Although intended as a cold dish for warm weather, my daughter also likes it served warm.

INGREDIENTS:

2 cups dry tricolor rotini
¼ teaspoon dry oregano
½ teaspoon salt
2 tablespoons olive oil
1 small red onion; diced finely
1/3 cup celery leaves and finely sliced celery stalks
1 tomato; diced

PREPARATION: Boil the rotini in 4 quarts of water with a rounded teaspoon of salt and a small amount of olive oil, until the pasta is "al dente", cooked, but still firm. Check the recommended cooking time on the box of pasta, and cook it for the lower range of minutes indicated. If it is too hard, check it again every minute. Drain the rotini in a colander, and briefly rinse it with cool water.

Move the rotini into a large mixing bowl. Sprinkle with the dry oregano and salt and gently "toss" the rotini, by sliding a wooden spoon along the inside of the bowl and lifting the macaroni, to avoid breaking it. Sprinkle on 2 tablespoons of olive oil, the onion, celery, and tomatoes and again toss the macaroni to mix well. A small amount of additional salt may be added to taste. Cool in the refrigerator before serving.

Espagueti con Calamar en Salsa de Coco y Ajo

SPAGHETTI WITH COCONUT CALAMARI SAUCE

INGREDIENTS:

1 pound of calamari
1 tablespoon coconut oil
3 cloves garlic
1 cup coconut cream
¼ teaspoon salt
1/8 teaspoon saffron
½ pound spaghetti
1 teaspoon coconut oil

PREPARATION: Clean and prepare the calamari as described on page 52, slicing the mantle into rings, and set aside.

Cook the spaghetti in the usual manner (see page 109) drain it and return it to its pot and cover to keep it warm.

Place the oil in a saucepan. When it is hot, sauté the garlic for about one minute until it turns golden. Add the coconut cream and simmer for about 10 minutes on low heat. Add the saffron and the salt. Add the calamari rings and tentacles and simmer for 60 to 90 seconds, and then remove the sauce from the heat. Do not overcook, as the calamari will become tough and rubbery.

Immediately, pour the sauce into the spaghetti and gently blend it in with a wooden spoon. This will cool the calamari down some, ending its cooking, and allows the spaghetti to soak up the flavor of the sauce. Serve immediately.

Serving suggestion: Serve with a green salad with avocado and tomatoes.

Pa'lo' Berro

PASTA WITH WATERCRESS

There was a spring in which watercress grew wild near my hometown. It was also a favored swimming hole. When we kids were headed there to swim, we would say we were going "pa' lo berro"; to the spring where watercress grows.

INGREDIENTS:

2 cups uncooked pasta (penne)
2 tablespoons olive oil
1 tablespoon garlic, minced
2 cups watercress, chopped
1 vegetable bouillon cube (5 grams)
1 heaping teaspoon capers
¼ cup white wine

PREPARATION: Cook the penne or other pasta as direct on the box and drain it in a colander, and place it back into the pot and cover it to keep it warm. Heat the oil over medium heat in a deep saucepan, and add the garlic. Sauté the garlic until the edges begin to turn light golden colored. Add and sauté in the bouillon and the capers for about 30 seconds and then stir in the wine. Add the watercress and sauté it for another 30 seconds. Mix in the pasta. Cover the pan and cook over low heat long enough for the pasta to absorb the flavors from the sauce, about 2 minutes.

Serve immediately while piping hot.

Pasta Solar

PENNE WITH SUN-DRIED TOMATOES AND MINT

INGREDIENTS:

8 oz macaroni such as penne
1 teaspoon salt
Water

2 tablespoons fresh mint leaves, cut into bits
1 tablespoon fresh basil leaves; cut into bits
2 tablespoons red wine
1 vegetable bouillon cube (5 grams)
4 cloves garlic; sliced thin
2 tablespoons olive oil
1½ tablespoons butter
2 tablespoons sundried tomatoes,
    cut into ¼ inch strips
Freshly grated Romano or Parmesan cheese

PREPARATION: Place about a quart of water into a medium-sized saucepan and bring it to a boil. Add one teaspoon of salt. There should be enough water to easily cover the pasta. Add the pasta. Stir to make sure that the macaroni does not stick to itself. Allow the water to return to a boil and gently stir again. Turn down the heat to maintain a quick simmer. Loosely cover, keeping the lid ajar.

While the pasta is cooking, place the oil and butter in a saucepan and place it over medium heat. Add the sliced garlic and sauté it for a couple of minutes until it starts to turn golden. Add the sun-dried tomatoes and bouillon, stirring to dissolve the bouillon in the oil. Add the basil leaves, the mint leaves and the red wine just before adding the cooked macaroni.

Drain the pasta in a colander, gently shake it to remove excess water and immediately place it in the sauté pan with the sauce that has been prepared. Gently mix the pasta into the sauce.
Serve immediately. Makes 2 or 3 servings.

Note: One teaspoon of red wine vinegar can be substituted for the 2 tablespoons of red wine.

Palitos y Piedras

Sticks and Stones Pasta

INGREDIENTS:

5 oz penne pasta (about 1/3 of a pound or 2 cups of dry pasta)
1 teaspoon salt
1-quart water

3 tablespoons olive oil
½ cup onions, chopped
3 cloves of garlic, chopped
1 Plum tomato, diced
¼ cup diced red bell pepper
¼ cup diced Anaheim pepper
¼ cup tomato based spaghetti sauce
1 tablespoon capers

PREPARATION: Put about 1 quart of water into a medium-sized saucepan and bring it to a boil. Add 1 teaspoon of salt. The water in the pan should be deep enough to easily cover the pasta being cooked. Stir in the penne to make sure that it does not stick to itself. Allow the water to return to a boil and gently stir again. Turn down the heat to maintain a quick simmer. Loosely cover, keeping the lid ajar.

While the pasta is cooking, place the oil in a saucepan over medium heat. Add the onions and sauté them for a couple of minutes until they start to become clear and then add the garlic. Sauté until the garlic turns golden. Add the tomato, and peppers and sauté them until the tomato disintegrates and forms a sauce. Add the tomato sauce and the capers. Turn the heat to a very low setting and cover to keep the sauce hot.

Cook the pasta for the time marked on the box, usually for about 8 minutes, stirring every couple of minutes to ensure that the pasta is not sticking and watching to make sure that it does not foam over. Removing a piece of pasta and test it to see if it is done. Pasta should be soft on the outside, but inside should remain firm.

Drain the pasta in a colander over a second pot to retain the water. Gently shake it to remove excess water and immediately place the cooked pasta into the sauté pan with the sauce that has been prepared. Do not allow the pasta to cool, as this limits the absorption of flavors into the pasta. Gently mix the penne into the sauce. Add a couple of tablespoons of the water in which the pasta was cooked turn up the heat and simmer, gently turning the pasta until most of the water has evaporated.

Serve immediately. Makes two to three servings.

Pasta con Carne de Res

PASTA WITH BRAISED BEEF

INGREDIENTS:

1 pound boneless beef
5 cloves garlic, minced
½ small Cuban pepper, chopped
½ cup onions; chopped finely
1 teaspoon fresh lemon juice
1¼ teaspoons salt
1/8 teaspoon dry oregano

1 glass of wine (optional)
½ pound penne pasta
2 tablespoons vegetable oil
1 tablespoon light brown sugar
1 pound plum (Roma) tomatoes

PREPARATION: Cut the meat into bite-sized pieces. Rinse the meat in cool water, allowing the water to drain off, and place the meat in a bowl. Add the minced garlic, peppers, onions, lemon juice, salt, and oregano. Mix these ingredients together, cover the bowl and let it sit for 10 minutes. Begin slowly sipping and enjoying the glass of wine.

Place 2 tablespoons of oil in a sauté pan over medium high heat. When the oil is warm, add one tablespoon of brown sugar to the pan and mix it into the oil until it bubbles and begins to caramelize. Add the meat a few pieces at a time, stirring to coat the meat with caramelized sugar, and then add the vegetables and seasoning from the bowl, mixing it in. Lower the heat to low and cover, allowing it to steam until all the liquid has evaporated and the meat is cooking in the oil that remains. Turning it gently with a wooden spoon, cook for 2 minutes adding 2 tablespoons of water at a time to keep the mixture from sticking to the pan.

Mix in one pound (about 3 cups) of diced ripe plum tomatoes. Cover and cook for 5 minutes over medium-low heat.

In a separate pot, add 8 cups of water and a teaspoon of salt, and bring it to a rolling boil. Add half pound of pasta (penne) and cook it until it is a diente. Drain off the water. Add the meat and sauce to the pot with the cooked pasta. Add ½ cup of water. Mix and cook for 3 minutes over low heat.

30 to 40 minutes preparation time.

Pato Macho

ROTINI AND CLAMS

This seafood pasta dish gets its name from the resemblance of the spiral macaroni to a curious feature of male duck anatomy.

INGREDIENTS:

6 cups water
6 to 8 oz. spiral macaroni
3 cloves garlic, finely sliced
1 tablespoon olive oil
2 tablespoons butter
1 can chopped clams
1 vegetable bouillon cube (5 grams)

PREPARATION: Boil the macaroni using 1 to 1½ quarts of water, for the amount of time listed on the spiral macaroni package. Cook until the macaroni is "al dente". Drain the pasta in a colander, gently shake it to remove excess water, and immediately place the pasta in the sauté pan with the sauce that has been prepared (below).

While the pasta is boiling, add the olive oil and butter into a saucepan, over medium to medium-low heat. Sauté the garlic until it is golden, and then add the clams along with the juice, and the bouillon. Stir and allow to simmer until the bouillon has dissolved. Add the drained macaroni and allow to simmer for a couple of minutes, and serve warm.

Serve along side of a green salad and garnish with shredded Romano or Parmesan cheese.

Side Dishes - Platillos

Espinaca Marinera

SPINACH WITH CLAMS

INGREDIENTS:

2 tablespoons butter or olive oil
4 cloves garlic; sliced thin
2 teaspoons ají dulce, minced,
    or substitute with ripe Anaheim pepper
½ lb. spinach, chopped, fresh or frozen
1 can (6.5 oz) chopped clams in clam juice
¼ teaspoon salt

PREPARATION: Lightly sauté the garlic and the peppers in butter in a sauté pan over medium heat for about one minute. Add the salt and spinach and sauté for about 3 - 4 minutes, until the spinach turns soft and dark green. Add the can of chopped clams with the clam juice, and mix it into the spinach. Let the spinach simmer in the clam juice for one minute.

Serving ideas: Serve as a side dish or serve over rice or pasta.

Ensalada de Tayota

CHAYOTE SALAD

INGREDIENTS:

1 chayote
1 teaspoon olive oil
½ teaspoon salt
¼ teaspoon red wine vinegar

PREPARATION: Peel the chayote, cut in half and remove and discard the seed. Cut the chayote into ½ to ¾ inch cubes. Place then in a saucepan with water and boil the chayote until a fork passes easily through the pieces. Drain the water.

Place the cooked chayote on a serving dish.

In a small glass, mix the oil, vinegar, and salt. Drizzle this dressing over the chayote and serve it with a meal.

Ensalada de Tomate Verde

GREEN TOMATO SALAD

INGREDIENTS:

2 breaker green tomatoes (See page 9)
1 teaspoon olive oil
A pinch of salt
A pinch of dry oregano

PREPARATION: Slice the tomatoes into wheels ¼ inch thick. Lay the slices out on a serving plate and dash with olive oil, salt, and oregano.

Ensalada de Aguacate

AVOCADO SALAD

INGREDIENTS:

1 ripe Mexican avocado (the small variety with thick dark, bumpy skin)
½ teaspoon olive oil
1/16th teaspoon salt
1/16th teaspoon ground dry oregano

PREPARATION: Slice the avocado into wedges about ½ inch wide in the center, and then remove the skin. Cut the strips into ½-inch sections.

In a small bowl, place the olive oil, salt, and oregano and blend them together. Add the avocado pieces, gently turning them so that they get coated with the olive oil. If using a larger avocado, increase the proportions of the other ingredients.

Serve with yellow rice, moro, or in a sandwich.

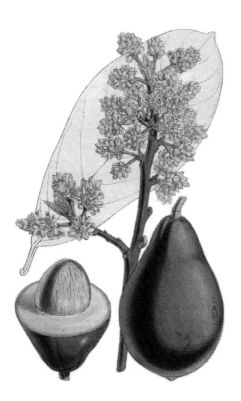

Ensalada de Mango

MANGO SALAD

INGREDIENTS:

1 barely ripe mango
½ teaspoon olive oil
1/16th teaspoon salt
1 teaspoon vinegar

PREPARATION: Peel the mango and slice the flesh away from the large seed. Cut the mango into wedges about ½-inch wide sections.

In a small bowl, place the olive oil, salt and vinegar and mix them together. Add the mango pieces, gently turning them so that they are coated with the olive oil.

Serve alone or with tostones as a snack.

VARIATION: Dice the mango into 1-inch pieces and add a tablespoon of toasted sunflower seeds.

Ensalada

DOMINICAN SALAD

The traditional Dominican salad that accompanies a meal is not a large bowl of lettuce with a few chunks of tomato hiding out from predators at the bottom. It is rather a serving tray with slices of ripe or green tomatoes, shaved cabbage, sliced boiled beets, sprigs of watercress, sliced carrots, radishes, onion rings or other seasonal fresh vegetables. The sliced tomatoes and beets are laid out in overlapping wheels to display their color, and the other vegetables are displayed for easy access. Avocado slices are also often added. A light dressing of olive oil and vinegar may be sprinkled on, and a light sprinkle of salt may be placed on the tomatoes and avocados.

INGREDIENTS:

½ small red onion
1 pound ripe red tomatoes
1 medium green tomato*
6 radishes
2 medium beets
½ cucumber
2 cups of lettuce leaves, torn into 2-inch pieces
2 cups of cabbage (green or red)
1 large avocado

2 tablespoons red wine vinegar
1 tablespoon olive oil
¼ teaspoon salt

PREPARATION: Steam the beets, allow them to cool and peel them. Slice the beets along their axis about one-eighth inch thick. Thinly slice the onion along the axis into thin sections, and separate it into rings. Slice the red tomatoes ¼ inch thick into wheels, and the green tomatoes about 1/8th inch thick. Slice the radishes thinly. Peel the cucumber and cut it into wheels. Halve the avocado, discard the seeds, and cut the fruit into about 8 wedges and remove the skin. Narrowly shave the head of cabbage, into eighth-inch wide ribbons. Mix the oil, vinegar and salt together to make the dressing.

On a serving tray, make a bed of lettuce and cabbage in the center. Lay the avocado out in the center on the lettuce like spokes in a wheel. Lay the beets out in a circle surrounding the lettuce so that each piece overlaps. Surround that with the cucumber and radish slices. Around the periphery lay out the red and green tomato slices, alternating them and overlapping to complete a circle. Cover with plastic food wrap and refrigerate until served.

Prepare the avocados with oil as described on page 116 to keep them from oxidizing. Sprinkle a pinch of salt onto the avocados and tomatoes, followed by sprinkling the oil and vinegar dressing.

* The green tomato should be just beginning to turn pink (See green tomatoes on page 9)

Salsa Fresca

SPICY GARDEN SALSA

INGREDIENTS:

6 ripe plum tomatoes; diced into ½ inch cubes
3 tomatillos; diced into ¼ inch cubes
4 green onions
½ medium red bell pepper; diced small
½ medium yellow bell pepper; diced small
2 or 3 jalapeño peppers, minced
4 cloves garlic, finely minced
1 teaspoon salt
2 teaspoons olive oil
3 tablespoons fresh lime juice

2 tablespoons chopped fresh cilantro
½ teaspoon chopped fresh mint leaves

PREPARATION: Dice the bell peppers into ¼-inch cubes. Cut the bulbs of the green onions into thin rings, and cut the greens into ½-inch lengths. Add all ingredients to a bowl and gently mix them together. Use 2 or 3 jalapeños depending on how hot you like it. Combine and chill before serving. Better the next day. Serve as a salad for the daring. Use as salsa or garnish.

Ensalada Rusa

PINK POTATO SALAD

INGREDIENTS:

2 lbs. (preferably fresh harvested) potatoes
4 cups water
1 teaspoon salt
½ cup diced cooked beets
½ small red onion, quartered and sliced
    into ½ by 1/16-inch pieces
1 cup green peas
1 cup sweet cut corn
2 eggs
1 tablespoon olive or sunflower seed oil
2 tablespoons mayonnaise

HARD COOKED EGGS: *Do not boil the eggs.* Place six cups of water into a medium-sized saucepan. It should be at least deep enough to cover the eggs by ½ inch, or use a smaller pot. Heat the water until it begins to simmer. Use eggs that have been allowed to warm to room temperature, or warmed for a few minutes in warm water to avoid cracking the eggs when placed in hot water. Using a large spoon gently introduce eggs into the hot water. Allow to cook at a low simmer for six minutes. Turn off the heat and allow the water and eggs to cool for at least 10 minutes, before removing the eggs from the water.

NOTE: At sea level a low simmer is about 180°F (82°C) degrees, a temperature high enough to harden the yolk of the egg and kill bacteria, but not high enough to make the egg rubbery or to cause the yolk to turn green. At higher altitudes 180°F (82°C), degree water will have a more active simmer, but still be below boiling.

PREPARATION: Cut the potatoes into one-inch cubes. Peeling the potatoes is traditional. Cutting the pieces into similar sizes will help the pieces to finish cooking at the same time. Place the potatoes in a saucepan, cover with water and add the salt. Bring the water to a boil. Allow the potatoes to boil for about 5 to 8 minutes until a fork passes through a piece of potato easily, splitting it. Turn off the heat and add the peas and corn, allowing them to sit for about 5 minutes. This will cool the water, but warm the peas and corn. Do not use a pot cover for boiling or blanching the vegetables.

Drain the water from the pot, and transfer the potatoes, corn and peas in a bowl. Add the mayonnaise and oil, gently mixing it into the vegetables, avoiding crushing the potatoes.

Peel the boiled eggs, and dice them into ½-inch cubes. Add the onions, beets and half of the diced eggs and gently mix them into the vegetables, until the color of the beets begins to stain the potatoes. Place the potato salad in the serving dish and garnish with the remaining cubed eggs. Although it can be served immediately while still warm, it is usually placed in the refrigerator and chilled before serving.

About Cruciferous Vegetables and Cancer Prevention

Consumption of cruciferous vegetables (broccoli, Brussels sprouts, cabbage, and other closely related vegetables) has been found to decrease the risk of cancer in many studies, and even to slow the progression of cancer in individuals who have already been diagnosed with it[19,20]. These benefits were most pronounced in people who ate at least 2 servings a week of these vegetables. These vegetables also protect the heart and prevent inflammation.

SCIENCE ALERT: Cruciferous vegetables contain certain (isothiocyanate) compounds that help the body detoxify and rid itself of carcinogenic HCA compounds that can be formed during the cooking of meat. The most active of these compounds, sulforaphane, is additionally thought to help eliminate cancer cells by a process called apoptosis[21]. This compound further protects the body from oxidative stress[22]. Sulforaphane is not only an anti-carcinogen; it is cardioprotective[23], lowers LDL cholesterol and has anti-inflammatory effects[24].

Sulforaphane is not stored in these vegetables but is present rather as its precursor, glucoraphanin. Glucoraphanin is enzymatically converted to sulforaphane by the enzyme myrosinase, which is held in a different cellular compartment of the plant. Glucoraphanin is activated by myrosinase when the cells are crushed or chewed. Thus, sulforaphane is not present until the plant's cells are disrupted, as occurs with chewing, cutting, freezing, cooking, or juicing[25]. Even then, however, most of the glucoraphanin is converted to a different compound, that is inactive.

If these cruciferous vegetables are heated to 140°F (60 °C) and then eaten or liquefied into juice, the amount of sulforaphane produced is greatly increased[26]. But cooking these vegetables at simmering or boiling temperatures denatures the enzyme myrosinase, inactivating it. These temperatures also destroy sulforaphane[27, 28]. Fully cooked cruciferous vegetables contain almost no sulforaphane and have minimal anti-carcinogenic activity.

To maximize the health benefits of cooked cruciferous vegetables, they should be very lightly heated to an internal temperature of 140°F (60 °C) and eaten while still warm to maximize sulforaphane availability.

Broccoli, for example, can be:

• Heated in 140°F (60 °C) water for 10 minutes

• Broken into florets and steamed with a cover above boiling water for 3 minutes

• Heated in a microwave for 45 seconds.

The health benefits from sulforaphane are also available when cruciferous vegetables are eaten raw or they can be juiced, preferably after heating them to 140°F (60 °C), and then cooling the juice with ice or refrigeration.

Purple and red cabbage and broccoli inflorescences are excellent sources of sulforaphane[29].

Radishes and radish seed sprouts, watercress and arugula, are other cruciferous vegetables that have the advantage that they are usually eaten raw. Radish seedlings and watercress have pleasant spicy flavors and can be added to salads.

Other cruciferous vegetables include cauliflower, mustard, napa, Brussels sprouts, turnip greens, collard greens, and kohlrabi. When possible these greens should be heated as described above, to provide the most health benefits.

About Tubers

Starchy tubers play an important role in African and Caribbean diets, as they do in many cultures. Some are harvested nearly year round in the tropics, so they have been food for times of scarcity and famine. The names for the tubers vary according to the country, and this causes confusion – that I will try to rectify.

The word potato is the anglicized form of the Taíno Indian word *batatas*, the Taíno word for sweet potatoes, a tuber that originated in Central America. Later, however, this name was applied by the English to the potato, a tuber that originated in the Andes Mountains of South America. The sweet potato is still called batata in the Spanish Caribbean. Since this plant enjoys wide cultivation, it has many names, including camote in Central America and kumara in Polynesia.

In the U.S., Africans brought as slaves called the sweet potato yam from the word *nyama* after the large tuber they were familiar with from the *Dioscorea* genus that are also called Yams in English. *Nyama* got turned into Ñame in Spanish (pronounced nya-may). Some of the name confusion about the name yam comes from the wide variety of sweet potatoes that are available, and the name yam is often incorrectly applied to the yellow to orange-fleshed varieties. Batata skin color ranges from red, brown-purple, and white, and the flesh can be white, yellow, orange, and purple. They are all sweet potatoes. The boniato variety of sweet potato, which is popular in the Caribbean, has a white to cream flesh, red to purple skin, is less sweet and has a texture more similar to a potato.

The Potato has been cultivated for over 7,000 years by the people of the Andes mountains. The Spanish word *papa* for potato is the Quechua word used by the Incas for this tuber.

Ñame (yam) is grown and used for cooking in the Caribbean. Yams were traditionally used in Africa to make a dish called fufu. However, the yam varieties grown in the Caribbean do not seem to be the correct type for preparing fufu. In the Spanish Caribbean, the analogous dish for fufu is made from plantains and is called Fufu de Plátano, Mofongo or Mangú. Yautia (page 122) is now grown in some areas of West Africa and used to make fufu.

SWEET POTATO: BATATA *(Ipomoea batatas)*

For most Dominican recipes that ask for sweet potatoes (batata) look for fat brown sweet potatoes with orange flesh.

SELECTION: Look for sweet potatoes that have smooth dark, unblemished skin. They should be hard. Often when I go to the market, they are rubbery and bendable. These should be rejected. Any defects in the skin can allow in fungal disease. Cutting out a bad spot will not cure the impaired flavor that a decayed spot imparts to the entire tuber.

STORAGE: Sweet potatoes are subject to chilling injury that makes the tubers susceptible to rot and pulp browning and shriveling. They should be stored between 61° and 65°F (16° to 18°C) and suffer chilling injury at 55°F (12.5°C) or below. Thus, do not place them in a refrigerator as it will give them a poor taste and texture. Do not wash them until you are ready to cook them. Unless you have a cool place to store them, it is probably best to buy what you plan to use within a week as you would with other perishable vegetables.

PREPARATION: Raw sweet potatoes contain a substance that inhibits an important digestive enzyme, so they should not be eaten raw. Any blemishes should be removed with a centimeter of the surrounding area to remove toxins.

SCIENCE ALERT: Plants use chemical weapons as a defense against attacks. When injured many plants increase the amount of defensive toxins they make to prevent further attack from insects. If one leaf is injured, the other leaves on the plant may increase the amount of defensive chemicals they produce. In potatoes, for example, if the tuber is injured during harvest, the tuber will produce more of the toxic chemicals solanine and chaconine that have fungicidal and pesticidal properties. Certain fungal attacks will also cause sweet potatoes to form toxins.

These toxins are also toxic to humans and other animals. Animals have developed taste sensors as a defense mechanism to avoid consumption of these toxins. Generally, they can be detected as having a bitter flavor.

Avoid tubers that show damage. Injured produce will not have as good a flavor, often being bitter, and will more likely have fungal growth that promotes the formation of more toxins. Onions (which are bulbs, not tubers) also tend to get bitter when exposed to light, while the bitter compound may not be toxic, it does not improve the flavor.

POTATO: PAPA (Solanum tuberosum)

SELECTION: When selecting potatoes look for undamaged skin and freshness. Fresh potatoes have much better flavor. The potato should be hard to thumb pressure and not rubbery. They should not be sprouting eyes, should not have any green under the skin, and should not be shriveled or wrinkled.

Bruises, cuts, and abrasions can be entry areas for bacteria and fungi that infect the tuber. Additionally, damage to potatoes during harvest increases the glycoalkaloids solanine and chaconine level and gives the potato a bitter taste. If a potato tuber is not covered by soil while it is growing, the exposure to light also causes an increase in these glycoalkaloids, to deter insects and animals from eating them. Light exposure also stimulates the production of chlorophyll, giving the exposed tuber a green color. Chlorophyll is harmless but is a good indicator that there is an increased production of solanine and chaconine in the tuber. Thus, avoid potatoes that have a greenish color under the skin. The glycoalkaloids, which can form even when there is no greening, have a bitter flavor, so discard any bitter potato even if it is not green. A higher level of the toxins may act as an irritant with a burning sensation similar to hot peppers. Cooking does not destroy the toxins. Most of the toxins will be just under the skin, so peeling potatoes decreases exposure to the toxins, if present. One green potato is enough to make an adult sick, and worse for children and pregnant women. Enough of the toxins can be deadly. Small greenish areas can be cut out, but better is to buy fresh, well-kept produce.

Potatoes also contain hemagglutinins and proteinases that are destroyed by cooking. They, like most tubers, should not be eaten raw. Other potato proteins that survive cooking can inhibit protein digestion, and may provoke an immune reaction in susceptible individuals.

STORAGE: Store potatoes in the dark to avoid production of the toxins and store in a cool place. Do not wash potatoes until you are ready to cook them to help prevent them from beginning to sprout. Potatoes should be stored between 45° and 50°F (7° - 10°C). Refrigeration of potatoes is not advised, as at temperatures below 40°F (4°C) the starch begins to turn to sugar and will cause the potato to darken when cooked. (Removing them from the refrigerator and leaving them in a cool place to slowly warm will allow the sugars to turn back into starch.) Gold-fleshed potatoes are naturally sweeter and can be stored in the refrigerator without browning. Chilling damage occurs at 36°F (2°C) or below. Freezing will cause them to become watery after cooking. The green giant has a trick for freezing potatoes – but he has not shared it with me.

YAUTIA AND TARO

Two related tubers are yautia *(Xanthosoma sagittifolium)* from the American tropics and taro *(Colocasia esculenta)* that originated in south Asia.

These plants can be found growing in gardens in the southern U.S. for their huge leaves that can be well over 2 feet across and twice as long. They are commonly called *Elephant Ears.* Yautia plants can be distinguished from taro by how the stem attaches to the leaf. The stem of yautia touches the notch in the leaf while the stem of the taro leaf is attached to the leaf away from the edges of the leaf. Also, the horns of the yautia leaves are pointed while taro has rounded ones. Taro can grow in waterlogged soil and becomes invasive. The leaves of either plant are among those leaves that may be used to make the Caribbean soup callaloo. Both plants produce lateral corms (tubers) that can be harvested without disturbing the main plant.

YAUTIA (MALANGA, TANNIA) *(Xanthosoma sagittifolium* and other species). In English, the tubers are called Tannia or New Cocoyam and in horticulture, they are called Arrow Leaf Elephant Ears. The leaves, especially young unfurled leaves, can be eaten.

Yautia tubers have shaggy hairs, but the scale does not cover the flesh between the rings of fibers. The main root is irregular, narrow and tapers. Yautia found in the U.S. usually white fleshed, but there are yellow and lavender fleshed varieties, and each has its own flavor and texture. Like taro, yautia has underground cormels that help support the central plant.

SELECTION: Look for fresh firm roots with light colored skin without soft spots, shriveling, mold, or sprouts. They should not be rubbery. If you pierce the skin with your thumbnail, the flesh should be juicy and crisp.

STORAGE: Yautia can be stored at 45°F (7°C) to extend its freshness, but should be allowed to warm to room temperature before using. Chilling damage occurs at 36°F (2°C) or below.

TARO *(Colocasia esculenta)* Taro has been cultivated in India for some 7,000 years, and is an important part of the cuisine of the Pacific islands, and used for making poi. Taro has about 1000 cultivars, and these are divided into two groups:

Dasheen with a large central corm and many small cormels, and *Eddo* with a small corm and large well-developed cormels. The rounded cormels do not have leaves, but help anchor the plant and gather water. The root has a fibrous skin with fibers arranged in circles around it.

The root, sap, stems and leaves of most taro cultivars, and particularly dasheens, contain irritants that are neutralized by cooking. No part of the plant should be eaten raw. When peeling the tubers, either wear gloves or peel them under running water to avoid skin irritation.

SELECTION: Check the roots to make sure that they are firm and without any soft spots, especially at the tips. If they are freshly harvested, the stem end of taro root may be pinkish or greenish. Choose medium to large tubers, with a dark muddy look, that are hairy.

STORAGE: Taro does not store well. Do not refrigerate it. Keep it in a cool ventilated area and use it within several days. The root should be stored at 60° - 65° F (16° - 18°C). They can be stored at 45° F (7°C), but need to be allowed to warm to room temperature before use. Chilling damage occurs at about 40°F (3-5°C).

CASSAVA: YUCA, MANIOC *(Manihot esculena)* Cassava grows well in poor soils with little rainfall, so it is an important food crop in some areas where little else does well. However, yuca contains cyanide forming compounds, and when the plant is stressed, as it is during a drought, the level of toxins can become dangerous.

During droughts, there is also little else to eat; thus it increases the amount of cyanide in the diet of people who depend on it for food. The cyanogenic glycosides are digested into cyanide in the gut, so the acute toxic effects are delayed for several hours. People, especially children, in this situation, are at risk of chronic poisoning resulting in permanent neurological injury causing spinal ataxia, optic atrophy, deafness, and peripheral neuropathy. Some varieties of cassava have as much as 50 times more toxins than others. The type sold for eating as tubers are referred to as "sweet" varieties. These are not sweet, but rather, just contain lower amounts of the bitter toxin.

Now that you can't wait to eat some yuca, please do wait until it is cooked, as cooking the sweet varieties is enough to eliminate most of the toxins. Never eat yuca raw. If it is bitter after cooking, it contains toxins and not worth eating in any case. Boiling the sweet cassava roots for twenty minutes removes about 90% of the toxins.

SELECTION: Pick fresh looking roots that are completely covered with the brown bark-like skin. Avoid roots with cracks, mold, damage or soft spots. Tubers that are mainly cylindrical and fat are preferable to long, thin or tapered tubers as these are more likely to be bitter and to be hard after cooking. If you open the skin with a finger nail, the flesh should be white and crisp, not yellowed. If you do this – you have opened a portal for damage, and should use it that day.

STORAGE: Without proper treatment, yuca has a very poor shelf life – only a few days from harvest. With pre and post-harvest treatment, it will last for several weeks. Most yuca sold in stores in the U.S. is coated with an antifungal wax that helps to hold in the moisture and seal the root from fungal and bacterial invasion. Cassava should be stored in a cool area between 60° and 65° F (16°- 18° C) with good ventilation. Cassava suffers from chilling damage at 54° F (12°C) or below. Chilling will make the yuca hard. When preparing yuca strip off the bark and remove the fibrous core in the center.

Yuca has a two-layer bark; the outer thin and like thick brown crepe paper and the inner, pink and thick. Cut the root into sections a few inches long, discarding the tip, and the stem ends. Slice deeply enough along the axis of the root to get under the inner bark and pull it back. It should come off cleanly. Discard the bark.

YAMS: ÑAME *(Dioscorea rotunda)* What is often called a yam in the United States is not a yam, but rather sweet potatoes (batata). True yams are unrelated plants with large tubers sometimes measuring over 6 feet in length, mostly from Africa. Some species of yam are sources of steroids used to make birth control pills and other pharmaceuticals and some yam species are bitter and toxic, and have to be heavily treated if they are edible at all. The aerial yam (*Dioscorea bulbifera*), which has become an invasive species in south Florida, has toxins that have been used to make poison arrows. It can be eaten after proper treatment. Bitter yam species must be treated by leaching and cooking before eating to remove toxins, and contact with uncooked yams can cause dermatitis.

The yams you are most likely to find in markets are the white or yellow yam *(D. rotunda),* which has about 200 cultivated varieties. Once the tubers are mature, they have little if any toxins, but should be peeled and cooked to be sure.

Selection: Yams are uncommon in the U.S. market. Because yams are so big, they are often sold in sections. In the U.S., I have seen smaller ones for sale. They should look fresh and be firm and disease free.

Storage: Ñame suffers from chilling damage at 54°F (12°C) or below. It should be stored in a cool, dry location from 55° to 65°F.

SOURCES: See citations:30, 31

Batata Horneada

Quick Baked Sweet Potato

INGREDIENTS:

Sweet potato
Salt
Black pepper
Butter or olive oil
Goat cheese

PREPARATION: Select an undamaged sweet potato (see page 120). Wash it and cut off both tips to act as steam vents. Do not prick the skin of the sweet potato, as is often done for baking, as it will cause it to dry out. Depending on the size of the sweet potato and the microwave power, it can take from 3 minutes to cook a small sweet potato to more than 10 minutes for a large one. The sweet potato should puff slightly when it ready. If overcooked the sweet potatoes will dry out and get hard.

Slice the sweet potato along its length to open it and reveal the orange flesh. If it remains undercooked and hard, cover it with a microwave safe bowl and place it back in the microwave for another minute. This will help retain moisture, but be careful; as the steam gets the bowl quite hot.

When the sweet potato is ready, slice it in both directions, using a fork to stabilize it as it will be too hot to handle. Cut it all the way through in both directions so that you end up with half inch pieces.

Add butter or drizzle with olive oil, and use a pepper grinder to sprinkle some fresh pepper and add some salt. For extra flavor, garnish with a tablespoon of crumbled goat cheese.

VITAMIN ALERT: There is a health reason for adding fat to the sweet potato, and to other vegetables beyond adding flavor and richness. Carotenoids, such as β-carotene, which forms vitamin A in the body, lutein, and zeaxanthin, which protect the retina, and other carotenoids which act as antioxidants, require bile for absorption. Bile is secreted to help with fat absorption. Less than 10 percent of these compounds are absorbed in a meal without fat, so these nutrients are mostly lost if vegetables are eaten in a meal by themselves. Vitamin K_1 from plants (phylloquinone) and vitamin E also require bile for absorption and so fat is required in a meal for them to be absorbed as well.

Vegans need to use vitamin B_{12} supplements as this vitamin is only found in animal products. The recommended daily allowance for vitamin B_{12} in adults is less than 3 micrograms, but if a supplement is used, it usually takes 1000 to 2000 micrograms of vitamin B_{12} a day as a supplement. The reason it that vitamin B_{12} is almost completely destroyed by stomach acid when swallowed as a pill. There is a protein in saliva; haptocorrin, which binds to B_{12} and protects it from stomach acid. This only works if food is chewed and mixed with saliva. Vitamin B_{12} lozenges and other forms that allow contact with saliva give much higher absorption rates; so much, so that they can cause problems, such as a rash or acne lesions, and may provoke other problems as well. If food is not chewed, Vitamin B_{12} is not absorbed.

Batata Asada

ROASTED SWEET POTATO

A sweet potato roasted in hot ashes then split open and filled with butter! Delicious, however, it is impractical most days of the year. Sweet potatoes can be prepared and eaten pretty much like a baked potato, but have more flavor and are more nutritious.

INGREDIENTS:

Plump, undamaged sweet potatoes.

PREPARATION: Prick the sweet potato in several areas with a fork to make vents for steam to escape as it cooks. The sweet potato is ready when a fork or a skewer passes easily through the tuber.

BAKED: Prick the sweet potato in several areas with a fork to make vents for steam to escape as it cooks. Place on the oven rack at 400°F for 40 minutes to one hour depending on the size of the tuber.

ROASTED IN ASHES: Do not prick the skin. Bury the potatoes into the hot ashes of a fire and roast until the batata is soft.

Serve: Split open lengthwise. Insert a tab of butter, or a dollop of sour cream. Sprinkle a dash of salt

FANCY BAKED: Select 4 unblemished small sweet potatoes. Make parallel slices along the length of the sweet potato, about ¼-inch wide, almost all the way through the sweet potato, leaving the bottom ½ inch intact. Place the 4 incised sweet potatoes in a baking pan with the cuts placed upwards in the pan. Place ¼-cup of butter in a cup and melt it in the microwave and then drench sweet potatoes with melted butter. Bake for 30 to 35 minutes at 400°F. The top edges should be slightly toasted. This recipe can be done with peel removed prior to cooking if preferred. For a holiday treat, add one tablespoon of brown sugar and 1/8 teaspoon ground cinnamon to the melted butter.

Batatas Fritas

SWEET POTATO FRIES

Better than French fried potatoes are fried sweet potatoes that have a sweet, earthy flavor and a golden orange flesh.

INGREDIENTS:

1 or 2 sweet potatoes (orange flesh)
2 tablespoons coconut oil
Salt (optional)

PREPARATION: Peel the sweet potato and slice into rounds about ¼-inch thick. Heat an 8-inch frying pan with a couple of tablespoons of heated coconut oil. Place the sweet potato rounds into the hot oil, turning them when they are golden brown on the underside. Cook the other side, remove and place them on paper towels to remove excess oil. If coconut oil is not available, other mild vegetable oil may be used. Sprinkle with a few grains of salt.

ALTERNATIVES: Rather than cutting into rounds, sweet potatoes can be cut into French fry style strips and fried. This works well in commercial kitchens where there is a deep fat fryer, and large amounts of fries are made. The wheel shape requires less oil and works where only a few people are being fed.

Fritas de Auyama

BUTTERNUT SQUASH FRIES:

Oooh! These are even tastier than sweet potato fries. Use the neck area of the butternut squash above where it becomes hollow. Peel it, and cut the neck into ¼-inch thick rounds, and fry them as for sweet potato fries.

Serving suggestion: These make for a great, almost guilty pleasure, a side dish that goes with seafood or with eggs.

Mazamorra - Puré de Auyama

BUTTERNUT SQUASH PUREE

INGREDIENTS

1 large butternut squash
2 tablespoons olive oil
3 tablespoons butter
¼ teaspoon salt
1 small red onion, quartered and sliced.
4 cloves garlic

PREPARATION: Cut the neck from the rest of squash and cut the base in half. Remove the seeds and fiber from the hollow center. Peel the skin from the flesh of the squash, and then cut the squash into 1-inch cubes. Simmer the squash in a covered pan for about 10 to 15 minutes until a fork easily passes through the squash. As the squash is cooking, sauté the onion and garlic in the oil and butter over medium-low heat. Add the salt.

When the squash is soft, drain off the water, and place it in a bowl. Puree the squash using a wooden spoon. Take half of the sautéed onion and garlic and blend it in with the squash. Serve the squash with the rest of the onions, garlic and oil as a garnish. Traditionally served with eggs (Sunny inside, page 31) and with fried salami.

Bollitos de Yuca

CASSAVA BALLS

INGREDIENTS:

1½ pounds of yuca
5 tablespoons butter
¼ teaspoon salt
1 egg yolk
1/3 cup vegetable oil

PREPARATION: Peel the yuca, and cut it along it's the long axis to reveal the fibrous center core. Remove the woody core and discard it. Cut the yuca into 1½-inch pieces. Place the yuca in a saucepan with sufficient water to cover it and set it to a low boil. Cook it until a fork passes easily through the pieces. Drain the water. Mash the yuca as for mashed potatoes. Add the butter and the salt. Allow to cool to room temperature before adding the egg yolk. Blend the ingredients together until it forms a smooth dough.

Using your hands roll one inch balls (about ½ oz.) and lay the balls on a tray.

Put the oil in an 8 - 10 inch cast iron pan, over medium heat. The oil should not be hot enough to smoke, but should look glassy, and should be about ¼" deep. When the oil is hot, add about a dozen balls to the pan. Use a spoon to roll then around so that they get cooked on all sides, until they are golden brown.

Serve while still hot and crispy.

Bollitos de Yuca Rellenos

FUFU

PREPARATION: Take the unfried balls as formed in the recipe above, and with your fingers, make a depression in the center 2/3 the way through. Fill with a teaspoon of meat or fish filling, or a ½ inch cube of cheese. Reform the ball so that the filling is in the center of the ball, and surrounded by dough and fry it as described in the recipe above.

For the meat filling, use the recipe for Empanadas de Maíz on page 136. A fish filling can be made using a can of spicy sardines with its liquid blended together to form a paste. This spicy sardine paste is also used as a street food to complement yaniqueques, a Dominican snack similar to native American fry bread

Puré de Papa

MASHED POTATOES

INGREDIENTS

3 pounds potatoes
1 teaspoon salt
5 tablespoons olive oil
4 tablespoons butter
1/8 teaspoon salt
1 small red onion, quartered and sliced.
2 cloves garlic

PREPARATION: Peel the potatoes and cut into one-inch cubes. Boil them in enough water that they float with one teaspoon salt for about 8 minutes. When ready, they should split easily when a fork is inserted them. Drain the water off.

Puree the potatoes. Add 2 tablespoons of butter and 2 tablespoons of olive oil and mix together.

In a separate pan, sauté the onions and garlic in 3 tablespoons of olive oil, until golden brown. Add 1/8th teaspoon of salt and 2 tablespoons of butter, and turn off the heat. Serve the sautéed onions over the mashed potatoes.

About Plantains and Cooking Bananas

The banana and plantain are natives of tropical Africa and Southeast Asia but were brought to the tropical areas of America during Spanish colonization. Both plantains and bananas are used as starchy vegetables when they are green, and can be eaten as fruit when they are ripe. They are an important part of the African heritage of Caribbean cuisine.

SELECTING PLANTAINS: Green plantains should be heavy, dense, firm and without damage or spliting. They can still be used when they are yellow and speckled for cooking, but will be softer and sweet. When ready to be eaten ripe, the skin of the plantains will be black.

SELECTING GREEN BANANAS FOR COOKING: If buying bananas for cooking, they must be deep green and very firm. Since bananas are usually sold for eating as fruit, they are usually sold in grocery stores ready to turn yellow; these are usually too ripe. If you ask the produce manager at your local grocer which day of the week he gets bananas in, you can often get them green enough for cooking. Keep the green bananas in the open and not enclosed with other fruit, as this encourages quicker ripening. Try to use them within a day unless you want to allow them to ripen. Bananas can be used for cooking like plantains, but must be deep green to match a green plantain. A speckled ripe yellow banana compares to a black plantain.

STORAGE: Green bananas and plantains can be stored at 56-58°F (13.3 to 14.4 °C) to delay their ripening. Colder temperatures (a refrigerator) will damage them. Ripe bananas and plantains can be peeled and frozen, and used for baking, or for smoothies.

PEELING PLANTAINS: Green plantains do not give up their peel easily. Plantains usually have more angular ribs along their length than do bananas. To peel a plantain, insert the tip of a paring knife about ¼ to ½ inch deep and about ¼ inch to the side along one of the ribs on the outside curve of the plantains, making a slit along its entire length. The knife should be angled so that it runs along the rib, and so that it runs between the peel and the fruit. Then run your thumb between the peel in the slit you have made, widening it. This will allow you to free the skin from the plantain, usually in a single piece.

PLANTAIN STAINS!: When fresh, the peels of the plantain will stain hands and clothing. When the skin is cut open, white sap can be seen to ooze out of the peel. To avoid dark brown staining of the skin, lubricate your hands and knife blade with vegetable oil before cutting the plantain. When finished dry your hands with a paper towel, and then wash your hands. Lemon juice, lime juice and vinegar followed by liquid soap can be used to help get rid of plantain stains from skin.

It is best to avoid staining clothes with plantain sap as it is usually permanent. If you do get a stain, soak the clothing in a mix of half white vinegar and warm water for half hour, and then apply vinegar directly to the stained area. Then wash the garment as usual.

Tostones, also called fritos, are fried (usually double fried) plantains. This is the most common way the plantains are eaten. They are used much like French fries or potatoes are, accompanying fish or meat in a meal. Tostones can also be made with ripe or semi-ripe plantains (Fritos de Plátanos Maduros).

MANGU AND MOFONGO:

Mofongo is a dish generally prepared from mashed baked or fried green plantains. In Cuba, it is called fufu, showing the African origin of this dish. Typically the cooked plantains are formed into a ball and stuffed with meat and covered with sauce. When I was growing up, we baked peeled plantains in the ashes of our cooking fire for making mofongo, which gives it a different flavor than frying does.

Mangu is similar to mofongo but generally prepared from mashed boiled rather than fried plantains. It usually served in a mound, like mashed potatoes, and topped with sautéed onions, and served with fried eggs, fried salami, or fried cheese. It is sometimes mashed with milk or butter.

Mangú de Plátano

MASHED PLANTAINS

INGREDIENTS:

1 medium green plantain
2 cups water
1/8 teaspoon salt

2 tablespoons butter
1 tablespoon olive oil
½ small red onion, quartered and sliced so that little onion strips are formed.
1/8th teaspoon salt

PREPARATION: Boil the plantain in salted water for about 10 minutes until they are soft and break with the insertion of a fork. Cooking hints are given in the recipe for boiled plantains below.

In a separate saucepan, melt the butter and add the oil. Sauté the onion until the pieces are just turning clear, then golden along the edges. Turn off the heat and sprinkle an eighth teaspoon of salt over them.

Remove the plantain pieces from the pot and place them in a bowl. Mash the plantains into a course puree. If it seems too dry, add about 1 tablespoon a time, water the plantains were boiled in.

Serve, covering the mashed plantains with the fried sautéed onions and oil.

Makes two servings.

This dish is usually prepared as a breakfast. Often served with eggs and fried salami.

Plátanos y Guineos Hervido

BOILED GREEN BANANAS AND PLANTAINS

INGREDIENTS:

2 green plantains or 4 green bananas
1 quart of water
¼ teaspoon salt

PREPARATION: To prepare boiled plantains or bananas, peel them (see page 128 for instructions on peeling plantains) and cut the plantains in half. Bananas can usually be left whole. Splitting the plantain lengthwise will make it more likely for them to get hard.

Boil plantains and bananas as you would a potato; set them in enough water that they can float, add the salt and boil them for about 10 to 12 minutes and then remove the pan from the heat. When cooked a fork should enter the plantain easily and break it, and the color should look creamy.

Boiled green bananas are often served with sautéed onions and eggs cooked sunny side up. Both boiled plantains and bananas are served much as boiled potatoes are - with chicken, meat, or fish that has been cooked in a sauce, where they are drizzled in the sauce.

Boiled plantains and bananas can easily become hard and unpalatable. Allow the plantains to cool some submerged in the water, as removing them hot will cause the plantains to get hard. To speed cooling, a couple of cups of cool tap water can be added to the hot water in the pot. This also helps keep the plantains from turning dark.

If allowed to sit in the water too long the boiled plantains will turn brown and unattractive. This brown layer can be scraped off with a butter knife.

Empanada de Plátano

PLANTAIN CHEESE POCKETS

Empanadas are small flat pastries made by doubling dough over itself to enclose a filling. These can be either baked or fried. These are also known as pastelones or empanadillas. They are often sold freshly prepared by street cooks on corners as an evening snack.

INGREDIENTS:

2 medium plantains (green to yellow)
¼ teaspoon salt
1 egg
1 clove garlic, minced
½ cup cheese, cut into ¼ inch cubes
2 tablespoons coconut oil

PREPARATION: Peel the plantains, cut into 3-inch sections and place them in a saucepan with enough water that they float. Place on the stove over high heat, and bring them to a boil. Lower the heat to medium and cook at a simmer for about 10 minutes. Cook until a fork can easily penetrate the plantains. Remove the pot from the heat.

Set the pot aside to allow the plantains to cool while sitting in the water they boiled in. While they are still warm (but not too hot to handle) drain off the water and mash the plantains. Beat an egg adding the minced garlic and salt, and add it to the plantains, and mash it all together.

Separate the mash into 8 equal-sized portions and roll them into balls.

Either roll each ball flat or use the bottom of a plate to flatten each ball into a disk about 3½ inches in diameter and ¼ inch thick. Put about one tablespoon of cheese in the center of each disk.

Fold the disk over onto itself to form half circles with the cheese inside of a pouch. You can wet the top edge of the disk by dipping your index finger into a cup of water to moisten the area where the plantain disk will fold over and meet, to help seal the pouch.

Add the oil to the sauté pan over medium heat. Fry the pouch on each side until they are deep golden brown. Serve while still hot.

Variations:
- Use plantains that are getting speckled, and almost ripe, but still firms to make a sweeter version.
- Use pepper jack or other spiced cheese for extra flavor.
- Leave out the garlic, and use a mild cheese.

Tostones

DOUBLE FRIED GREEN PLANTAINS

Tostones are for us Dominicans what French fries are to Americans and what chips in fish and chips are to the British. We even drizzle them with ketchup sometimes.

INGREDIENTS:

Green plantains
Olive oil
Salt (Coarsely ground sea salt)

PREPARATION: Peel the plantains as explained on page 128. Slice the plantain into ½-inch thick wheels for round tostones, or do a French cut (angled) to make longer ones.

Place the oil in the frying pan about one-eighth inch deep and heat over medium heat. The oil should be hot enough to lose some viscosity, but never hot enough to smoke.

Place the plantain pieces in the oil and allow them to fry for about 2 minutes, turn them over to cook on the other side for 2 minutes and remove them from the pan. If making more than fit in the pan at once, you can continue to cook more.

Place the fried tostones on a plate with a paper towel to soak up excess oil, and allow them to cool enough to handle. Here comes the part for a special tool, a tostone press, but don't worry if you don't have one. Use the press to flatten the tostones to about ¼ inch thick. If you don't have a tostone press handy, place the fried plantain slices on a cutting board and flatten them with the bottom of a flat saucer, cup or another utensil.

When you have a batch flattened, fry them again for 30 seconds on each side until they begin to brown lightly. Again place them on a paper towel to soak up excess oil. Transfer them to a serving plate, and sprinkle a pinch of coarse salt onto the tostones and serve hot.

Serve with fried eggs, fried fish, salad, or with almost any Caribbean dish.

Plátanos Rellenos

After cooking, press into a bowl shape and fill with sardines or meat as described for fufu on page 127 or empanadas de maíz on page 136.

Fritos de Plátanos Maduros

FRIED RIPE PLANTAINS

Plantains can be fried in varying degrees of ripeness. When riper, they are sweeter and more translucent. Fried ripe plantains, (where the skin is yellow with black patches or darker) are a sweet side dish.

INGREDIENTS:

1 ripe plantain
2 tablespoons vegetable oil

PREPARATION: Peel the plantain, and cut it in half, and slice each piece lengthwise into 4 slices. Heat the oil in a skillet, and lay about half the sliced plantain in the heated oil. Turn the pieces over as they cook until they are golden and just begin to have a toasted brown color along the edges, allowing them to caramelize some, for about 2 to 4 minutes. Remove the plantain and cover the pieces to keep them warm, while you cook the other half.

SERVING IDEAS: Ripe plantain fritos are sometimes eaten as an afternoon snack, or with fried eggs. Some people like them with salt. They are also eaten along with supper.

Mofongo

CARIBBEAN PLANTAIN FUFU

Fufu is a traditional African dish, usually prepared from yam, or cassava. In the new world, plantain fufu is more common. The traditional fufu was made from starchy tubers, mashed and formed into a ball. A depression would be made into the ball so that it could be filled with meat, and sometimes closed. In this recipe, the mofongo is formed into a bowl and filled with fried meat or sautéed shrimp, with onions and garlic.

INGREDIENTS:

3 green plantains
Olive oil (for frying tostones)
2 medium cloves of garlic
1 tablespoon oil
¼ teaspoon salt

PREPARATION: The filling for fufu should be ready before cooking the plantains. Mofongo should be served hot. If allowed to cool, it will get hard and lose its magic.

Suggested fillings:
• Sautéed (small) shrimp with butter, garlic, and onions.
• Sauté pork, beef, chicken, salami or sausage, with onions and garlic.

Prepare tostones from green plantains as directed on page 131. Do not allow them to brown. Cover them to keep them warm. Place one clove of garlic and 1/8th teaspoon salt in a large wooden mortar and smash it. (See below if you do not have a mortar). Add a few tostones at a time to the mortar smashing them and blending them with the garlic. If the plantains are too hard, ½ tablespoon of olive oil or butter may be added. Use about half the tostones, mashing them together until it forms a stiff dough that can be molded. Use the pestle to form the mofongo into a bowl about 3 inches across at the bottom of the mortar. Use a butter knife to free the edges of the bowl to remove it from the mortar. Fill the mofongo bowl with the meat or shrimp filling. Place it in a toaster oven set to 150°F to keep it warm. Repeat the process with the remaining tostones to make a second bowl. Serve hot. Makes 2 servings.

Serve along with a fresh garden salad.

If you do not have a large mortar and pestle, a wooden spoon can be used to mash the tostones and mix in finely mince garlic. Small bowls can be modeled using the fingers.

Notes:

Mazorca

CORN ON THE COB

While I was in college, I would sometimes buy corn on the cob from a street vendor with a three-wheeled bicycle with a large heated cauldron in front, filled with water, cooking corn on the cob near one of the entrances to the campus. At home, we cooked our meals over fire or charcoal. To cook corn, we would bury the ear, still in its husks in the hot ashes. This remains my favorite method with a campfire, as I like the smoky flavor from the husks. Oven roasted or grilled corn on the cob is also excellent.

The secret to sweet, tender, juicy corn on the cob is fresh, never frozen corn on the cob, and that is not overcooked. Look for fresh corn that the cobs are filled nearly to the tip. The husks should be bright green and snug. You should be able to feel the rows of corn kernels under the husks. Cooking corn too long will make it tough and starchy rather than sweet and tender.

Corn on the cob can be cooked in the husk or without. Cooking with the husk is easier, as it is easier to remove the silk after cooking than before. The outer layer of the husk can be removed, and the exposed silk trimmed before cooking.

INGREDIENTS: Fresh ears of corn on the cob.

BOILED: Use a large pot with enough water to cover the corn, and deep enough that it will not overflow after adding the corn. Bring the water to a boil, and carefully slide the ears into the water or use tongs to avoid splashing the hot water. Cover and cook for 3 to 5 minutes depending on how tender or how dense you enjoy your corn. Remove from the hot water using tongs or a skewer fork. Allow enough time for the corn to cool enough to handle.

ROASTED: Presoak the ear of corn in its husk in water for 15 - 30 minutes, leaving more time if the corn is not quite as fresh as you would wish. Place the corn on the oven rack at 350°F for 30 minutes. Serve with the husk. When eating it, pull back the husk, and use the inverted husk as a handle.

GRILLED: Presoak the ear of corn as for roasting. Grill for about 20 minutes, turning occasionally. The outside husks and silk will get toasted or even charred. Allow to cool for about 10 minutes before serving.

MICROWAVE: If cooking in the husks, presoak the ear of corn as for roasting. Microwave for about six minutes, depending on the power of your microwave.

Serve with butter, and sprinkle with a bit of salt, cayenne pepper powder.

ALTERNATIVE: Before cooking, peel back the husks and remove the silk. Butter the cob, and spice with salt and pepper, paprika, or cayenne pepper. Pull the husks back over the cob, and tie shut with cotton string. Roast, grill or microwave as above.

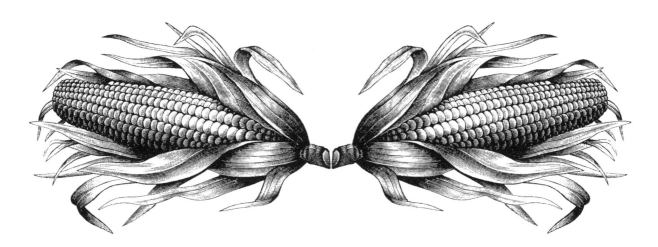

Chacá

MAIZ NIXTAMALIZADO CON HABICHUELAS Y COCO

COCONUT CORN STEW

This vegetarian stew was a special treat at home. I would be lucky to have this dish once a year and most people did not make it. It was just too much work, as it required 2 days of preparation. The corn had to be cooked in ashes or soaked in calcium hydroxide solution (lime water) until the skin of the corn kernel were removed. The coconuts had to be gathered, the copra removed from the shell, finely grated and the coconut cream expressed by hand. The beans were soaked overnight and cooked over a wood fire. But here in the U.S. nixtamalized corn is available in a can and called hominy. One could cook this dish in 8 minutes including opening the cans – but the flavor improves with slow cooking and is even better when reheated the next day after sleeping in the refrigerator. Meat or other ingredients can be added to vary this recipe.

INGREDIENTS:

2 cups coconut cream (or one 13 to 14 oz. can)
1 20 oz. can of beans (black or red) drained
1½ cups white hominy corn – drained
1½ cups yellow hominy corn – drained
5 cloves garlic, sliced
½ small red onion, chopped
1/8 teaspoon salt
1 tablespoon fresh chopped cilantro

PREPARATION: Place all ingredients except the cilantro in a pot and heat over medium heat until the liquid boils. Turn heat down and cook over low heat, stirring occasionally for about 30 minutes until the stew gets creamy and thick. Stir in the cilantro before serving.

VARIATIONS: Carnivore edition: Add diced chicken breast and 2 tablespoons of whole, dried coriander seeds. When cooked into the stew, the coriander seeds give a crunch and burst of flavor.

Cafungi

INGREDIENTS:

1 2/3 cups cooked and drained red kidney beans
   (or one 15 oz. can)
14 oz. coconut cream (1 can, 20% fat)
3 tablespoons finely chopped garlic
1 cup water
1 teaspoon salt
1 tablespoon chopped fresh cilantro
2 cups yellow cornmeal
A banana leaf if available

PREPARATION: Place all ingredients together in a saucepan and mix them together. Place over medium heat, and cook at a simmer for about 10 minutes stir continuously to avoid having the cornmeal stick to the bottom of the pan. When this "porridge" gets thick, reduce the heat to low, cover the contents with a banana leaf and put a lid on the pan to retain the vapor. Cook for 40 minutes at low heat. Remove from the heat and remove the banana leaf and using a wooden spoon lift the contents from underneath to release some steam as done in cooking rice. Allow the porridge to sit for about 5 minutes with the lid in place.

Serve with carne guisada (goat stew) or shrimp in garlic sauce, or with avocado.

It is the sauce from the accompanying dish that brings cafungi to life.

Pan de Maíz con Coco

COCONUT CORN BREAD

INGREDIENTS:

3 cups yellow cornmeal
1 teaspoon anise seed
2 teaspoons salt
3 cups water
2½ cups coconut cream
2 tablespoons butter

PREPARATION: Place the dry ingredients in a deep pan and mix together. Stir in the water and coconut cream, making sure that there are no lumps. Place the pan over medium-low heat, stirring continuously while cooking for about 20 minutes. This should form a thick gruel.

Place the gruel in a buttered 8-inch baking pan and allow it to sit for a few minutes to thicken.

Melt 2 tablespoons of butter in a cup in the microwave, and use it to paint the surface of the batter. The back of a tablespoon dipped in the butter can be used to gently paint the surface of the corn bread with the butter, avoiding breaking or denting the surface.

Bake at 325 degrees for 25 minutes. The surface should be golden brown. Paint on a second coat of butter on the bread while it is still hot.

Precolumbian taíno village life

Empanadas de Maíz

Corn Pockets

Ingredients: Dough:

2 cups yellow stone ground corn meal
½ teaspoon salt
1 1/3 cups coconut cream
1/8 teaspoon anise seed

Preparation: Dough:
Using a deep bowl, mix the ingredients together, making the dough. Knead the dough for about 5 minutes, and then let it rest for 10 minutes.

Meat Filling:

½ pound ground beef
1 plum tomato; diced
1 clove garlic; diced finely
1 teaspoon olive oil
¼ teaspoon salt
½ small jalapeño pepper; diced

Preparation: Meat Filling:
Place all ingredients in a sauté pan and mix together over medium heat. The ground beef should be crumbled into little grains. Cook until the meat is well browned.

Veggie Filling:

4 oz. cheese; diced into ¼ inch cubes
1 Plum tomato minced
1 small clove garlic minced
¼ teaspoon oregano minced
Pinch of salt

Preparation: Cheese Filling:
Mix ingredients together in a bowl. Use 2 tablespoons as filling for the empanadas.

Pouches:
Form the dough into balls, each about two oz., or about 1¼" (4 cm) diameter. Place a dough ball on top of a sheet of wax paper or plastic wrap and using a rolling pin, roll it out into a disk about 5 inches in diameter.

Place 2 tablespoons of filling in the center of the dough. Lift one edge of the wax paper or plastic wrap and fold the dough over so that it makes a half circle. Peel back the wax paper, and then press the dough edges together to seal the half circle pouch.

Fry the empanada in a sauté pan filled ¼ inch deep with vegetable oil at a temperature of 350° to 375°F; medium heat. Fry the empanada on one side until it browns and then turn it over to brown the other side. Serve while still hot and crispy.

Notes:

The American Crocodile

Lasagne de Berenjena

Eggplant Lasagne

Ingredients:

1½-pound eggplant
Salt
½ cup olive oil (for frying)
2 eggs
2 tablespoons milk
½ teaspoon salt
¼ teaspoon garlic powder
2 cups pasta sauce
½ pound medium sharp cheddar cheese, shredded
½ cup ricotta cheese

Preparation: Remove the stem and peel the eggplant (Page 10). Cut the eggplant in half lengthwise. Slice each half lengthwise into strips about ¼ of an inch thick. Lay a layer of the eggplant slices in a colander, and evenly sprinkle with salt. Add a layer and repeat this process until all the eggplant is in layers with salt. This helps remove moisture and bitterness from the eggplant. Allow to rest for about an hour. Rinse the salt off of the eggplant slices in cold running water, and blot them dry with paper towels.

In a mixing bowl add the eggs, milk, ¼ teaspoon of salt, and garlic powder, and beat together to form a batter.

Place the olive oil in a cast iron skillet, and heat the oil over medium heat. There should be just a little more than a ¼ inch of oil in the pan. It should not be hot enough to smoke. Dip an eggplant slice in the batter, allow the excess to drain off and place in the hot oil to fry. Allow each slice to cook for about 30 seconds on a side, flipping it over with a spatula and cook the other side. The oil should be about 300 to 350° F, which is below the smoke point of olive oil. After cooking each slice, lay them aside on a plate to be used later.

When done frying the eggplant, take a 8 x 8-inch baking pan and pour in one cup of your favorite off the shelf pasta sauce. Place a layer of eggplant slices to pave the bottom of the pan. Add a layer of shredded cheese and a thin layer of ricotta cheese. Now add another layer of eggplant, but lay them in the opposite direction. Add a thin layer of shredded cheese and of ricotta cheese, estimating the amount of material you have so that there will be extra cheese to top the top layer of eggplant. With each layer, change the direction of the eggplant so that the crisscross. When all the eggplant has been used, pour a second cup of pasta sauce, the rest of the ricotta cheese, and then sprinkle with the remaining shredded cheese.

Place in an oven heated to 350° F for 30 minutes. Allow to cool for several minutes before serving.

Notes:

Salsa de Berenjena con Coco

EGGPLANT IN COCONUT SAUCE

INGREDIENTS

14 oz. coconut cream
4 cloves garlic; minced
1 large shallot; minced
1½ teaspoons salt
¼ teaspoon saffron
½ cup of water
1½ pounds of eggplant; peeled and diced.
1 teaspoon achiote (bija)
2 teaspoons minced cilantro

PREPARATION: Directions for peeling eggplant are given on page 10. Place the coconut cream in a saucepan with the water, garlic, shallot, saffron and salt. Bring the liquid to a simmer and add the eggplant. Stir occasionally.

Place the achiote seeds in a small bowl. Add a tablespoon of hot water, and press the seeds up against the wall of the bowl with the back of a spoon to release the color into the water. Add this juice to the eggplant mixture after cooking for about 10 minutes. Cook for another 15 minutes. Add the cilantro, and remove from the heat.

Serve this over boiled green plantains, boiled green bananas or over white rice.

Alternative: Also good as a thick soup; add an extra cup of water at the beginning and one cup cut corn at the same time as the achiote. Garnish with grated cheese.

Notes:

The palmchat, (Dulus dominicus) is the national bird of the Dominican Republic

Lechosa Verde con Tomates

GREEN PAPAYA WITH TOMATOES

In this dish, papaya is used as a vegetable, much as potatoes would be used. It is lighter and more succulent than potatoes.

INGREDIENTS:

A green papaya, about 2 pounds
1 teaspoon salt
2 tablespoons olive oil
1 small onion; diced
3 cloves garlic; sliced
2 plum tomatoes; diced
2½ vegetable bouillon cubes (5 grams each)
2 tablespoons butter

PREPARATION: Prepare the papaya: Halve the papaya, and remove the seeds and the lining on the inside of the seed cavity. Cut off the stem area.

Peel the papaya and cut into 3/4 to 1-inch cubes. Boil the papaya in a saucepan with about 1½ quarts of water and 1-teaspoon of salt until it is tender, about 7 minutes as you would for potatoes, and then drain off the water.

Place the olive oil in a sauté pan over medium heat. Add the diced onions and sauté them until they begin to get clear. Add the garlic and sauté for about 2 minutes until they begin to turn golden. Add the tomatoes and the bouillon cubes and sauté for about three minutes or until it forms a sauce. Add the butter and melt it in. Stir in the boiled papayas and cook over low heat for a couple of minutes to allow the flavor to soak into the papayas. Serve hot.

Molondrones a la Vinagreta

OKRA A LA VINAIGRETTE

Okra is well known as an ingredient to thicken stews such as gumbo. It is less appreciated as a vegetable. Unless okra is being used to thicken a soup or stew, they should be lightly steamed to avoid their getting slimy.

Okra is commonly eaten as a green vegetable on the islands. Okra is easy to grow in the garden and has pretty, pale yellow hibiscus flowers. They need to be harvested daily as the seed pods grow surprisingly quickly and get stringy and hard if left on the plant a couple of extra days. Okra is at its best when it is small and tender, no more than 3 and a half inches long.

INGREDIENTS:

2 cups whole okra
1 cup water
1 tablespoon olive oil
1 tablespoon wine vinegar
A pinch of salt
Fresh ripe tomato slices (optional)

PREPARATION: If you have a vegetable steamer, place a half inch of water in a saucepan below the steamer, add the okra to the steamer, cover and bring the water to a low boil. Steam the okra for about 4 minutes.

Alternatively, place the water and okra into a saucepan with a well-fitting lid. Bring the water to a boil, and turn off the heat. Allow the okra to steam in the covered pot for 2 minutes. Drain off the water.

In the pan with the steamed okra add the olive oil and vinegar and gently turn the okra so that it gets covered with the dressing. Add a pinch of salt to taste. Serve immediately while the okra is still hot.

Serving suggestion: Serve the okra in the center of a serving tray surrounded by tomato slices.

Beverages ~ Jugos y Bebidas

About Fruit Beverages

Fresh fruit juices and smoothies are part of life in the Caribbean. They are served to guests in the afternoon or with light evening meals.

Traditionally "comida" or supper, the main meal of the day, was served midday, followed by a nap and shower before returning to work. This helped avoid working during the hottest part of the day. The evening meal was light, and Dominican or Cuban sandwich and juice or a smoothie did nicely.

In recent years, as people urbanize, and there is air conditioning, the midday meal has become lighter, and siestas are fading away. Fortunately, juices remain.

SCIENCE ALERT:

Papaya and pineapple (and also melons, figs, and kiwi fruit) contain proteolytic enzymes that help break down proteins into fragments call peptides. When these fruits are mixed with milk, the milk proteins get cut up by these enzymes into peptides, exposing bitter tasting amino acids. This causes papaya and pineapple smoothies to become bitter within a few minutes of making them and is why when you go back for a second cup, the smoothie can look lumpy and have an unpleasant taste. This process also changes the texture of the smoothie.

These enzymes can be denatured by heating the fruit to around 149°F (65° degrees C), for one minute. Depending on the power of the microwave, this can be done by microwaving one cup of fruit for about 70 seconds; enough to get it very hot throughout. After heating, place the fruit in the refrigerator to chill. Canned fruit has already been heated, so it will not cause the milk to turn bitter.

SMOOTHIE SECRET: If you make smoothies with frozen fruit, e.g.; frozen bananas, strawberries or blueberries, you can leave out the ice and get a richer, thicker smoothie that requires much less and often no added sugar.

Batida de Piña

PINEAPPLE SMOOTHIE

INGREDIENTS:

2 cups of fresh pineapple or a 20 oz. can
   of pineapple in juice; crushed or bits
1 cup evaporated milk
½ cup of sugar
2 cups of ice cubes

PREPARATION: Liquefy the ingredients together in a blender at high speed for 2 minutes and then serve. If using fresh pineapple, it is best not to use the core, as it leaves too much fiber in the drink.

Note: If replacing evaporated milk with whole milk, use 1½ cups of whole milk and decrease the ice to 1½ cups.

Jugo de Lechosa

PAPAYA SMOOTHIE

INGREDIENTS:

2 cups of papaya fruit
1/3 cup sugar or 1 tablespoon honey
2 cups ice
1 can of evaporated milk (12 oz.)
½ teaspoon vanilla extract

PREPARATION: Clean a ripe papaya, removing the seeds and the skin. (See section on fruits). Place the papaya and other ingredients in a blender and liquefy for 2 minutes at high speed. You can add one tablespoon of sugar as needed according to the sweetness of the papaya. Sugar brings out the flavor of the fruit, but too much sugar will overwhelm it.

For variety, add a ripe banana or one cup of pineapple or pineapple juice to the smoothie.

Note: The 12 oz of evaporated milk (and 2 cups of ice cubes) can be replaced with 2 cups of milk and 1½ cups of ice cubes.

Note: See the Science Alert on the previous page to avoid smoothies turning bitter.

Jugo de Fresa

KICKIN' STRAWBERRY SMOOTHIE

INGREDIENTS:

1½ cups of cut strawberries
1 cup milk
1/3 cup sugar
½ teaspoon vanilla extract
1 cup of ice cubes

PREPARATION: Place the ingredients into a blender and liquefy for about 60 to 90 seconds. Add an extra tablespoon of sugar if needed to bring out the strawberry flavor. Makes 3 servings

Jugo de Níspero

SAPODILLA SMOOTHIE

When perfectly ripe, this fruit has a flavor between caramel and brown sugar. In some areas, this fruit is also known as zapote.

INGREDIENTS:

1 cup ripe sapodilla fruit pieces
1 cup evaporated milk
1 cup of ice cubes
3 tablespoons sugar

PREPARATION: Cut the níspero in half, top from bottom, and remove the shiny black seeds and discard the skin. Place the ingredients in a blender, blend for one minute, and serve.

Note: If replacing evaporated milk with whole milk, use 1¼ cups of whole milk and decrease the amount of ice to 3/4 cups.

Jugo de Guayaba

GUAVA JUICE

It is often difficult to find fresh guavas for making juice. This is a recipe for making guava juice from guava paste, which is much easier to find than fresh guavas, and easier to keep at home.

INGREDIENTS:
1/3 cup of guava paste, or 4 oz. by weight
2 cups water
Ice

PREPARATION: Dice the guava paste into several small pieces and place in a small saucepan with the water. Bring the water to a boil, stirring constantly, and then turn off the heat as soon as it boils. The paste should be dissolved. If not, cover it and allow to rest for a few minutes. Chill the juice in the refrigerator. Serve it poured over ice.

Jugo de Naranja Cocolada

COCONUT ORANGE SMOOTHIE

INGREDIENTS:
2 cups orange juice
1 cup coconut cream
1 medium orange
1/3rd cup sugar
1 cup of ice cubes

PREPARATION: Add the orange juice and coconut cream to the blender. Peel the orange. If the orange has seeds, cut the orange in half, across the sections, and remove all the seeds before adding the orange to the blender. Add the ice cubes and ¼ cup of sugar. Blend for about 2 minutes at high speed. Adding the orange adds fiber and gives more body to the smoothie, but it takes more time to liquefy. Taste the smoothie. Depending on how sweet or acidic the orange is, you will likely need to add another 2 to 3 tablespoons more sugar to bring out the flavors. Blend for another 15 seconds, as it takes several seconds for the sugar to dissolve completely in a cold smoothie.

Jugo de Tamarindo

TAMARIND JUICE

This is a quite refreshing drink for hot summer days; tart and sweet.

INGREDIENTS:
2 quarts water
4 oz. tamarind paste (by weight)
2 cups white sugar

PREPARATION: Place the water and the tamarind paste in a pitcher. Allow to sit for about an hour to soften the tamarind paste. Stir the tamarind. Pour the juice through a strainer, and use a spoon to express as much paste from the pulp as possible. Add the sugar to the juice, and stir. Use a container that allows the juice to be shaken before serving, as the pulp tends to settle. Place in the refrigerator to cool. May be served with ice.

Batida de Limón

LIME SMOOTHIE

This is a smoothie that we could make before we had a blender!

INGREDIENTS:

2 cups milk
½ cup sugar
3 tablespoons fresh lime juice
1/8th teaspoon vanilla extract
2 cups ice cubes

PREPARATION:

1: USING A BLENDER: Blend the milk, sugar, ice and vanilla together in a blender at high speed for one minute. Add the lime and blend for another minute and serve.

2: NO BLENDER: Add the milk, sugar and vanilla together in a pitcher, and stir together making sure that the sugar dissolves completely before adding the ice, as it will be difficult once the ice is added. Stir in the ice for about 30 seconds to get the milk cold. Continue stirring as you slowly add the lime juice, and the milk will thicken. It is then ready to serve.

Morir Soñando

ORANGE SMOOTHIE

This highly esteemed beverage's name translates as "to die dreaming".

INGREDIENTS:

2 oranges
1 cup evaporated milk
1 cup of ice cubes
2 tablespoons sugar
½ teaspoon vanilla extract (optional)

PREPARATION: Peel the oranges. If they have seeds, slice them in half (top from bottom) and remove all the seeds. Place the oranges with the rest of the ingredients in a blender and liquefy for 1 ½ minutes. Serve.

NOTE: If replacing evaporated milk with whole milk, use 1¼ cups of whole milk and decrease the amount of ice to 3/4 cups.

Jugo de Avena

OATMEAL LIME SMOOTHIE

INGREDIENTS:

1/3 cup rolled oats
2½ cups water
6 oz. evaporated milk
2 cups whole milk
1 cup sugar
A small pinch of salt
½ teaspoon vanilla extract
3 tablespoons fresh lime juice

PREPARATION: Boil the oatmeal in the water for 2 minutes, and then let it sit to cool and thicken. When cool, place the cooked oatmeal in a blender adding the milk and evaporated milk, sugar, salt and vanilla. Place in a pitcher and then stir in the lime juice, and chill in the refrigerator. It is ready to serve as soon as it is chilled. The smoothie can be served more quickly by adding ice. If allowed to chill overnight, it will become very thick.

Makes 6 servings.

Jugo de Berro

WATERCRESS JUICE

Here is a distinctive juice with a refreshing bite. It is used as a folk remedy to treat colds and the flu.

INGREDIENTS:

½ cup of watercress leaves and stems
1 cup orange juice (chilled)
2 tablespoons sugar

PREPARATION: Place the orange juice, watercress and sugar in a blender and liquefy for one minute at high speed. Serve directly or over ice.

Jugo de Remolacha

BEETLE JUICE

INGREDIENTS:

3 medium size beets (uncooked)
2 cups orange juice
2 tablespoons sugar (optional)
Ice

PREPARATION: Wash the beets with running warm water before peeling them. Cut the beets into small cubes. Place the beets, orange juice, and sugar in the blender. Blend at high speed for about 2 minutes. Pour through a strainer to remove excess pulp. Serve over ice.

Makes 2 servings.

HEALTH ALERT: About 10 to 15 percent of the population is subject to Beeturia, a condition in which the consumption of beets is followed, several hours later, by red urine (and sometimes red stools). Although disconcerting, the condition itself is harmless and does not indicate a problem with the kidneys or other acute medical problem. It appears, however, to occur more often in individuals with unusually avid iron absorption, as found in individuals with anemia[32].

Jugo de Aguacate

AVOCADO SMOOTHIE

Avocado and smoothie may seem strange words to place next to each other, but this is a rich mild and creamy smoothie.

INGREDIENTS:

One ripe avocado (about 1 cup flesh)
2 cups milk
1/3 cup sugar
½ teaspoon vanilla extract
2 cups of ice cubes
Small pinch of salt

PREPARATION: Place the avocado flesh, milk, sugar, and vanilla in a blender and liquefy. Next, add the ice, and blend it in. Add a small pinch of salt and mix it in. Serve fresh.

Variations: To notch up the flavor add a cup of strawberries. If you want to maintain the unusual green smoothie color, add a couple of peeled kiwifruit instead. For a pleasant surprise try avocado smoothie as above and blend in a tablespoon of chopped mint or lemon mint leaves.

Avocado smoothies can also be made without milk. The milk can be substituted with fruit juice, for example, orange juice.

Cocobana

COCONUT BANANA SMOOTHIE

INGREDIENTS:

2 large ripe bananas
6 oz. coconut cream
¼ cup water
1 tablespoon sugar
1 cup of ice cubes

PREPARATION: The bananas should be yellow with many dark speckles to show that they are ripe. Combine the ingredients in a blender and blend at high speed for 2 minutes, and serve.

Jugo de Chinola

PASSION FRUIT JUICE

Passion fruit is named for its flower, but this acidic and refreshing, fruity beverage earns its name.

INGREDIENTS:

10 – 12 passion fruits
3 cups water
½ cup sugar

PREPARATION: Split the passion fruit open, pulling them apart as you would an egg and empty the seeds into a blender. The shell is not edible and is discarded. Add the water and sugar and blend for 20 seconds. Don't over blend as you don't want to liquefy the seeds. Pour the juice through a strainer. Serve the juice poured over ice.

Batida de Mango

MANGO SMOOTHIE

Mangoes are very large trees that produce a huge number of fruits. Different mango varieties produced over a fairly long season and during those months there is an abundance of the fruit. Growing up, we would take a daily walk to one of many trees and gather a bag of fruit, sometimes eating a dozen mangoes as we collect them. My grandfather's land, as many other local farms, had excellent large trees, guarded only by a 3 strand barbed wire fence meant to keep the cattle from roaming too far. The cattle also enjoyed eating the mangoes. In my mind, I can still see the tree I had to hurriedly climb to escape a rather annoyed bull. I sat in the tree for nearly an hour eating mangoes hoping the bull would get bored with me and wander away. Finally, I climbed out along a thick branch that extended towards the fence, jumped down and rolled under the fence to escape.

INGREDIENTS:

1 large ripe mango
1 cup evaporated milk
2 cups of ice cubes
¼ cup sugar
1/8th teaspoon vanilla extract

PREPARATION: The mango should be fragrant and smell ripe and delicious. Using a paring knife, cut the fruit parallel to the mango's large flat seed, and separate the fruit from each side of the seed. Then peel the skin away from the flesh of the 2 pieces of fruit that have been removed. Next, peel the ring of skin away from the remaining fruit around the seed. Cut the rest of the flesh away from the seed. Add the mango flesh to the blender. Add the milk and liquefy for one minute. Add the sugar and vanilla and then the ice cubes, one cup at a time. If it is too thick and not mixing well, try blending at a lower speed.

Note: If replacing evaporated milk with whole milk, use 1½ cups of whole milk and decrease the ice to 1½ cups.

MANGO HEALTH ALERT: People who are allergic to poison oak, poison ivy, or poison sumac can get an allergic reaction to another relative, the mango, as the skin of the fruit and sap of the tree contain the same allergen (urushiol). For those with this allergy, eating mangoes can cause itchy rashes with blisters around the lips and swelling, or it can worsen an ongoing reaction to poison oak.

Most people allergic to urushiol can eat the peeled fruit without any problem, as long as they do not come into contact with mango skin or sap at the tip of the stem. Cashews are also related and eating them can cause or worsen an allergic reaction to urushiol.

Té de Canela y Jengibre

CINNAMON GINGER TEA

This is a sweet and spicy tea for cool winter evenings, or it can be used as an ice tea for the summer.

INGREDIENTS:

3 six inch cinnamon sticks
1 tablespoon fresh ginger cut into 3 or 4 pieces
1 quart of water
4 teaspoons sugar per 8 oz. of tea

PREPARATION: Place the cinnamon, ginger and water in a medium-sized saucepan, and place over high heat. Allow to boil for 2 to 3 minutes and allow it to steep for a couple of more minutes.

Serve with four level-teaspoons of sugar per cup of tea. The sugar brings out a spiciness that you can feel, and the tea is bland without it. The tea can be cooled and served as ice tea.

Don't throw out the cinnamon and ginger yet. Add more water and make another batch. The cinnamon and ginger should be useful for a second or even third batch of tea, with the second batch better than the first, especially if you allow the tea to steep in cold water before heating it.

For a milder flavor use cinnamon sticks alone.

Pera-Piña

PINEAPPLE-PEAR JUICE

Here is another traditional recipe (in addition to pineapple mabí) for a beverage that utilizes parts of a pineapple that are usually discarded. When it comes out right, it tastes and has the mouth feel of pear juice.

INGREDIENTS:

1 pineapple
7 cups water
1/3 cups white rice
1 cup sugar
Small pinch of salt

PREPARATION: Select a ripe, fragrant pineapple, and wash it in running tap water. Remove the green top and the stem end of the pineapple.

Cut the skin of the pineapple just deep enough so that the skin comes off in long strips, and not in little pieces.

Place the skin of the pineapple, water, rice and salt in a saucepan that will hold at least 4 quarts, and throw out the rest of the pineapple (Only joking. Use the pineapple as you please.) The core can be cut in half along its axis and be added to the skin in the pot for making the juice a bit more flavorful).

Cover the pot and bring it to a boil. Allow to boil for a minute, and then lower the heat to a simmer for 30 minutes. Turn the heat off, and allow the pot to cool to room temperature

Remove the pineapple skin and core from the pot and discard them. Pour about half the rice and pineapple broth into a blender and add half the sugar. Blend at medium speed for about a minute, and then pour the juice through a strainer into a pitcher. Repeat with the other half of the rice and broth. Taste it to make sure that it is mildly sweet. Chill in the refrigerator. It will thicken and taste sweeter after it cools and rests for a while.

Frío~Frío

SNOW CUPS

A frío-frío (cold-cold) is similar to a snow-cone and is a favorite of children young and old on hot summer days. They are sold on the street by vendors with wooden carts with a one hundred pound block of ice, often covered with a burlap sack, and bottles of brightly colored syrup. They are also known as yun-yun, "guayao" (grated) "cepillao" (brushed). The vendors shave the ice with a metal scoop with a blade, pop it into a cup and flood it with sweet syrup. The two most popular flavors are "mabe" and frío-frío rojo, which is raspberry syrup.

To get the right fluffy texture, the ice should be shaved, not crushed or ground. A couple of inexpensive electrical ice shavers are the Hamilton Beach Ice Snowman, and the Victorio Electric Ice Shaver. Ice in a blender will give fine grains, better for slushies than for frío-fríos.

PREPARATION: To prepare the frío-frío, use about one ounce (two tablespoons) of syrup over six ounces of shaved ice in a cup. If the syrup is freshly made, be sure to cool it down to room temperature or cooler before using it to keep it from melting the ice.

Frío~Frío Rojo

RASPBERRY SNOW CUP

Frío-frío Rojo (red) is probably the overall favorite and is raspberry flavored.

RASPBERRY SYRUP:

INGREDIENTS:

10 oz. frozen raspberries
¾ cup water
1½ cups sugar

PREPARATION: Place the thawed berries and water into a blender, and blend at medium speed for one minute. Strain the juice through a sieve to remove the seeds and pulp. Extra juice can be expressed using the back of a spoon. Place the juice in a saucepan with the sugar. Stirring, bring the juice to a boil, and allow it to boil for one minute. Cool the syrup before using it. Store it in a glass container in the refrigerator.

OTHER FLAVORS: Many other syrup flavors for frió fríos can be made; here are a few examples, in addition to cocolimón that is given on page 148.

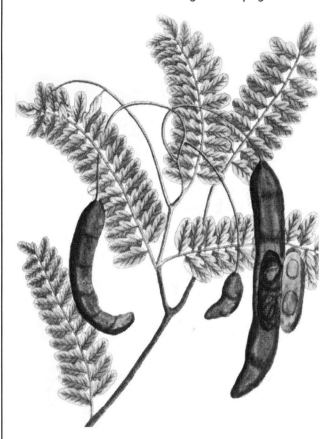

TAMARINDO; TAMARIND SYRUP

INGREDIENTS:

1 cup water
¾ cups sugar
3 oz. tamarind paste

PREPARATION: Stir the sugar into the water in a small saucepan while bringing it to a boil. Allow it to boil for about 30 seconds to get the sugar to dissolve completely, and turn off the heat. Tear the tamarind paste into small pieces to make it easier to dissolve, and stir it into the hot sugar water. Allow it to sit for about 15 minutes to soften, and stir it some more to get the paste to dissolve. Pour the syrup through a strainer and use a spoon to mash through the pulp, and separate out the seeds or seed coats. Allow the syrup to cool before using it. Makes about 8 oz. of syrup.

148

GUAYABA; GUAVA SYRUP

INGREDIENTS:

1/3 cup guava paste (about 3.5 oz. by weight)
¾ cups water
1 tablespoon sugar

PREPARATION: Simmer the guava paste, water and sugar together in a small saucepan, stirring for about 2 to 3 minutes until the paste dissolves. Allow to cool before using.

LIMÓN; LEMON OR LIME SYRUP

INGREDIENTS:

Zest from 2 lemons or limes (See page 167)
¼ cup of lemon or lime juice (2 medium lemons)
½ cups water
¾ cups sugar

PREPARATION: Juice the fruit and set the juice aside.

Bring the water to a boil in a small saucepan and stir in the sugar. Allow it to boil for about 30 seconds to make sure the sugar is completely dissolved, remove it from the heat and stir in the zest. Allow the zest to steep for one minute, and then strain the syrup, but do not press on the zest or it may get too bitter. Allow the liquid to cool and then stir in the lemon or lime juice.

To make different quantities: Zest the fruit you will use, and then juice them. Measure the amount of lemon or lime juice made. Use twice the amount of water and 3 times the amount of sugar as juice.

Notes:

Guayao de Cocolimón

COCONUT LIME ICY

INGREDIENTS:

1 oz. coconut cream
1.5 oz. lemon or lime syrup (on this page)
2 oz. finely crushed or shaved ice

PREPARATION: Mix the coconut cream and limeade mix together. Pour into a glass with ¼-cup of crushed ice and serve.

Crushed ice can be prepared by placing ice into cold water in a blender. Make sure that there is sufficient water so that the ice floats at least 2 inches above the blades. Blend on high until the ice is finely ground. Pour the resulting ice slurry through a sieve to get rid of the water.

Alcoholic Beverages

Leche Batida

WINE SMOOTHIE

Traditionally, red wine is used for this party smoothie, and a bold cabernet Sauvignon or merlot work well. A word of caution: this alcoholic smoothie goes down as easily as chocolate milk, but this drink is not for kids. A lactose-free form is given below.

CONTAINS ALCOHOL

INGREDIENTS:

1 cup whole milk
½ cup sugar
4 oz. red wine
1 cup of ice
Pinch of salt

PREPARATION: Add the ingredients in a blender and liquefy. A thick foam will form on top.

Makes two servings. This drink will store in a closed jar overnight in the refrigerator, but the foam will disappear.

Vino Coco

COCONUT WINE SMOOTHIE

This wine smoothie is made with coconut cream.
CONTAINS ALCOHOL.

INGREDIENTS:

1 cup coconut cream
¼ cup sugar
¾ cup merlot or other red wine
1 to 1 ½ cups of ice cubes
A pinch of salt

PREPARATION: Add the ingredients in a blender and liquefy, and serve. Makes three servings.

Piña Colada

PIÑA COLADA

No drink seems more Caribbean!
CONTAINS ALCOHOL.

INGREDIENTS:

1 cup coconut cream
1 cup pineapple juice
1 cup pineapple pieces
¼ cup evaporated milk
¼ cup sugar
½ cup rum
3 cups ice

PREPARATION: Place the coconut cream, pineapple juice and pieces, evaporated milk, sugar and rum in the blender at a middle speed and blend for one minute. Add the ice and blend until the ice is finely and evenly crushed. Serve in stemmed glasses. Makes 6 servings

The rum can be left out to make a treat that kids will enjoy.

Ron con Limón

LIME COCKTAIL

INGREDIENTS:

¼ cup lemon or lime syrup (see page 148)
1 oz. rum
1 cup ice cubes

PREPARATION: Mix the ingredients, relax and enjoy.

Cocolimón con Ron

COCONUT LIME COCKTAIL

"Put de lime in the coconut, drink them both togedda. Put de lime in the coconut, den you feel betta"

Harry Nilsson

INGREDIENTS:

1 oz. (2 tablespoons) rum
    (Caribbean dark rum such as Brugal Añejo)
2 tablespoons coconut cream
3 tablespoons lemon or lime syrup (page 148)
3 ice cubes

PREPARATION: Put the limeade mix, coconut cream, and rum in a glass and mix together. It may take a few seconds to melt the frozen concentrate. Add ice and enjoy. Also very pleasant when prepared with crushed ice as for Guayao de Cocolimón but adding rum.

ALCOHOL HEALTH WARNING: Alcoholic beverages have been a part of the Dominican culture for centuries. Slaves were brought to the Caribbean from Africa to work on sugarcane plantations for the production of rum. The Dominican Republic produces high-quality rum and fine pilsner beers. Unfortunately, there is nothing quite as effective as alcohol in acting as a solvent for extracting the joy from paradise.

The health benefits of alcohol are limited to red wine consumed in moderation. Moderation means no more than one ounce of red wine per 30 pounds of ideal body weight per day. This is 3 to 4 ounces for most women. Higher amounts of alcohol increase the risk of many diseases including depression and cancer[33]

While small amounts of red wine lower the risk of heart disease and some other diseases, distilled spirits and beer do not provide this benefit, nor do sweet wines such as port. In fact, adding sugar to wine (as in the wine smoothie recipe) prevents any health benefits. The health benefits of red wine come from phenolic compounds that are also available in fruits, herbs, coffee, tea, and chocolate; much safer sources. The most benefit seems to come from the consumption of small amounts of various phenolic compounds from a variety of foods.

Even moderate consumption of alcohol is damaging during pregnancy. Alcohol can cause lifelong behavioral problems for the offspring of women who drink even small quantities of alcohol during the last 3 months of gestation, the time when the brain is developing quickly. Alcohol also increases the risk of breast cancer in the offspring[34]. In men, heavy alcohol consumption damages the DNA of the sperm, which decreases fertility and can harm the child. Men should lay off alcohol for two months before impregnating.

To minimize cancer risk, it is not imprudent to enjoy as much as one ounce of red wine per day/30 pounds of ideal body weight. It should be consumed slowly or with a meal to avoid a rapid absorption and a high peak alcohol level. This amount should have little effect on behavior other than mild relaxation. If the alcohol decreases inhibition, gives a sense of euphoria or inhibits concentration, it has likely reached levels that increase the risk of cancer, depression, and inflammatory diseases.

Mabí de Piña

PINEAPPLE CHAMPAGNE

"With the express'd Liquor of either the red or the white (sweet) Potato is made what we here call Moby, or a Sort of cool Drink answering to small Beer in England. The Method of making this, is to mix the raw express'd Juice of the (sweet) Potatoes with a certain Quantity of Water; this in a seasoned Vessel will soon ferment, and in about four and twenty Hours be ready for Use; it tastes cool and sharp, and it is generally esteem'd a healthy Liquor."

Rev. Griffith Hughes 1750

Mabí is a refreshing fermented beverage that usually only contains an insignificant amount of alcohol.

Mabí was likely a Taíno beer, made from sweet potatoes (as noted above) and other plants. Usually, the name mabí refers to the bark of the mabí tree (Seaside Buckthorn: *Colubrina elliptica*). The bark is boiled in sugar cane juice, and allowed to ferment for a few days, chilled and enjoyed for more than just its flavor. Mabí made from seaside buckthorn has some psychotropic effects; thus large amounts are best avoided.

Many other flavors of mabí are also made.

Mabí de Piña is a refreshing fermented beverage that takes its name from Mabí, which does not contain Mauby bark, but rather "pineapple bark". It uses the skin from a pineapple, a part that is usually discarded.

STARTER RECIPE

Take a large ripe fresh pineapple. If it does not have a pleasant pineapple fragrance and it does not have fresh green leaves in the store, don't bother with it.

Rinse the pineapple under running water. Cut off the top with the green leaves, and plant it if you'd like. Cut the "bark" off the pineapple, slicing down from the top, rotate and then cut down again. When cutting, the skin, cut it about half-inch thick so that it comes off in slabs, not little pieces. Cut off the base of the pineapple. Put all the pineapple skin in a half-gallon container with 2 cups of sugar, and cover with water and stir. If the core of the pineapple is not otherwise used, it too can be added. Put this in the refrigerator and wait for three to five days, and enjoy the champagne. More traditional is warm (room temperature) fermentation, but I have success with cold fermentation, which gives a fruitier flavor. The container should be able to vent, as some gas production occurs.

When the beverage is gone, the pineapple skin can be reused with more water and sugar, but the pineapple flavor will be milder the second time around.

This is a fermented beverage, and its quality depends on the yeast and bacteria that came with the pineapple. If it comes out well, you will want to save the fermentation starter, "el pie" so that you can make more, as described below.

Warning Migraineurs: Fermentation takes yeast and bacteria. If you get the wrong bacteria in the mauby (or in other fermented products) it can cause a migraine (just like with some grape champagne). If this occurs, throw it out and start with a new pineapple. To get a better class of bacteria, make the environment more acidic, by adding less water with the pineapple and by adding one or 2 tablespoons of yogurt whey, the clear liquid that separates from plain yogurt.

MABÍ DE PIÑA; RECIPE 2: Now that you have the mauby starter, you can make mauby even if you can't find a good pineapple at the market:

INGREDIENTS:

A 20 oz. can diced pineapple in juice
2½ cups sugar
½ to 1 cup of starter juice from the previous batch
Water to complete a gallon

Café Dominicano

DOMINICAN COFFEE

We love dark, sweet, rich coffee. It's grown in mountainous areas, where "summer" vacation for school kids is in November and December so that they can help with the coffee harvest. The sweet red coffee cherries are collected, piled into a mound, and allowed to ferment for a few days, producing a delicious sweet fragrance. The fruit is then cranked through a mill that separates the coffee beans from the pulp. The green coffee beans are washed in mountain streams and then spread out in the sun to dry before being sold to coffee exporters. Coffee that is kept for personal use is usually dark roasted, often with sugar to help caramelize it, and then ground using a large wooden mortar made from a tree trunk and heavy wooden pestle larger than a baseball bat.

Coffee should never be bitter. Bitterness is the result of oxidation. The best coffee is made from fresh green coffee beans, roasted ground and brewed within a couple of days. The next best choice is to buy roasted beans in a vented pack and grind them just before brewing. If you buy vacuum-packed ground coffee, the pack will be best in the first days after you open it. Buy small amounts of coffee that you expect to use within a few days. Store it in a cool area, sealed, with the excess air removed from the pack, to avoid oxidation and loss of aromas. Do not freeze or refrigerate coffee, as this drives off essential oils and flavors.

Dominican coffee is usually made in Italian stove-top espresso makers we call "greca de cafe."

INGREDIENTS:

1 cup water
¼ cup scoop of finely ground espresso coffee
8 teaspoons sugar

PREPARATION: Put the ingredients into a clean gallon jug, and add enough water to fill the container. Refrigerate for four to five days. Enjoy the beverage, but save either the fruit or some juice for the next brew. This can be frozen for later use.

The excess fruit can be eaten, may be placed on ice cream, and has a nice sparkly sensation.

PREPARATION: Place the water in the base of the espresso maker, and the coffee in the funnel. Rotate the filter plate to spread and then lightly tamp down the coffee grounds. This slows the coffee's ascent some and gives more flavor, but don't pack it hard. Screw on the top until you feel the gasket seal.

Place the espresso maker on the stove on high heat and remove as soon as it completes the wake-up song. Add 2 level teaspoons of sugar to a demitasse and fill the cup. Makes 4 demitasse (¼ cup) servings.

Chocolate

DOMINICAN HOT CHOCOLATE

INGREDIENTS:

2 cups milk
1 six-inch cinnamon stick
1/16th teaspoon freshly grated nutmeg
A one ounce square of Dominican chocolate
1 tablespoon sugar

PREPARATION: Place the milk in a saucepan over medium heat. Break the chocolate into pieces and add them along with the other ingredients. Stirring continuously, heat it until it begins to simmer and then turn the heat to low and allow it to cook for 5 minutes.

We usually enjoy this hot beverage with breakfast or in the evening with a snack.

Te de Jengibre y Chocolate

TAÍNO HOT CHOCOLATE

"Take one hundred cocoa beans, two chilies, a handful of anise seed and two of vanilla (two pulverized Alexandria roses can be substituted), two drams of cinnamon, one dozen almonds and the same amount of hazelnuts, half a pound of white sugar and enough annatto to give some color. And there you have the king of chocolates."

Antonio Colmenero de Ledesma, 1631

The original Aztec use of chocolate was a beverage using hot water, cocoa beans, and chili peppers. I cannot verify the origins of this Dominican recipe, but it is easy to imagine that the Taíno Indians made this spicy hot cocoa beverage. The Dominican Republic is the largest producer of cocoa in the Caribbean, yet somewhat surprisingly; the traditional use of chocolate is limited to only three recipes I am aware of, two forms of hot cocoa, and a form of sweet Arepa (Indian corn bread) made by very few people.

Some of the best chocolate I have ever tasted came in a baseball-sized sphere from the farm of a girl I knew. The beans were allowed to ferment and were very much unrefined, with light and dark specks. It had rich wine flavor with a hint of vanilla. Chocolate bars do not do well in stores in tropical climates without air conditioning, and Dominican chocolate is grainy and dissolves rather than melts.

Taíno Hot Chocolate is rich, sweet and very spicy hot. It is prepared for holidays, especially around Christmas and to bring in the New Year, often in the home, or sold on street corners at night. The chocolate would be grated from the ball into the boiling water mixed with spices. This recipe calls for commercially available Dominican Chocolate, which may be found in Hispanic grocery stores or on the internet. Mexican chocolate, which is easier to find, can be substituted as described at the end of the recipe.

INGREDIENTS:

1 quart of water
2 tablespoons freshly grated ginger
2 six inch cinnamon sticks
8 tablets Dominican chocolate
  (Chocolate Embajador, 0.92 oz each)
2 tablespoons sugar
A pinch of salt

PREPARATION: Heat the water in a medium saucepan that has a well-fitting lid. Bring the water to a boil and then add the ginger and cover it, adjusting the heat to maintain a steady boil. A well fitting lid and a low boil help to reduce the loss of water and flavor as vapor. After 10 minutes add the cinnamon sticks broken into 2 or 3 pieces, and cook at a low boil for 5 more minutes. Strain the tea into a second pot. Discard the ginger, rinse off the cinnamon sticks and return them to the tea. Add the 8 tablets of chocolate, the sugar and salt to the ginger cinnamon tea and allow them to simmer for about 1 minute. The tablets should be softened, and you can now stir them and they will dissolve. Place the lid on the pot again. If it is not simmering, raise the heat until it comes to a boil, and then turn the heat down to maintain an active simmer for 10 minutes. Serve hot, or allow to cool some and serve.

Makes about six servings. Recipe can be easily halved to make a smaller amount. If you can't stand the heat, use half as much ginger.

SUBSTITUTION: In place of the Dominican Chocolate, 3 Mexican Chocolate Tablets (about 3 oz. each) may be used, along with an extra one tablespoon of sugar.

Desserts and Sweets ~ Dulces

About Sweets, Siestas, and Evening Desserts

We don't really eat much dessert; we eat fruit in its place and cut fruit is served with most meals. We do enjoy sweet snacks, though.

In the Dominican Republic, it is still traditional in many areas to eat the main meal of the day at noon, followed by a long, leisurely, two-hour midday break. This often includes a siesta, followed by a shower and coffee before returning to work for the afternoon. In the tropics, a nap in the shade is a better use of time than sweating at work during the hottest part of the day.

It is hard to stay awake after a large meal. In North America, Thanksgiving and Christmas feasts are special days for midday overeating, that often includes turkey, and many people succumb to drowsiness and the urge to nap after the feast. The amino acid tryptophan has been identified as causing this drowsiness.

There is actually more to it. Turkey is a low-fat meat that is high in protein, but it is only an average source of tryptophan. The drowsiness that ensues the feast is greatly affected by the rest of the meal – particularly the carbohydrates. A Thanksgiving feast can easily exceed 3500 calories, with many of those calories in the form of carbohydrates. This load of carbohydrates promotes the release of insulin, which increases the uptake of glucose and of branched chain amino acids into the muscles, but leaves tryptophan behind, which is then available for conversion to serotonin[35]. Serotonin can enter the brain, where it acts as a calming neurotransmitter and can be converted into melatonin, a hormone that makes us drowsy and promotes sleep[36].

If your job does not accommodate siestas, and you want to stay alert after lunch, it may be best to avoid large meals, especially ones loaded with simple and readily available carbohydrates (sugars and starches), and instead, eat a light meal high in protein.

Milk is high in tryptophan, calcium, and sugars. This may be why milk based desserts high in protein and carbohydrates help us relax, and are comfort foods, and why we enjoy desserts in the evening. The calcium helps convert serotonin to melatonin in the brain. Cake with ice cream, a bowl of cereal with milk, milk and cookies, or just a glass of warm milk (especially with a spoon of brown sugar) an hour before bedtime gives a chance to serve some extra serotonin to the brain that make us feel relaxed. In the pineal gland, serotonin can be converted into melatonin, which helps with sleep.

Chocolate, however, contains caffeine and a similar compound, theobromine. Both of these compounds promote wakefulness. Coffee and chocolate desserts may make it difficult to fall asleep if consumed late in the day.

Arepa con Dulce

Coconut Corn Cake

Arepa is the Taíno Indian word for unleavened corn cake. This Dominican style arepa is a rich and sweet unleavened cornbread that can be found sold on the street by vendors early in the morning. When I was a student, one of my friends paid his way through college by making and selling arepa on the street. He made his, in a cast iron Dutch oven that he would bury in a bed of glowing charcoal, embers covering the lid with more hot charcoal. Traditionally, we line the pan with banana leaves that keep the bread from burning or sticking to the pan and added a distinctive flavor.

There are many variations of arepa; this recipe is adapted for cooking in an oven. It sometimes has cinnamon, anise or other spices, raisins or flavorings. It can be prepared with chocolate as described below. The preparation time is about one hour.

Ingredients:

1 can (13 oz) coconut cream
1½ cups evaporated milk
¾ cup sugar
¼ teaspoon salt
¼ teaspoon vanilla extract
2 cups yellow (stone ground) corn meal
1 tablespoon butter

Preparation: Combine the coconut cream, one cup of evaporated milk, sugar, salt and butter in a saucepan. Stir in the cornmeal. Stirring constantly, cook over low heat for about 20 minutes until the combination has a thick porridge like consistency. When it gets thick add the evaporated milk little by little, continuing to stir over low heat for another 10 minutes as it thickens. Stir in the vanilla.

Pour the contents into an 8 or 9-inch cake pan, or for thicker bread use a bread pan. Bake at 350 degrees for thirty minutes until the top is just starting to turn golden brown. This bread does not have leavening, and it cannot be tested by inserting a fork or knife as can be done with a cake; to tell when it is done. The bread should have a crust on it, which will soften over a few hours as it cools.

Arepa con Chocolate:

Chocolate Coconut Corn Cake

Using the recipe for arepa con dulce, pour about half the batter into the baking pan. Grate about 3 oz. (3 tablets) of Dominican Chocolate, and sprinkle the crumbs evenly over the layer of batter. Slowly spread the remaining batter over the layer of chocolate. Use a fork to make a single long spiral from the edge into the center to give a chocolate swirl design. Bake as for the recipe above. Mexican chocolate may be used as a substitute if Dominican chocolate is not available.

Arepa Fría

CORN PUDDIN' PIE

This is another traditional form of Taíno sweet arepa. This form is not baked and is more delicate.

INGREDIENTS:

1½ cups coconut cream
2 cups evaporated milk
½ cup sugar
½ teaspoon vanilla extract
1/8 teaspoon salt
1 cup corn meal

Topping:
Fruit pieces (mango, strawberries or blueberries)
¼ cup white chocolate chips
1 tablespoon butter

PREPARATION: Place the combined milk in a saucepan and stirring, slowly mix in the cornmeal to avoid lumping. Stir in the other ingredients. Turn on the heat to medium, bring to a simmer, and then lower the heat and cook for 30 minutes stirring continuously. Pour the cream into a non-stick pie dish, and place in the refrigerator to chill. Before serving, invert the arepa onto a plate, and cut into pie shaped wedges. Serve with a garnish of fruit and a drizzle of white chocolate.

DRIZZLE: Melt chips and butter together. Drizzle the melted glaze over the arepa and fruit.

Arroz con Leche de Coco

COCONUT RICE PUDDING

INGREDIENTS:

2½ cups water
½ cup white rice
2 three inch cinnamon sticks
1½ teaspoons butter
1½ cups coconut cream
½ cup sugar
1/8th teaspoon salt
¼ cup raisins
1 teaspoon vanilla extract

PREPARATION: Place the water, salt, and cinnamon sticks in a 4-quart pot, and bring it to a boil. Add the rice and cover the pot. Lower the heat to medium-low and simmer the rice for 15 minutes. Add the coconut cream and continue to simmer the rice for 10 more minutes. Stir the rice every couple of minutes to prevent it from sticking to the bottom of the pan. As it gets thicker, it will need to be stirred more frequently.

Add the sugar butter and raisins, cover the pan, and cook over low heat for 10 minutes until it is creamy and thick, and the raisins are fat and plump. Mix in the vanilla just as it is taken off the heat.

Serve warm or chilled.

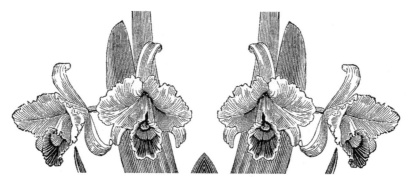

Vanilla comes from the seed pod of an orchid native to the gulf coast of Mexico

Arroz con Leche

RICE PUDDING

INGREDIENTS:

5 cups water
½ cup white rice
2 cinnamon sticks
1 can of evaporated milk (12 oz.)
½ cup sugar
3 tablespoons butter
¼ teaspoon salt
¾ cup raisins
½ teaspoon vanilla extract

PREPARATION: Place the water and cinnamon sticks in a 4-quart pot, and bring it to a boil. Add the rice and cover the pot. Cook over low heat until the rice splits open and most of the water is gone. Add the evaporated milk, sugar, salt, and butter, and cook at low to medium heat for about 5 minutes. Stir every minute or so to keep it from sticking to the bottom of the pot. As it gets thicker, it will need to be stirred more frequently. Add the raisins, and cook over low heat for 10 minutes until it is creamy and thick and the raisins are fat and plump. Mix in the vanilla just as it is taken off the heat.

Serve warm, or chilled.

Pan de Batata

SWEET POTATO LOAF

This sweet loaf is delicious as a warm dessert. Traditionally, like an arepa, it is cooked in a cast iron Dutch oven, buried in charcoal, with the inside of the pot lined with banana leaves.

INGREDIENTS:

4½ cups of grated peeled sweet potatoes
1 can coconut cream (13-14 oz)
1 can of evaporated milk (12 oz.)
½ cup milk
1 cup stone ground yellow cornmeal
1 teaspoon ground cinnamon
1 cup sugar
¼ teaspoon salt
½ teaspoon vanilla extract

PREPARATION: Mix ingredients in a pot on the stovetop, and cook at a simmer, stirring constantly until the mixture thickens. This should take about 20 minutes. When the sweet potato is cooked, and the cornmeal is soft, place in a casserole bowl and bake 375° for 45 minutes or until the bread turns light brown. The edges of the loaf should have a slightly caramelized crust. Remove the loaf from the baking bowl by turning it upside down onto a plate. It can be served still warm, or cooled.

Guanimos Dulce

TAÍNO CORN BREAD

In Mexico, there are perhaps a thousand local variations of tamales, a steamed corn dough bread, usually prepared in corn husks. Along the Caribbean coast of Mexico, in Central America and parts of South America and the Caribbean, these breads are often cooked in banana leaves rather than in corn husks, and rather than using masa harina, stone ground cornmeal is used.

The Dominican and Puerto Rican version of the tamale are the guanimo (or guanime depending on the region). It is a favorite comfort food and often sold by vendors walking along the streets in the morning from trays carried on their heads as they make change with their hands free. Guanimo is a quick breakfast snack, sometimes filled with meat or fish (guanimos rellenos). In Puerto Rico, they are often made with cheese.

This recipe is for a sweet Guanimos made with coconut cream.

INGREDIENTS:

2½ cups stone ground cornmeal
½ cup sugar
1/8th teaspoon salt
1 cup coconut cream
½ cup water
½ teaspoon vanilla extract
Banana leaves (or aluminum foil)

PREPARATION: Combine the dry ingredients in a mixing bowl and blend them. Then add the coconut cream, water, and vanilla and blend the ingredients together to form a thick dough. Allow this dough to sit for 10 minutes.

If banana leaves are available: Cut the banana leaf blades from both sides of the midrib so that there are sheets to use for wrapping the guanimos. Cut the leaf blades into 10-inch lengths to form sheets. Place about 1/3 of a cup of dough onto the banana leaf and shape the dough so that it can be folded in the direction of the leaf veins to form a rectangle about 2 inches wide, 3½ inches long and ½ inch thick. Fold the edges over first and then fold over the long direction. Tie string around the leaf-like wrapping a gift to hold it together.

If banana leaves are not available, use sheets of aluminum foil and fold the edges of the foil over about a ½ inch and then fold them over a second time to form a tight seal.

Wrap all the dough until it is used up. Place the guanimos in a steamer with the seals downwards, so steam runs off, not into the wrappings. Use about ¾ inch of water in the pot and cover. Steam the guanimos for 35 minutes. They are best served warm.

Bombón

MOLASSES BARS AND COOKIES

During my college years, this was a highly affordable breakfast favorite sold on trays by vendors walking the streets crying out "Bonbon! Cinco cheli!" (Bombón! 5 cents!). This is more of a dense dark sweet quick bread than a cookie; made with bread flour rather than pastry flour, without eggs, and with molasses to activate the baking soda. Depending on the region, they were either baked as individual 4" diameter cookies or as a non-chocolate brownie usually cut into diagonally shaped bars. They are often made with bits of coconut.

NO WHEAT – NO EGGS – NO DAIRY: These cookies or bars can be made with gluten free flour, do not require eggs, and the butter can be replaced by vegetable oil, preferably coconut oil, as coconut oil has a similar melting temperature to butter.

COOKIE STYLE BOMBÓN

INGREDIENTS:
2¼ cups flour (unbleached, bread flour preferred)
1 teaspoon baking soda
¼ teaspoon salt
¼ teaspoon ground cinnamon
2 tablespoons unsweetened coconut flakes
¼ cup sugar
½ cup water
¼ cup melted butter
½ cup molasses
½ teaspoon freshly grated ginger

PREPARATION: Combine the flour, soda, salt, cinnamon, and coconut flakes in a mixing bowl and blend them together.

In a separate container, dissolve the sugar in the water, add the melted butter, and mix together. Next add the molasses and ginger and mix them in. Pour the liquid into the bowl with the dry ingredients and mix together with a wooden spoon to form the dough. Mix for at least 5 minutes to eliminate any lumps of ingredients. The resulting dough will be wet and sticky. Cover the bowl and place it in the refrigerator for about one hour.

The cooled dough should be firm enough to roll. Oil clean hands with a bit of butter or salad oil, and pinch off bits of the dough, enough to roll the dough into balls about 1½ in diameter. Place the balls on a cookie tray greased with butter about four inches apart. Flatten them to about ¼ inch thick. Place on a rack in the middle of the oven and allow them to bake at 375°F for 10 to 12 minutes.

BROWNIE STYLE BOMBÓN

INGREDIENTS:
2¼ cups flour
1 teaspoon baking soda
¼ teaspoon salt
¼ teaspoon ground cinnamon
½ teaspoon ground fresh ginger
2 tablespoons coconut flakes

¼ cup sugar
¾ cup water
¼ cup melted butter
1 cup molasses

PREPARATION: Combine the flour, soda, salt, cinnamon, ginger and coconut flakes into a mixing bowl and blend them together.

In a separate container, dissolve the sugar in the water, add the molasses and melted butter and mix it together. Pour the liquid into the bowl with the dry ingredients and mix them together with a wooden spoon to form the batter.

Pour the batter into an 8 x 8 buttered baking dish. Bake on a middle rack at 350°F for 30 to 35 minutes. Allow to cool enough to handle comfortably, remove the bread, and slice it into bars.

Condolías / Habichuelas con Dulce

Condolías is a traditional dish served on Good Friday. The name translates to condolences or sympathies. It is also called "Habichuelas con Dulce." The traditional recipe takes several hours to prepare and it is usually made in the largest kettle available, so that it can be shared with neighbors; if you are going to spend the time required to prepare it, you might as well make enough to go around.

Two recipes are included. The first recipe is more traditional, and the second a quicker version.

The traditional method for making condolías took two days. On the first day wood would be gathered, and the coconuts were broken opened and grated. Anything that made noise had to be done the day before Viernes Santo (Good Friday). On that day, we were not allowed to talk above a whisper. The radio stations had nuns reciting the rosary for hours; no music was played. We were not allowed to go to the river to swim; we were told that if we swam on that day that we would turn into half fish/half human creatures.

If you have not had this dish before - it is a rather strange idea; bean soup as a dessert, but it is a quite pleasant treat. In recent years, it has become better known and served in some restaurants as a dessert throughout the year. Good Friday is also no longer a day of quiet and Easter weekend is the most popular time to enjoy swimming at the beach.

WARNING: It is very easy to scald sweet beans and ruin the entire pot if you do not stir frequently enough!

Condolías / Habichuelas con Dulce

TRADITIONAL SWEET BEANS:

INGREDIENTS:

1 pound dry red beans
2½ cups water
½ teaspoon finely ground epazote
3 cups coconut cream (See pages 18-19)
   or use two 14 oz. cans coconut cream
2 cans evaporated milk
1 pound sweet potatoes
2 six inch cinnamon sticks
3 oz. raisins
2 ¼ cup sugar
2 tablespoons butter
1 teaspoon vanilla

PREPARATION: Soak the beans in water overnight. On the next day, rinse the beans and replace the water. For quicker cooking, cook the beans in a pressure cooker with 2 inches of water covering the beans, adding the epazote. Cook the beans until they split open and are very soft. Without a pressure cooker, you may need to add water during cooking to make sure they remain covered in water. With a pressure cooker, it should take 15 to 20 minutes. This should yield about 12 cups of cooked beans and broth. Discard extra broth, or add water to get a total of 12 cups of beans and broth. In batches, blend the beans and broth in a blender. Pour through a wire strainer, and use the back of a spoon to press out the bean paste, straining out and discarding the skin.

Place the bean soup in a large deep pot over medium heat and bring it to a boil, stirring frequently. Lower the heat to medium-low and stir in the evaporated milk and the coconut cream. Cook for 20 minutes, stirring constantly. Lower the cooking temperature to low and cook at a slow simmer for another 40 minutes stirring at least once a minute. (Yes, it is a lot of time and stirring.) Then place lid on the pot ajar on the pot over low heat, to vent vapor, stirring every few minutes.

Sweet Potatoes: Peel and cut the sweet potatoes into ½-inch cubes. In a separate pot, simmer the sweet potatoes with enough water to cover them over medium heat with the cinnamon sticks, with the pot covered to retain the cinnamon flavor. Cook for 15 minutes.

Add the sugar, raisins, butter, and sweet potatoes with the cinnamon water to the beans. Cook for one more hour at low heat. Uncover for the last 20 minutes. Add the vanilla. Serve warm or chilled.

Condolías / Habichuelas con Dulce

QUICK SWEET BEAN SOUP

INGREDIENTS:

2 No. 1 cans of red beans – drained
2 cups water
¼ teaspoon finely ground epazote leaves
   (no stems)
1 can coconut cream (14 oz.)
2 pounds sweet potatoes
2 six inch cinnamon sticks
¾ cups sugar
½ cup raisins
1 cup evaporated milk
Pinch of salt
¼ teaspoon vanilla extract

PREPARATION: Peel the sweet potatoes and cut them into 1-inch cubes. Boil the sweet potatoes in 2½ cups of water with the cinnamon sticks.

CAUTION: Condolías are easy to scald and burn the bottom of the pot. Be careful to stir frequently throughout the preparation and to avoid using cooking temperatures that are too high. Even with this quick recipe, it is a slow process.

Place the beans in a blender with 2 cups of water. Liquefy for 2 minutes at high speed. Strain the bean juice into a 4-quart pot. Discard the skin that is caught in the strainer. Add the coconut cream and epazote to the pot, and set the heat to medium until the soup begins to boil. Turn the heat down to a simmer, stirring constantly for at least 10 minutes, and then lower the heat to a low simmer, and cook for another 30 minutes. Add the sugar. Add the sweet potatoes with their cooking water, and cook for 10 more minutes. Add the raisins and cook for 15 minutes. Add the evaporated milk and cook for 20 minutes. Add the vanilla at the very end, so it's flavor is not cooked off.

Serve it hot, or cold. The soup will thicken into a pudding if allowed to chill. It may be placed in custard dishes and allowed to thicken overnight in the refrigerator.

Helados

ICE CREAMS

Nearly any of the smoothies described in the beverages section can be adapted to make ice cream in an ice cream maker. To change a smoothie recipe into an ice cream recipe, replace the volume of ice plus the volume of evaporated milk that is used in the smoothie recipe with milk or milk substitute (coconut milk, almond milk, or soymilk).

Helado de Guayaba

GUAVA ICE CREAM

INGREDIENTS:

2 cups milk or milk substitute
1/3 cup guava paste (4 oz. by weight)
2 teaspoons lemon juice
1 tablespoon semisweet mini chocolate chips

PREPARATION: Slice the guava paste into pieces about ¼-inch thick. Add the milk and guava paste pieces to the blender. It takes about a full minute to liquefy the guava paste to the point where little pieces are no longer visible.

Taste the smoothie. If it does not have a fruity flavor, add one teaspoon of lemon juice at a time to give it more tang. Vitamin C can also be used to give tanginess. A tablespoon of sugar may also be added; however, the guava paste is usually sweet enough by itself.

Pour the smoothie into the ice cream maker and get it started. When the ice cream begins to congeal, add the chocolate chips.

Mini-chips work best, as chocolate chips get hard when frozen, and the small ones soften more quickly in the mouth and need to melt to give their flavor. Small chips also are less likely to hurt the teeth than larger ones that stay frozen longer.

Helado de Sapote

SAPOTE ICE CREAM

The name sapote comes from the Aztec Nahuatl word *tzapotl,* for a soft, sweet fruit, and this name has been applied to at least 7 distinct fruits. There are four that are in the sapote family: mamey. abiu, sapodilla, and canistel. There are two fruits in the persimmon family called sapote, and there is another unrelated fruit from South America also called sapote. Adding to the confusion, the same fruit may have different names even in the same language; sapodilla is also called níspero in Spanish. Mamey is also called sapote de Santo Domingo. Fortunately, almost any of these fruits makes for excellent ice creams and smoothies. For this recipe, mamey was used.

INGREDIENTS:

4 cups sapote; diced
1½ cups milk
½ cup cream
¼ cup sugar
A small pinch of salt

PREPARATION: Blend the ingredients together in a blender for one minute. Place the mixture in the ice cream maker, and churn until congealed. Serve immediately or place in a freezer for later enjoyment.

Helado de Coco

COCONUT POPSICLES, OR ICE CREAM

Ice cream makers were not available, but when there was electricity, we could make popsicles. These are creamy and rich, like ice cream, rather than hard like a frozen juice popsicle. In this recipe, the milk is heated.

INGREDIENTS:

1 can coconut cream (14 oz.)
½ cup milk
½ cup sugar
Pinch of salt
1 egg yolk
2 tablespoons milk
½ teaspoon vanilla extract

PREPARATION: Place the coconut cream, ½ cup whole milk, ½ cup of sugar, and a pinch of salt in a saucepan over medium heat, stirring constantly,

being careful not to allow the milk to scald or boil. When it just begins to simmer, lower the heat allowing it to cook at a very low simmer, stirring constantly. Cook for 15 minutes, and remove from the heat.

Place the egg yolk in a mixing bowl with 2 tablespoons of milk, and beat it until they are blended together. Beat the egg mixture into the heated milk, adding a very little bit at a time so that it does not coagulate. Allow it to cool to room temperature. Stir in the vanilla extract.

Pour the mixture into popsicle molds or small custard dishes. Place in the freezer for about 5 hours to harden. Makes about 16 oz. of dessert, or 4 half-cup servings.

One quart of ice cream can be made by doubling the recipe and freezing it in an ice-cream maker.

Helado de Guineo

ICE CREAMED BANANAS

This simple, creamy, cool dessert requires fully ripened speckled bananas as described on page 3 so that this dessert will be rich and sweet.

INGREDIENTS:

2 ripe bananas

PREPARATION: Peel the ripe bananas making sure to remove the threads that sometimes cling to the banana, as they are bitter. Slice the bananas into 1-inch thick wheels. If you plan to make the dessert the same day, you can freeze them on a plate in the freezer for 1-2 hours. If setting aside ripe bananas for later use, place the banana slices in a plastic storage bowl separated into layers with plastic wrap so that they stay separate pieces and do not form a large block of frozen bananas.

The frozen bananas then just need to be creamed in a food processor or a blender at low speed. Add a few pieces at a time. You will likely need to use a spatula to push some of the banana spray down

from the sides of blender. This can be a workout for the blender. If it is too much for your machine, add a tablespoon of liquid: orange juice, water, coconut cream, milk....

As soon as it is smooth and creamy, it is ready to serve. If a more traditional ice cream rather than "soft serve" texture is preferred, it can be put back in the freezer to solidify.

EMBELLISHMENTS: Add one cup of frozen strawberries (my favorite) or frozen blueberries when making the ice cream.

Alternatively use fresh berries or diced mango pieces as a topping. Or, when the ice cream is almost ready, blend in a tablespoon of semisweet mini chocolate chips or 2 tablespoons of almond butter.

If there is any bitter aftertaste, a small pinch of salt can cut it. Embellishing the ice cream with a bit of fat: coconut cream, almond or peanut butter, or adding another fruit can masks bitterness. Alternatively, try slightly riper bananas, however, they will give the ice cream a darker color.

Flan de Leche

CARAMEL CUSTARD

Flan is one of the most popular desserts in Latin America. This delicate, rich and creamy dessert has many variations. In Cuba, flan is often prepared with egg whites and cinnamon and served with vanilla ice cream (Copa Lolita). It is sometimes topped with shredded coconut or raisins that have been soaked in rum. In other countries, it is served with dulce de leche. Flan is also known as crème caramel.

INGREDIENTS:

Caramel Topping:
¼ – $^1/_3$ cup sugar

Custard:
1 can of evaporated milk (12 oz.)
½ cup fresh whole milk
1 large egg, room temperature
5 egg yolks, room temperature
¼ cup sugar
¼ teaspoon salt
½ teaspoon vanilla extract

PREPARATION: CARAMEL: Have six heat-proof single serving (e.g. 175 ml or ¾ cup size) custard bowls ready. Preheating the bowls on a dry baking tray to about 200°F in the oven makes them less likely to crack when the molten sugar is added, although I have not had a problem with cracking using Pyrex bowls. Prepare the caramel by heating ¼ to $^1/_3$ cups of sugar in a dry pan over medium heat, stirring it constantly with a wooden spoon. It will begin to get sticky and then quickly turn to a golden brown liquid. As soon as it liquefies into a clear honey yellow liquid, pour a small amount of the liquid into the bottom of each bowl, dividing the syrup evenly. If you heat the sugar for even a few seconds too long, it will turn dark. There should be enough syrup to cover the bottom of each bowl. Set them aside to cool so that the melted sugar candies and adheres to the bowls.

CAUTION: Although fun to play with, the melted sugar is very hot, will adhere to the skin and burn.

CUSTARD: Add whole milk to a can of evaporated milk so that the total amount of fluid is 2 cups (usually 12 oz. evaporated milk and ½ cup whole milk). Heat the milk over medium heat, stirring constantly, until it forms a skin on top, but not enough to scald. You want to heat the milk to just below a simmer and keep it there. As an alternative, the milk can be heated in a microwave for about two minutes depending on the power of the microwave. Heating denatures the protein in the milk, changing the flavor and texture of the flan. After heating, the milk needs to cool to a tepid (body) temperature, to avoid it cooking the eggs when they are mixed together.

In a separate large mixing bowl, beat the whole egg and the yolks from 5 large eggs together until they begin to foam. Room temperature eggs will whip better than eggs just out of the refrigerator. Next, beat in the sugar. Now slowly add in the milk, while continuing to beat the mixture, adding the salt and vanilla.

Pour this liquid into the custard bowls over the candied sugar, filling the bowls evenly. Place custard bowls in a shallow rectangular baking pan and fill it with water to just below the level of the custard mix in the bowls. Place it on the middle shelf of the oven. Bake at 350 degrees for 45 minutes. A knife should come out clean when finished baking. Chill for several hours.

Separate the edge of the flan from the side of the custard dish with a knife and flip it onto a saucer, serving the flan upside down. The crystallized sugar turns into a liquid during cooking, and pulls water from the custard, making it denser and creamier, and provides syrup for the flan. The flan is denser and creamier after a night in the refrigerator.

Flan de Coco

COCONUT FLAN

A delicious milk-free version of flan with coconut flavor may be prepared by replacing the 2 cups of milk in the recipe above with 2 cups of coconut cream. The coconut cream does not need to be heated and can be added directly to the beaten eggs.

Flan de Auyama

PUMPKIN FLAN

This flan can be made pumpkin, butternut squash or other yellow winter squash.

INGREDIENTS:

1 cup cooked puréed butternut squash
12 oz. evaporated milk (1 can)
5 egg yolks
1 egg
1/3 cup sugar
1 teaspoon vanilla extract
¼ teaspoon salt

Caramel:
1/3 cup sugar

PREPARATION: Set out six four-ounce heatproof custard dishes. Make the caramel syrup by melting 1/3 cup of sugar in a sauté pan. It only takes a few seconds, stirring the sugar with a wooden spoon. Remove immediately from the heat when the sugar liquefies and turns golden yellow, and pour about an eighth inch of melted sugar into each custard dish. Be careful not to overcook the sugar, and have it turn dark. Also be careful as the molten sugar is very hot and will adhere to the skin.

Blend the milk and squash in the blender. Then slowly add the egg yolks and the egg, followed by 1/3 cup sugar, salt, and vanilla extract, giving time for the ingredients to mix thoroughly.

Within a couple of minutes, the melted sugar should harden in the custard dishes, and the custard mix can be poured over the hardened sugar. Place the custard dishes in a deep tray in the oven, and fill the tray about ½-inch deep with water. Bake at 350°F for 40 minutes. Allow the flan to cool, and then place in the refrigerator to chill. Chilling for several hours gives the flan a firmer texture.

To serve, place the blade of a knife at the edge of the flan at the wall of the bowl, and separate the flan from the bowl all the way around to free it. Invert a serving plate over the bowl, and then flip the plate and bowl over. The flan should come free and be drenched in caramel syrup. Sometimes the inverted bowl needs to be gently jiggled to get the flan to release from the bowl.

Dulce de Leche

Thick, creamy, sweet, and delicious, dulce de leche is a great topping for ice cream and desserts. More complex and sublime than caramel, dulce de leche results from a Maillard reaction involving the proteins in milk, rather than caramelization in which sugar is toasted.

The traditional recipe is a long, slow, process taking 8 to 12 hours, as most of the water needs to be carefully removed from milk. This recipe uses evaporated milk, which has had 60% of the water already removed, and thus most of the work has been done for you.

INGREDIENTS:

1 can of evaporated milk (12 oz.)
1 cup sugar (See note)
1/16 teaspoon baking soda
A small pinch of salt

Optional: a 3-inch cinnamons stick or ½ teaspoon vanilla extract

PREPARATION: Place the evaporated milk, sugar, salt and soda and cinnamon stick if used, in a small saucepan over medium heat and stir almost constantly. Use enough heat to keep the milk at a low simmer. After about 30 minutes, you will notice that the milk begins to thicken and begin to yellow. Remove the cinnamon stick, and lower the heat to medium-low. Add the vanilla if desired. Stir constantly until the dulce de leche becomes so thick that it is difficult to stir. Remove from the heat and allow to cool.

Note: When we make dulce de leche at home, we use about half as much sugar to get a less sweet product. I would make this less sweet version as a spread for toasted bread when I was in college.

Majarete

Traditional Sweet Corn Pudding

INGREDIENTS:

5 ears fresh sweet corn on the cob
14 oz. coconut cream (1 can)
1 cup water
1 cinnamon stick (6-inch or ¼ oz.)
½ teaspoon whole allspice
1/8 teaspoon salt
¼ teaspoon vanilla extract
5 tablespoons light brown sugar (packed)

PREPARATION: The first step is to milk the corn: Grate the corn from the cobs and reserve the grated ears in a bowl as you go. This should yield about 2½ cups of corn mash. Place the mash in a strainer and squeeze out as much liquid as possible into a second bowl. Pour the one cup of water over the cobs in the first bowl, and wring out the "corn milk" from the cobs. Discard the cobs, and take the squeezed mash from the strainer and mix it with the "corn milk" from the cobs. Again use the strainer to express as much liquid as possible and collect it in the second bowl.

In the traditional method, where coconut cream is being made at the same time, the grated coconut and the corn mash can be mixed together and "milked" together.

Add the corn milk and the coconut cream together in a 2-quart saucepan and place over medium heat. Stir in the brown sugar and the salt and the spices. Continue stirring. When it begins to simmer lower the heat and continue stirring. Cook it for about thirty minutes (stirring continuously) until it begins to thicken. Pour into custard dishes. It can be eaten as warm pudding, or if allowed to cool, it will thicken into a custard-like consistency.

Makes 5 to 6 half cup (4 oz.) servings.

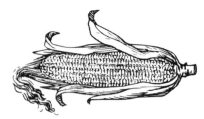
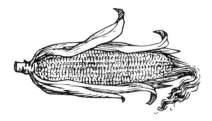

Easy Sweet Corn Pudding

INGREDIENTS:

2½ cups cut corn (frozen)
1 cup water
1 cinnamon stick (6-inch or ¼ oz.)
¼ teaspoon salt
1/3 cup light brown sugar (packed)
14 oz. coconut cream (1 can)
¼ teaspoon vanilla extract

PREPARATION: If using frozen cut corn, allow it to thaw or thaw it in a microwave, but not long enough to get it hot. Place it in a blender with one cup of water, and blend it for about 30 to 40 seconds at a low to medium speed. The intent is to grate it, not to liquefy the mash. Use a strainer to separate out the liquid into a saucepan. A large spoon can be used to express the liquid through the strainer. About 2 cups of corn milk should be produced. The dry mash can be discarded.

Place the pan over heat, add the cinnamon and salt and bring it to a boil, lower the temperature to a simmer for about 10 minutes. Add the brown sugar stirring it in, followed by the coconut cream. Continue to simmer, stirring frequently. Avoid boiling, as it may cause the coconut cream to curdle. Continue cooking until the pudding thickens. Stir in the vanilla extract. Total cooking time is about 35 minutes.

Pour into custard dishes. It can be eaten as warm pudding, or if allowed to cool and set for about 12 hours it will thicken into a custard-like consistency.

Makes 5 half-cup (4 oz.) servings.

Note: Canned corn can be substituted, but has a different flavor. Pour the contents of 2 cans of corn including the liquid into the blender blend as above. Separate out the milk as above.

Pastel de Coco y Zanahoria

COCONUT CARROT CAKE

This is a simple twist for baking a cake that adds a rich coconut flavor. Here it is done using a carrot cake mix from a box, but it will work for other cake recipes as well.

INGREDIENTS:

1 box carrot cake mix
1½ cups coconut cream
3 eggs

PREPARATION: Prepare the cake batter as directed in the recipe, but use coconut cream to substitute for the total volume of milk, water, and vegetable oil called for in the recipe. Bake as directed.

RICH CREAM CHEESE FROSTING:

INGREDIENTS:

¼ cup butter
¼ cup light brown sugar
8 oz. cream cheese, warmed to room temperature
1 teaspoon vanilla extract
1 cups sifted powdered sugar

PREPARATION: Melt the butter in the microwave and blend in the brown sugar. Blend these together with cream cheese and vanilla in a mixing bowl until smooth and creamy. Sift the powdered sugar, adding about ¼ cup of powdered sugar at a time, blending until the mixture gets smooth.

For a more delicate flavor, substitute the ¼ cup brown sugar with ¼ cup powdered sugar. Soften the butter and cream it together with the cream cheese, rather than melting it.

Note: Since real cream cheese is used for the frosting in this recipe, it is best to cover the cake and store in the refrigerator to keep it fresh.

LOW FAT CAKES: When baking cakes, oil is used to keep the cakes moist. To make low fat cakes, oil that is called for in the recipes can be replaced with the same volume of apple sauce, to replace the fat and maintain moisture. To make a low-fat frosting, use a glaze. A recipe for the lemon glaze is provided.

Glacé de Limon

LEMON GLAZE:

INGREDIENTS:

¼ cup fresh lemon juice
Zest from one large lemon (See below)
1¼ cup powdered sugar

PREPARATION: Mix the glaze ingredients together until smooth in a saucepan, heating it to a simmer, but do not allow it to boil. Drizzle or gently brush onto the cake while the cake is still warm.

MAKING LEMON ZEST: Wash the fruit to remove any agricultural residues, oils and waxes that may be used to keep the fruit fresh. Use a small amount of dishwashing detergent in warm water, and scrub the fruit with your hands or a cloth and rinse well with tap water to remove any detergent. The lemons should squeak when you rub them with wet fingers.

Zest the fruits with a fine grater or zester tool, to collect the colored part of the skin, and avoiding the bitter white pith. A vegetable peeler can also be used if caution is used to avoid cutting into the bitter pith. A medium sized lemon should give about one tablespoon of zest. Other citrus fruit can also be used to make zest. Zest can be frozen, or dried on a plate for a few days then stored in a sealed bottle for later use.

Caution: In the United States, oranges are often colored with Citrus Red No. 2 dye that is a known carcinogen. Orange peel should not be used for zest or other foods (such as marmalade or to flavor tea) unless you are certain that the fruit has not been dyed.

Dulces ~ Candies

Bolitas de Batata y Coco

SWEET POTATO AND COCONUT BALLS

INGREDIENTS:

2 pounds of sweet potatoes
1 can of evaporated milk (12 oz.)
1½ cups coconut cream
1 cup sugar
¼ teaspoon vanilla extract
¼ teaspoon salt
Sweetened shredded coconut

PREPARATION: Peel the sweet potatoes and discard the skin. Shred the sweet potatoes, and place them in a saucepan with the sugar, coconut cream, salt and evaporated milk. Place the pot over medium heat and bring the contents to a simmer, stirring constantly. After about 10 minutes, lower the heat to maintain a low simmer, stirring constantly. It will take about one hour and 45 minutes to get thick. Add the vanilla extract. When the mixture is thick enough to hold its shape, remove from the heat and allow to cool.

Form the dough into 3/4-inch diameter balls and roll them in sweetened shredded coconut. You can butter your hands to keep the dough from sticking to your fingers.

TIP: A half cup of sweetened shredded coconut can be placed in a blender for several seconds to cut it into fine bits for rolling the balls into so that they do not stick to each other.

Dulce de Coco

COCONUT FUDGE

INGREDIENTS:

One fresh "new" coconut
½ pound of sweet potatoes
2 cups evaporated milk
1 cup sugar
½ teaspoon vanilla extract

PREPARATION: This sweet is made using fresh young coconuts that have a light colored shell, and with a light brown inner skin, where the coconut flesh is still moist. Finely grate the coconut. It should yield 3 to 4 cups of shredded coconut.

Peel the sweet potatoes and discard the skin. Cut the sweet potatoes into one-inch pieces, place them in a saucepan with an inch of water and steam them until they are soft, and set them aside.

In another saucepan, place the shredded coconut, milk, and sugar over medium heat and simmer stirring frequently. After 10 minutes, lower the heat to medium-low and cook for 10 more minutes.

Drain the sweet potatoes, mash them with a fork and then add them to the other pot. Cook them together for 15 minutes stirring continuously. Blend in the vanilla when the mix becomes thick and stiff, and remove it from the heat and allow it to cool enough to handle.

Spoon the candy out onto buttered wax paper. Take a second sheet of buttered wax paper (butter side down) and cover the candy. Roll the candy to about ¼-inch thickness, and then remove the top sheet of wax paper. Allow to cool in the refrigerator for about 15 minutes, and then cut into one-inch squares.

ALTERNATIVE: Sweetened shredded coconut (7 oz.; 2 2/3 cups) can be used in place of fresh coconut; decrease the sugar from 1 cup to ¾ cups.

Turrones de Coco

HAYSTACKS

INGREDIENTS:

4 cups shredded coconut
1 14 oz. can sweetened condensed milk
½ teaspoon vanilla extract
A large pinch of salt (1/16th teaspoon salt)

PREPARATION: Mix ingredients together. If they are too wet to form into a ball, allow the dough to rest for a while. The coconut will absorb some of the moisture. Divide the dough into about 32 balls, and place them on a greased cookie sheet. Bake at 375°F for 15 minutes. Remove from the cookie sheet while they are still very warm.

VARIATION: Replace salt with baking soda to enhance Maillard reaction to give more "dulce de leche" flavor

TIP: Evaporated milk plus 1 cup sugar may be used in place of sweetened condensed milk.

Mermelada de Plátano

PLANTAIN JAM

INGREDIENTS:

1 fully ripened plantain
¼ cup sugar
½ cup water
1/8 teaspoon vanilla extract

PREPARATION: A fully ripened plantain will have its skin at least mostly if not completely black. Peel the plantain and slice it into one-inch lengths. Place the pieces in a small saucepan with the other ingredients, over medium heat, and stir, until the ripe plantain forms a paste. Cook for about 10 minutes.

Use: Eaten as a sweet dessert.

Jalea de Batata

SWEET POTATO JAM

INGREDIENTS:

1½ lbs. sweet potatoes
1 cup sugar
Pinch of salt
2 cups evaporated milk

PREPARATION: Peel the sweet potatoes and discard the skins. Shred the sweet potatoes with a grater or food processor.

Place the shredded sweet potatoes, and the other ingredients in a saucepan and heat. Stir the contents. As soon as it begins to boil, lower the heat to a simmer, and stir while cooking it for 10 minutes. Lower the heat to low and continue cooking and stirring for another 30 minutes. The resulting jam should be thick and smooth.

Use for spreading on toast or it can eaten by itself as a dessert.

Dulce de Piña

COCONUT PINEAPPLE FUDGE

INGREDIENTS:

3 cups of sweetened grated coconut flakes
1 can of evaporated milk (12 oz.)
1/8 teaspoon ground cinnamon
¼ cup sugar
1 cup drained canned pineapple tidbits
¼ cup milk
½ teaspoon vanilla extract

PREPARATION: Place the coconut flakes, evaporated milk, cinnamon, sugar, and drained pineapple tidbits in a saucepan. Cook at a medium simmer, *stirring constantly* to avoid burning, until it becomes a smooth paste. This should take about 15 minutes. Turn the heat to low. Add the vanilla to the milk, and then stir the vanilla-milk mixture into the paste, about one tablespoon at a time.

Allow to cool for several minutes. Place tablespoon sized dollops on foil or an oiled cookie sheet.

Dulce de Leche y Piña

CREAMY PINEAPPLE FUDGE

INGREDIENTS:

1 can of evaporated milk (12 oz.)
1 cup white sugar
1/16 teaspoon of baking soda
¼ cup drained canned crushed pineapple
Small pinch of salt

PREPARATION: Place the evaporated milk, sugar, soda and salt in a small saucepan over medium heat, stirring almost constantly. Use enough heat to keep the milk at a low simmer. After about 25 to 30 minutes, you will notice that the milk begins to thicken and begins to yellow. Add the pineapple and cook for another 5 minutes. Reduce the heat to low and cook for another 5 minutes. The mixture should be thick and stiff. Remove from the heat, but continue mixing for a couple of minutes more.

Place spoon sized dollops of the candy on a sheet of wax paper while still warm. They can be eaten warm, or allowed to cool.

NOTE: If fresh pineapple is used, it needs to be heated prior to use in this recipe to avoid curdling the milk (See note on page 140 under smoothies.)

Cucurucho

COCONUT TAFFY

INGREDIENTS:

2 cups sweetened shredded coconut
1 can of evaporated milk (12 oz.)
¼ cup sugar
¼ teaspoon vanilla extract

PREPARATION: Place the coconut flakes, sugar and evaporated milk in a saucepan over medium heat and stir constantly. Use enough heat to keep the milk at a low simmer. After about 5 minutes, lower the heat to medium-low. Continue mixing the candy constantly for about 20 more minutes. Remove from the heat and mix in the vanilla extract.

VARIATION: In Cuba these candies are made into a cone shape and wrapped in banana leaves. If no banana leaves are available, place tablespoon sized balls of the candy on a buttered cookie tray and allow them to cool. This candy is often flavored with bits of fruit: At the same time that the vanilla is added, ¼ cup of finely diced pineapple may be added.

Dulce de Ajonjolí

SESAME SEED BARS

This sweet is made in many Mediterranean countries and is also traditional in the Caribbean. These are called Turrón de Ajonjolí in Puerto Rico. In the Dominican Republic, this treat is often given to new mothers, as it is believed to increase milk production.

INGREDIENTS:

1 cup sesame seeds
¼ cup honey
¼ cup light brown sugar
¼ teaspoon salt
¼ teaspoon cinnamon
¼ teaspoon fresh finely ground ginger
2 sheets of buttered wax paper

PREPARATION: The first step is to toast the sesame seeds. Place them in a sauté pan or cast iron pan over medium-low heat, and stir constantly. There will be little color change until they get hot enough and then they will begin to change quickly, and give a nice toasted aroma. The time between toasted and burned is pretty quick, so as soon as they are light gold colored, empty the seeds onto a dish to cool. If they overcook they become bitter.

Prepare 2 sheets of wax paper, coating one side with a thin layer of butter.

Now add the honey and brown sugar, salt and spices into the pan and place over medium heat. Stir the contents constantly. Bring the sugars to a slow boil, and keep stirring for 2 minutes. If the boiling gets too vigorous, turn down the heat and lift the pan off the fire for a few seconds. As soon as the 2 minutes of boiling are complete, turn off the heat and add the toasted sesame seeds. Mix them in completely with the sugar mix.

Allow the sesame seed mix to cool for about a minute, and then empty it onto one of the sheets of wax paper. Take the second sheet of wax paper, and with the buttered side down begin to flatten the sesame seed candy into a sheet. A rolling pin or cylindrical wine bottle can be used to roll the candy into a ¼-inch thick sheet. Allow the candy to cool for 10 minutes, and remove a layer of wax paper. Use a large knife to cut the candy into one inch squares rectangles or diamonds. Remove them from the other sheet of wax paper. Allow them to cool to harden and enjoy.

Makes about 2 dozen one-inch candies.
Note: Sesame seeds may be found at lower prices at international grocery stores.

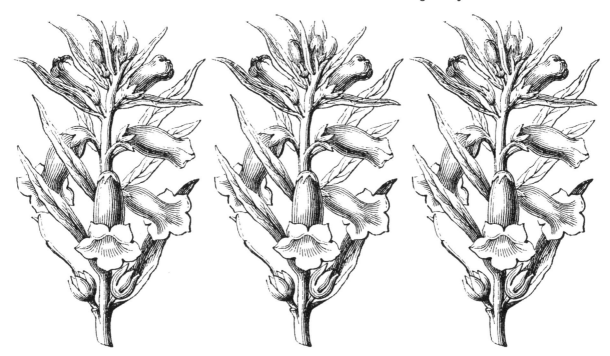

Glossary

Caribbean, Spanish and Taíno terms:

A la Parrilla: Grilled

Arepa: Unleavened corn cake. The word originates from the Arawak language.

Asado: A method of roasting meats on a grill (*parrilla*) or open fire. Carne (meat) asado is not covered during cooking. Also refers to cooking in hot ashes. This technique is used to cook corn on the cob (still in its husk) and for cooking plantains (in their skin) for making mofongo.

Asopao: A thick rice soup, often with large chunks of chicken, but which also can be made with seafood, green pigeon peas, vegetables or salted codfish.

Barbacoa: Barbequed, cooked over hot charcoal coals, buried or otherwise covered during cooking.

Bolitas (or Bollitos) de Plátano Maduro y Queso: Ripe plantain mofongo (Fufu) made from ripe plantains and filled with cheese.

Cena: An evening meal. The evening meal is usually a light meal in the Caribbean, often a snack, or a sandwich with juice. If dining in a restaurant, cena is often a relaxed conversation with friends over food and drinks lasting from nine P.M. until past eleven.

Chimichurris: A type of hot sandwich made in a bun, made by street vendors, usually with a hamburger patty but also made with eggs.

Colmado: A shop, usually a single room of a house facing the street, which sells a few grocery items, often in single-use quantities.

Comida: Meal. The largest meal of the day, traditionally at served at midday and followed by a siesta and shower before returning to work.

Conuco: A small piece of land outside of town that is cultivated with a mix of food crops and fruit trees for family use and often to provide extra income. Likely an Arawak word.

Criollo: Originally referred to colonists, but now used to refer to those born in the Caribbean or natives of the Caribbean.

Epazote: (*Dysphania ambrosioides*), also known as Mexican tea. This herb, when cooked with beans, prevents the formation of intestinal gas. Native to South and Central America, this invasive weed can be found growing in 46 states in the U.S.

Escabeche: Pickled fish and other meat. Differs from Ceviche in that the fish or meat is cooked prior to marinating it in vinegar or acid fruit juice.

Escalfado: Poached.

Frito: Fried.

Fufu: A food made of starchy vegetables made into a ball, often eaten with a filling. A traditional African dish made from African Yams. It is usually made from plantains in the Caribbean.

Guineo: Banana.

Guanimes or Guanimos: Unleavened bread made of cornmeal, in the form of a small round ball, similar to a tamale. Prepared with cheese, filled with meat, or prepared as a sweet.

Guisado: A method of lightly stewing meat in a thick savory sauce.

Habichuelas: Beans.

Hervido: Boiled.

Horneado: Baked.

La Bandera Dominicana: (The Dominican Flag) The traditional basic supper time meal (midday), consisting of red beans stewed beef and white rice. If you can't afford this, you are considered truly poor and deprived.

Lechosa: Papaya.

Locrio: A rice dish (sometimes substituting cracked wheat) cooked with small pieces of seafood, fowl or meat, similar to a Spanish paella.

LOS TRES GOLPES: A traditional breakfast combination consisting of Mangú, Fried Salami with onions and Fried Cheese.

MABÍ: A traditional fermented sparkling beverage with a low alcohol content.

MANGÚ: Similar to mofongo, mangú is generally prepared from mashed *boiled* rather than fried plantains, and is topped with sautéed onions, and served with fried eggs, fried salami, or fried cheese. Sometimes it is mashed with milk or butter.

MOFONGO: Generally prepared from mashed *fried or baked* green plantains. In Cuba, it is called fufu, showing African origin of this dish. Often made into a ball and stuffed with meat, and covered with sauce.

MORO OR MOROS: Rice and beans cooked together. Originally "Moros y Cristianos", referring to dark-skinned Moors and white Christians; dark beans with white rice.

PASTEL EN HOJA (Pie in Banana Leaves): Similar to empanada, but rather than fried, the pie is made rectangular, and wrapped in a banana or plantain leaf and steamed as in the preparation of guanimos dulce.

PASTEL: Another form of Pastel en Hoja is made from green bananas, green plantains, or yautia tuber dough. These are also prepared by steaming the dough in banana or plantain leaves.

PASTELONES: A regional term for empanadas, usually baked rather than fried.

RANCHO: A stew made of what is available, often on a picnic to the countryside, using leaves and vegetables, fish, or meat that can be gathered.

REFRITO: Refried.

REHOGADO: Braised or Browned.

SALTEADO: Sautéed.

SANCOCHO: A stew usually with meat, with plantains, yuca, or other starchy tubers.

SOFRITO: A thick sauce that is the basis for many dishes, and that may be used to sauté meat. There are many local variations, but it often contains plum tomatoes, Cubanelle or sweet peppers, onion, and garlic. A general recipe for sofrito is given on page 90.

SANCOCHO: A traditional soup (often considered a stew). It usually consists of large pieces of meat and vegetables served in a broth.

TAÍNO: The Native American people who lived on the islands of Hispaniola, Cuba, Puerto Rico and other Caribbean islands. Their cooking influence is present in many of the recipes included in this book.

TRIFONGO - Mofongo, prepared with fried cassava, green plantains, and ripe plantains.

TOSTONES: Refried sliced plantains.

YANIQUEQUES: Johnnycakes. Originally an American Indian food made of corn and baked. The Dominican yaniqueque is made with wheat flour, baking soda, salt and water, and then deep fried in vegetable oil, very similar to frybread made by Navaho and other Native Americans. In both cases the dish likely evolved as an adaptation of traditional foods to make use of two non-native ingredients; flour and shortening, - provided by the American government. Yaniqueque is often enjoyed as a warm evening street food snack accompanied with a mabí de limón (sparkling lemonade).

174

Recipe Index

Índice de Receta

Citations

1 Screening for heterocyclic amines in chicken cooked in various ways. Solyakov A, Skog K. Food Chem Toxicol. 2002 Aug;40(8):1205-11.PMID: 12067585

2 An open-label pilot study to assess the efficacy and safety of virgin coconut oil in reducing visceral adiposity. Liau KM, Lee YY, Chen CK, Rasool AH. ISRN Pharmacol. 2011:949686. Epub 2011 Mar 15. PMID:22164340

3 Coconut oil is associated with a beneficial lipid profile in pre-menopausal women in the Philippines. Feranil AB, Duazo PL, Kuzawa CW, Adair LS. Asia Pac J Clin Nutr. 2011;20(2):190-5. PMID:21669587

4 Evaluation of antihyperglycemic activity of Cocos nucifera Linn. on streptozotocin induced type 2 diabetic rats. Naskar S, Mazumder UK, Pramanik G, Gupta M, Suresh Kumar RB, Bala A, Islam A. J Ethnopharmacol. 2011 Dec 8;138(3):769-73. PMID:22041106

5 Intensive meditation training, immune cell telomerase activity, and psychological mediators. Jacobs TL, Epel ES, Lin J, Blackburn EH, Wolkowitz OM, Bridwell DA, Zanesco AP, Aichele SR, Sahdra BK, Maclean KA, King BG, Shaver PR, Rosenberg EL, Ferrer E, Wallace BA, Saron CD. Psychoneuroendocrinology. 2011 Jun;36(5):664-81. Epub 2010 Oct 29. PMID:21035949

6 Chicken soup inhibits neutrophil chemotaxis in vitro. Rennard BO, Ertl RF, Gossman GL, Robbins RA, Rennard SI. Chest. 2000 Oct;118(4):1150-7.

7 Effects of drinking hot water, cold water, and chicken soup on nasal mucus velocity and nasal airflow resistance. Saketkhoo K, Januszkiewicz A, Sackner MA. Chest. 1978 Oct;74(4):408-10.

8 Isolation and characterization of collagen from squid (Ommastrephes bartrami) skin.Yan, M, Li,.B, Zhao,X. Journal of Ocean University of China, Volume 8, Issue 2, pp.191-196

9 Frequency and distribution of bacterial flora of Penaeus shrimp. Ricardo J Alvarez,. 19(3-4). 1983

10 Lin, C. S., C. Hung, and C. M. Park. "Quality and Microbial Safety for Shrimp Thawed Using a Constant Temperature Thawing Chamber."2000 IFT Annual Meeting, 51A-1Institute of Food Technologists, 2000.

11 Sirintra Boonsumrej, Saiwarun Chaiwanichsiri, Sumate Tantratian, Toru Suzuki, Rikuo Takai Effects of freezing and thawing on the quality changes of tiger shrimp (Penaeus monodon) frozen by air-blast and cryogenic freezing. Journal of Food Engineering Volume 80, Issue 1, May 2007, Pages 292-299

12 Isolation and characterization of collagen from squid (Ommastrephes bartrami) skin.Yan, M, Li,.B, Zhao,X. Journal of Ocean University of China, Volume 8, Issue 2, pp.191-196

13 Heterocyclic amines: occurrence and prevention in cooked food. Robbana-Barnat S, Rabache M, Rialland E, Fradin J. Environ Health Perspect. 1996 Mar;104(3):280-8. PMID:891976613

14 Effect of cooking methods on the formation of heterocyclic aromatic amines in chicken and duck breast. Liao GZ, Wang GY, Xu XL, Zhou GH. Meat Sci. 2010 May;85(1):149-54. Epub 2009 Dec 23. PMID:20374878

15 Effect of marinades on the formation of heterocyclic amines in grilled beef steaks. Smith JS, Ameri F, Gadgil P. J Food Sci. 2008 Aug;73(6):T100-5. PMID:19241593

16 Effect of microwave pretreatment on heterocyclic aromatic amine mutagens/carcinogens in fried beef patties. Felton JS, Fultz E, Dolbeare FA, Knize MG. Food Chem Toxicol. 1994 Oct;32(10):897-903. PMID:7959444

17 Minimization of heterocyclic amines and thermal inactivation of Escherichia coli in fried ground beef. Salmon CP, Knize MG, Panteleakos FN, Wu RW, Nelson DO, Felton JS. J Natl Cancer Inst. 2000 Nov 1;92(21):1773-8.

18 Effect of meal composition and cooking duration on the fate of sulforaphane following consumption of broccoli by healthy human subjects. Rungapamestry V, Duncan AJ, Fuller Z, Ratcliffe B. Br J Nutr. 2007 Apr;97(4):644-52. PMID:17349076

19 Vegetable and fruit intake after diagnosis and risk of prostate cancer progression. Richman EL, Carroll PR, Chan JM. Int J Cancer. 2011 Aug 5. PMID:21823116

20 Prospective study of fruit and vegetable intake and risk of prostate cancer. Kirsh VA, Peters U, Mayne ST, Subar AF, Chatterjee N, Johnson CC, Hayes RB; Prostate, Lung, Colorectal and Ovarian Cancer Screening Trial. J Natl Cancer Inst. 2007 Aug 1;99(15):1200-9. PMID:17652276

21 D,L-sulforaphane-induced apoptosis in human breast cancer cells is regulated by the adapter protein p66(Shc). Sakao K, Singh SV. J Cell Biochem. 2011 Sep 28. PMID:21956685

22 Sulforaphane inhibits mitochondrial permeability transition and oxidative stress. Greco T, Shafer J, Fiskum G. Free Radic Biol Med. 2011 Sep 21. PMID:21986339

23 Comparison of the protective effects of steamed and cooked broccolis on ischaemia-reperfusion-induced cardiac injury. Mukherjee S, Lekli I, Ray D, Gangopadhyay H, Raychaudhuri U, Das DK. Br J Nutr. 2010 Mar;103(6):815-23. PMID:19857366

24 Sulforophane glucosinolate. Monograph. Altern Med Rev. 2010 Dec;15(4):352-60. PMID:2119425

25 The activity of myrosinase from broccoli (Brassica oleracea L. cv. Italica): influence of intrinsic and extrinsic factors. Ludikhuyze L, Rodrigo L, Hendrickx M. J Food Prot. 2000 Mar;63(3):400-3. PMID:10716572

26 Heating decreases epithiospecifier protein activity and increases sulforaphane formation in broccoli. Matusheski NV, Juvik JA, Jeffery EH. Phytochemistry. 2004 May;65(9):1273-81. PMID:15184012

27 Effect of meal composition and cooking duration on the fate of sulforaphane following consumption of broccoli by healthy human subjects. Rungapamestry V, Duncan AJ, Fuller Z, Ratcliffe B. Br J Nutr. 2007 Apr;97(4):644-52. PMID:17349076

28 Changes in glucosinolate concentrations, myrosinase activity, and production of metabolites of glucosinolates in cabbage (Brassica oleracea Var. capitata) cooked for different durations. Rungapamestry V, Duncan AJ, Fuller Z, Ratcliffe B. J Agric Food Chem. 2006 Oct 4;54(20):7628-34. PMID:17002432

29 [Sulforaphane (1-isothiocyanato-4-(methylsulfinyl)-butane) content in cruciferous vegetables]. Campas-Baypoli ON, Bueno-Solano C, Martínez-Ibarra DM, Camacho-Gil F, Villa-Lerma AG, Rodríguez-Núñez JR, Lóez-Cervantes J, Sánchez-Machado DI. Arch Latinoam Nutr. 2009 Mar;59(1):95-100. PMID:19480351

30 Roots, Tubers, Plantains and Bananas in Human Nutrition. Food and Agriculture Organization of the United Nations. Rome, 1990

31 Root Crops (Tropical Products Institute) by Daisy E. Kay 1973

32 Beeturia and iron absorption. Sotos JG. Lancet. 1999 Sep 18;354(9183):1032. PMID:10501390

33 Alcohol and postmenopausal breast cancer risk defined by estrogen and progesterone receptor status: a prospective cohort study. Suzuki R, Ye W, Rylander-Rudqvist T, Saji S, Colditz GA, Wolk A. J Natl Cancer Inst. 2005 Nov 2;97(21):1601-8. PMID:16264180

34 Fetal alcohol exposure increases mammary tumor susceptibility and alters tumor phenotype in rats. Polanco TA, Crismale-Gann C, Reuhl KR, Sarkar DK, Cohick WS. Alcohol Clin Exp Res. 2010 Nov;34(11):1879-87. PMID:20662802

35 Effects of normal meals rich in carbohydrates or proteins on plasma tryptophan and tyrosine ratios. Wurtman RJ, Wurtman JJ, Regan MM, McDermott JM, Tsay RH, Breu JJ. Am J Clin Nutr. 2003 Jan;77(1):128-32. PMID:12499331

36 High-glycemic-index carbohydrate meals shorten sleep onset. Afaghi A, O'Connor H, Chow CM. Am J Clin Nutr. 2007 Feb;85(2):426-30. Erratum in: Am J Clin Nutr. 2007 Sep;86(3):809. PMID:17284739

The Authors

Susana grew up in a small town in the Dominican Republic in a home without electricity. She learned the art of slow cooking over an open fire helping her aunts and grandmother prepare meals outside under a palm thatched cooking shelter. Coconut cream was prepared daily, grating the copra, and squeezing it by hand. Meat was either butchered the same morning in the market, or dried in the sun. Without refrigeration fish was limited to salted cod, dried herring or dried tilapia. Tilapia can still be seen hanging to dry on lines in many villages near where she was raised.

Like many people in her town, Susana's family raised goats and had a "canuco"; a plot of land near town where they cultivated vegetables, plantains, avocados, mangoes, coconuts and other fruits. Planting and harvesting was a community event with "plenas" sung as neighbors helped each other with planting and bringing in the crop.

In the days of her youth it was not unusual to pass the evening with friends and family members, shelling pigeon peas, exchanging local gossip and telling cautionary tales to the young. Other than some music on the radio there was little electronic interference to boisterous conversation and play with friends and extended family. Clothes were washed by hand, often on the river bank. Everyone had chores, but there was also opportunity to sneak off and play, to climb trees and to swim in nearby streams.

Susana moved to a provincial capital on the coast to attend college, and here she expanded her culinary experience to a wider variety of foods, including fresh seafood. Soon after coming to the United States Susana was selected to be a participant in the Betty Crocker composite portrait. She has worked as a business manager and has taught both elementary and high school.

Dr. Charles Lewis, MD, MPH, served as U.S. Peace Corps Volunteer in a isolated mountain village in the Dominican Republic and lived in that country for several years. He returned to the Dominican Republic after residency training and helped to organize public health efforts to improve children's health and survival, and worked at the regional hospital. He and Susana met at this time, when she was nearing completion of her college degree.

Dr. Lewis is board certified in Public Health and Preventive Medicine and has practiced medicine in Florida for over 20 years. He is also the author of a textbook on enteroimmunology, an emerging field of medicine, and is an expert on food-related diseases.

Made in the USA
San Bernardino, CA
24 April 2019